HELEN FRANKENTHALER

HELEN FRANKENTHALER

Painting History, Writing Painting

Alison Rowley

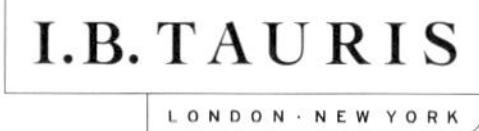

Published in 2007 by I.B.Tauris & Co Ltd
6 Salem Road, London W2 4BU
175 Fifth Avenue, New York NY 10010
www.ibtauris.com

In the United States of America and Canada distributed by Palgrave Macmillan
a division of St. Martin's Press, 175 Fifth Avenue, New York NY 10010

ISBN (HB): 978 1 84511 518 0
ISBN (PB): 978 1 84511 519 7

A full CIP record for this book is available from the British Library
A full CIP record is available from the Library of Congress

Library of Congress Catalog Card Number: available

Printed and bound in Czech Republic by Finidr, s.r.o., Cesky Tesin
From camera-ready copy edited and supplied by the author

For Anne

CONTENTS

ILLUSTRATIONS

Figures

Plates

Pl. 4 Vanessa Bell, *The Beach Studland,* c.1911, oil on board, 10 x 13 ½ in. (25.5 x 34.5 cm.) Private Collection, © 1961 Estate of Vanessa Bell, courtesy Henrietta Garnett. Photograph courtesy Sotherby's, London.

Pl. 5 Vanessa Bell, *Studland Beach,* c.1912, oil on canvas, 30 x 40 in. (76.2 x 101.6 cm.) Tate Gallery, London, © 1961 Estate of Vanessa Bell, courtesy Henrietta Garnett. Photograph © Tate, London 2005.

Pl. 6 Helen Frankenthaler, *With Blue,*1953, oil on canvas, 35 x 31 in. (89.9 x 78.7 cm.) Private Collection, © 2007 Helen Frankenthaler.

Pl. 7 Bridget Riley, *Winter Palace*, 1981, oil on linen, 83 ½ x 72 ¼ in. (212.1 x 183.5 cm.) Leeds City Art Gallery, © the artist.

Pl. 8 Andy Warhol, *Lavender Disaster,* 1963, acrylic and silkscreen ink on canvas, 108 x 82 in. (274 x 208 cm.) The Menil Collection, Huston; © The Andy Warhol Foundation for the Visual Arts, Inc./ARS, NY and DACS, London 2005.

Pl. 9 Morris Louis, *Salient,* 1954, acrylic on canvas, 74 ½ x 99 in. (189.2 x 252 cm.) Courtesy The Donald and Barbara Zucker Family Foundation.

Pl. 10 Helen Frankenthaler, *Hôtel du Quai Voltaire*, 1956, mixed media on paper, 15 ⅜ x 23 in. (38.1 x 58.4 cm.) Private Collection. © 2007 Helen Frankenthaler.

Pl. 11 Helen Frankenthaler, *Eden,* 1956, oil on unprimed canvas, 103 x 117 in. (261.6 x 297.2 cm.) Private collection. © 2007 Helen Frankenthaler. Image © Geoffrey Clements/Corbis.

Pl. 12 Helen Frankenthaler, *Landscape (Nice, France)*, 1956, watercolour on paper, 9½ x 12 ½ in. (22.8 x 30.4 cm.) Private Collection. © 2007 Helen Frankenthaler.

Pl. 13 Friedel Dzubas, *Early Grave,* 1957, oil on canvas, 96 ½ x 47 in. (240.9 x 120 cm.) Courtesy of the Elkon Gallery, Inc., New York City.

Pl. 14 Nicolas Poussin, *The Arcadian Shepherds,* also known as 'Et in Arcadia Ego', c.1638-40, oil on canvas, 33 ½ x 47 ¾ in (85 x 121 cm) Paris, musée du Louvre. Photograph RMN/ © René-Gabriel Ojèda.

Pl. 15 Helen Frankenthaler, *Mother Goose Melody,* 1959, oil on unprimed canvas, 82 x 104 in. (208.3 x 264.1 cm.) Virginia Museum of Fine Arts, Richmond. Gift of Sydney and Frances Lewis. © 2007 Helen Frankenthaler. © Photograph Virginia Museum of Fine Arts. Detail reproduced as the cover of the catalogue for the exhibition *After* Mountains and Sea: *Frankenthaler 1956-1959*, Solomon R. Guggenheim Museum, courtesy the Solomon R. Guggenheim Museum.

Pl. 16 Bracha Lichtenberg Ettinger, *Eurydice no. 13*, (1994-1996). Oil painting mixed with black photocopy toner and pigments on paper mounted on canvas. Private Collection. Photograph courtesy the artist.

The author and publisher are grateful to all those individuals and organisations listed above who have granted permission to reproduce pictures. Every effort has been made to obtain permission to use copyright material but if for any reason the request has not been received the copyright holder should contact the publisher.

ACKNOWLEDGEMENTS

I would like to thank Helen Frankenthaler for agreeing to discuss her work with me in the early stages of researching this book, and I am immensely grateful to Maureen St Onge for her assistance with enabling the images of paintings by the artist to be reproduced in the text. In New York John Elderfield generously shared his knowledge of Frankenthaler's work with me and provided access to the resources of the library of the Museum of Modern Art, Karen Wilkin kindly lent me material relating to Frankenthaler's works on paper, and Nanette Salomon assisted with locating a document vital to the logic of the opening chapter of the book, and was my guide in the archives and galleries of the Metropolitan Museum of Art. I have benefited enormously from Fred Orton's scholarship on the New York School and thank him for his help and advice at various points during the course of my research. My thanks go to David Lomas, Deborah Cherry, Barbara Engh, Judith Tucker, and Phyllis Tuckman all of whom read versions of the book at various stages of its development and offered helpful suggestions. An earlier version of part of Chapter 2 appeared in *Unframed: practices & politics of women's contemporary painting* edited by Rosemary Betterton, I.B.Tauris, 2004. Jenny Tennant Jackson gave me support, hospitality and understanding at crucial times during the years this book took to complete; I cannot thank her enough. Catherine Alder and Kristine O'Leary made me welcome in their home at Moondyne, Western Australia in the summer of 2005, where I worked at revising the manuscript. I thank them for yet another instance of their long-standing friendship and generosity. I want to acknowledge James and Shirley Marten and the North American Foundation at the University of Leeds for a scholarship that assisted a period of research in New York at the beginning of the project, and the British Academy for a Small Research Grant awarded in 2005 to support the acquisition of visual material for the book. I am grateful to Professor Kerstin Mey for making available the resources of Interface: Centre for Research in Arts, Technologies and Design at the University of Ulster, especially in the person of Chérie Driver without whom the task of securing images for the book would never have been completed, I am indebted to her calm, meticulous and tireless work. I would like to thank Audrey Daly, Anna Johnson, and Keith Connolly at Tonic Design, Belfast, for their assistance with preparing the manuscript for publication. Elizabeth Galloway at I.B.Tauris has been most helpful with production matters. My deepest thanks go to Susan Lawson for her enthusiastic response to the manuscript of the book, for understanding the importance of its unconventional turns, and for her patience guiding them into publication with sound editorial advice.

My debt to the rigorous feminist scholarship and endless intellectual generosity of Griselda Pollock are part of the fabric of the text: the dialogue continues. I have dedicated the book to Anne Patricia Gilbert without whom it would never have begun.

PREFACE

The challenge of writing this book has been to trust that its two initiating insights made sense. Starkly put, they were first, that the painting made by the character Lily Briscoe at the end of Virginia Woolf's 1927 novel *To the Lighthouse* is Helen Frankenthaler's 1952 painting *Mountains and Sea*, and second that the mountain in *Mountains and Sea* is Cézanne's *Mont Sainte-Victoire.* I had to trust that beyond their status as singular notions that arose for me nearly thirty years ago in the studio when, as a young painter, I first engaged with the work of Helen Frankenthaler, they were indicators of knowledge with wider cultural, social and political implications. At the outset the ideas seemed worth pursuing if for no better reason than that, together, they already possessed the value of enlivening the meaning-making potential of a painting utterly stultified by the sheer monotony of the critical literature's repetitive accounts of its genesis and effects. For sure, what has been written about *Mountains and Sea* gives it a certain visibility in the modernist canon, but what invariably gets shown is something that never quite has the status of a painting in and of itself.

Evidence to support a developed argument that *Mountains and Sea* registers a profound engagement with Cézanne's late *Mont Sainte-Victoire* studies was not hard to find. Establishing a logic that gave substance to the idea of *Mountains and Sea* as the delayed historical manifestation of Lily Briscoe's fictional painting in *To the Lighthouse* was another matter. It involved risking the loopy kinds of moves that expose the project to criticism analogous with that of *Mountains and Sea* itself in the Frankenthaler literature, that is to say, this writing never quite makes it as art history even though arts histories, social, semiotic, and feminist, are all mobilised. For instance, even in the various discourses of feminism's engagement with art history and criticism it is still unthinkable to set Martha Rosler's *Unknown Secrets (The Secret of the Rosenbergs)* beside Helen Frankenthaler's *Mountains and Sea* and *Eden.* The practice of a feminist, left-aligned political activist meets that of a representative of precisely the high bourgeois political conservatism it rejects. Conversely Frankenthaler and her formalist critics have rejected feminism and direct political action. This book works through and extends a body of feminist scholarship in art history which, informed by Freudian psychoanalysis, has identified art making and the formation of art historical canons as structurally Oedipal. A feminist canon is no exception, and it is the Oedipal mechanism of rejection or assimilation of the other that constructs as unthinkable a meeting between the work of Helen Frankenthaler and Martha Rosler even in feminism's political work of analysing the cultural significance of work made by women.

This book's specific intervention into the field of the study of Helen Frankenthaler's work in the 1950s is to read two paintings, *Mountains and Sea* (1952) and *Eden* (1956), against the grain of dominant formalist interpretations, as history paintings. They are read both for the inscription of major events that shaped the particular cultural and political environment in which the artist worked in the mid 1950s, and as engagements with correspondingly significant works in the history of western painting. The book explores how the two paintings *do* history in their own terms, that is to say, *as painting*. This involves a detailed analysis of the fundamental spatial and temporal structure of Frankenthaler's painting practice. Beyond its canonical designation as a 'the bridge between Pollock and what was possible' in a formalist account of the advance of American painting in the 1950s, here, for instance, *Mountains and Sea* comes into view as a painting of the Rosenberg era. I read it as a product of the years that witnessed the arrest, trial and execution of Julius and Ethel Rosenberg on the charge of atomic spying, and argue that the value and meaning of the formal innovation of the painting is connected, however indirectly, with those events.

My structural analysis of the work of history in painting in *Mountains and Sea* and *Eden* coincides with recent developments in feminist scholarship in the area of psychoanalysis and aesthetics in which the activity of painting is central to a different theorisation of the formation of human subjectivity: as encounter. Psychoanalyst and painter Bracha Lichtenberg Ettinger's post Freudian/Lacanian concepts of *matrix* and *metramorphosis* allow two moves to be made in the book. Firstly it provides a theoretical logic for the unconventional structure through which the text finally is able to makes 'sense' of the first of its initiating intuitions. I argue that in *To the Lighthouse* Virginia Woolf, in her imaginative formulation of Lily Briscoe's painting activity, prefigures in fiction a psychic structure theorised over sixty years later, traces of which I read inscribed in Helen Frankenthaler's practice. Key to this argument is the concept of *metramorphosis*, a psychic subjectivising process that corresponds with certain material and procedural characteristics of the activity of painting exemplified in Frankenthler's work.

Secondly, if feminist scholarship in art history has recognised the Oedipal nature of art making and the formation of art historical canons, academic practices themselves are no less Oedipal. An intellectual understanding of a psychic mechanism is no guarantee against its unconscious effects. Predictably, but no less avoidably, pressure to reject or assimilate antecedents in this text intensifies precisely at the point where I engage directly with a body of feminist work on women and painting in New York in the 1950s. This is also the point, however, where Bracha Lichtenberg Ettinger's theoretical speculations in the field of Freudian/Lacanian psychoanalysis offer the text the possibility of functioning differently as a site of the production of academic subjectivity and knowledge. She proposes that the Oedipal dimension of subject formation is supplemented by a different psychic mechanism in which subjectivity co-emerges in an encounter with (the) other(s). This text is marked in obvious ways by the Oedipal tensions of its status, at one level, as a feminist intellectual genealogy in process, at close quarters, in the discipline of art history. The decision to allow these tensions to surface in an attempt to acknowledge and monitor, as feminist politics, their destructive potential, leads to some embarrassing lapses of academic decorum. They are the price I am prepared to pay for attempting to forge a productive working relation beyond the Freudian Oedipal family structure in the unfamiliar, or more accurately non-familial, mode so suggestive in Lichtenberg Ettinger's theoretical work as a vital and revitalising resource for future feminist practice in cultural analysis.

It is, then, in unfamiliar company, categorically and temporally, that the 'understated' events, public and private, 'that are really present' in *Mountains and Sea* and *Eden* tip into view in this book.[1] The pleasure and violence, awkwardness, and indeed embarrassments of its passionate engagement, not only with the concerns of art, but also of the world at large, are palpably inscribed in Frankenthaler's work throughout the 1950s to a degree that makes the decorum that characterises much of its subsequent art historical treatment at best ridiculous, at worst deadly.[2] In 1954, however, Frank O'Hara was not afraid to point out the distinguishing quality of the artist's work in a review for *Art News*:

> She does not hesitate to deal with her subject with a frankness approaching sordidness, for the power of their impact is that of natural violence evoked in a lofty immaculate tone – the compacted sordidness of one of those 'unspeakable' characters in a Henry James novel.[3]

The desire in this study to reactivate the meaning-making potential of *Mountains and Sea* and *Eden* in the present represents a return to the spirit of that 1954 review.

1

MOUNTAINS AND SEA: CÉZANNE'S COUNTRY IN NEW YORK AND NOVA SCOTIA

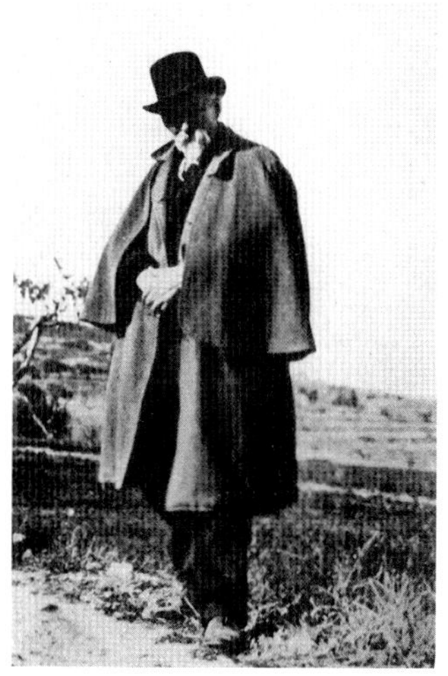

Fig. 1
Paul Cézanne on the hill of Les Lauves, c.1905

> It was as if I suddenly went to a foreign country but didn't know the language, but had read enough and had a passionate interest and was anxious to live there. I wanted to live in this land; I had to live there and master the language.
>
> Helen Frankenthaler[1]

A prologue

'Cézanne's Country' is the title of an article written by Erle Loran Johnson published in the April 1930 issue of the American journal *The Arts* (fig. 1).[2] It was in this article that photographs of Cézanne's motifs in the countryside of Aix-en-Provence appeared for the first time. Loran developed his initial article into a book called *Cézanne's Composition: Analysis of His Form with Diagrams and Photographs of His Motifs*. In the introduction he writes:

> The photographic material for this study was collected when, for more than two years, I lived in Cézanne's studio in Aix-en-Provence, painting in the Cézanne country and taking snapshots whenever I came upon motifs of Cézanne's paintings.[3]

Loran, an American, first arrived in Provence in 1927 and he describes the motivation for his visit as follows:

> As a young painter passionately devoted to the art of Cézanne, I was first of all bent on seeing what Cézanne's country looked like...At the time the photographs were taken, the primary objective was to show how closely Cézanne followed nature, because at first it seemed an astounding revelation that the paintings were so much like the subjects.[4]

But by 1943 and the publication of *Cézanne's Composition*, Loran's project had changed. The photographs are now presented as documentary evidence of the extent to which the pictorial space in Cézanne's paintings departs from what Loran calls 'space in nature'. On page after page of formal analysis they are placed for comparison alongside reproductions of single works by Cézanne and accompanied by clumsy diagrams swirling with directional arrows illustrating compositional organisation in terms of 'Static Planes' and 'Dynamic Planes', 'Axes of Volumes' and the like (fig. 2). All of which is fatally undermined by the fallacious premise upon which Loran founds his argument, namely, that the space recorded in a photograph is equivalent to that lived in the presence of the motif. This makes for an irritating and tedious read, but I can never pass the book on the shelf of an art library without taking it down to have another look at the photographs, in spite of their leaden context. Or perhaps it is precisely *because* they are lodged in the weighty paraphernalia of such a laborious and misconceived pedagogical exercise that Loran's pale blurry snapshots, taken with a Brownie 2A camera, resonate so compellingly as what they originally were – souvenirs of the initial urge of a young painter to see what Cézanne's country looked like.

In the catalogue for the 1978 exhibition *Cézanne: The Late Work* there is another set of photographs, this time taken by John Rewald; they accompany his essay called 'The Last Motifs at Aix.' In a postscript to the essay Rewald tells how he first came to Aix in the late spring of 1933 where he met the painter Leo Marchutz, who had been living and painting for several years at the Chateau Noir. Marchutz owned a copy of the April 1930 issue of *The Arts* with Loran's article and it had prompted him to search for other motifs around the Chateau Noir. Marchutz persuaded Rewald, who had just bought a new Leica camera, to photograph them and, to take up the story in Rewald's own words:

> ...we set out on a systematic hunt for Cézanne's motifs throughout the region of Aix, L'Estaque, Gardanne, usually on bicycles…Until 1939 I spent several months in Aix every year roaming around the countryside with Leo Marchutz.[5]

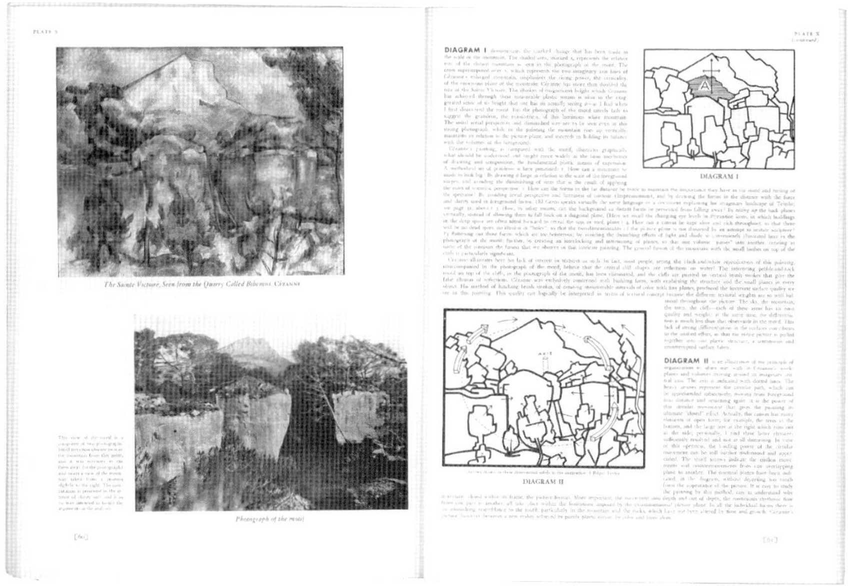

Fig. 2
Illustrations from *Cézanne's Composition: Analysis of his Form with Diagrams and Photographs of his Motifs*, by Erle Loran, 1947

The main body of Rewald's catalogue does read like a guided cycling tour through Cézanne's Country. This is just one example of several similar passages:

> What was then the 'Petite Route du Tholonet' leads from Aix eastward in the direction of Sainte-Victoire. The road bends frequently, rises and falls, until, after about a mile, at a sharp turn, the view is suddenly free over an undulating landscape that reaches the foot of the commanding gray rock. After one more gentle curve a small, slowly mounting path to the left of the road disappears into the forest. From a slight elevation near the path, one can look down over the road and see two umbrella pines that cast their shadows on it with Mont Sainte-Victoire looming over the whole scene. From here Cézanne painted two views of the mountain, of those pines, and of the road that loses itself in the distance.[6]

He even provides a map of Aix-en-Provence and its environs marked with routes to the Bibemus quarry, the Chateau Noir, the Jas de Bouffan and the Lauves studio. If the title of Loran's original article has a hint of the holiday brochure about it, then Rewald provides the pocket guide (fig. 3).

Rewald returned to Aix-en-Provence in 1947 to continue the photographic project with Marchutz. But by then building programmes were encroaching on and

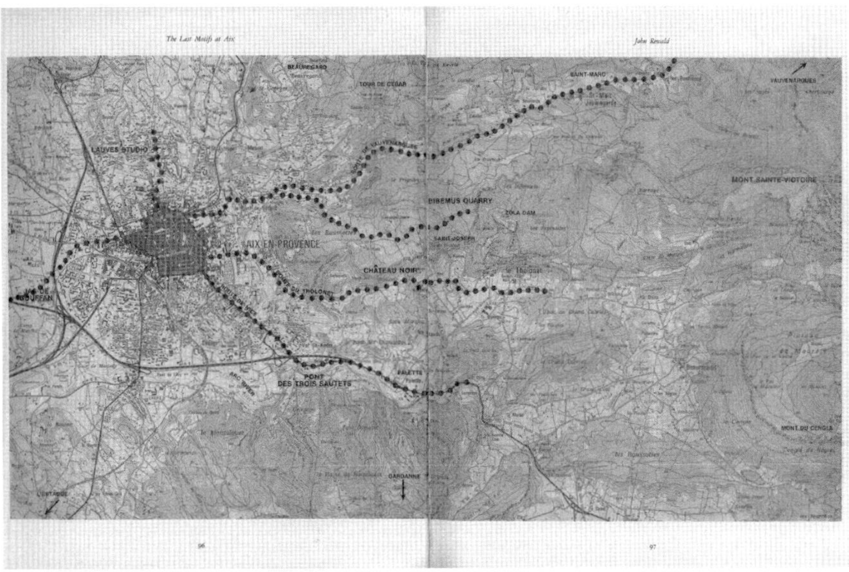

Fig. 3
Map of Aix-en-Provence, reproduced in 'The Last Motifs at Aix'
by John Rewald, 1983

obscuring the motifs, and in 1953 developers threatened Cézanne's Lauves studio itself. In response, Rewald formed an American committee of Cézanne admirers who raised the money to purchase it so that in 1954, what began in 1930 as an imaginative investment became a financial and a national one when the American committee bought a piece of Cézanne's Country.[7]

At home in New York

The sense of having suddenly gone to a 'foreign country' Helen Frankenthaler described to Barbara Rose had nothing to do with Cézanne. It was the effect of the painter's encounter with the work of Jackson Pollock at the Betty Parsons gallery, right on her own doorstep in New York. The Frankenthaler literature cites the artist's exposure to Pollock's work in exhibitions in 1950 and 1951, together with several visits she paid to Pollock's East Hampton studio during 1951, as key events that propelled her towards her 'breakthrough' in 1952 with the painting *Mountains and Sea* (pl. 1). What *Mountains and Sea* supposedly broke through to is now an art historical commonplace. Karen Wilkin in her review of the exhibition 'After *Mountains and Sea*: Frankenthaler 1956-59', shown in 1998 at the Guggenheim Museum in New York, sums it up neatly:

> There's a whole litany of quotations and anecdotes permanently lodged in the brain of anyone who has ever studied art history, truisms that gladden the

> heart and ease the jobs of people who write gallery guides and museum press releases...There is Cézanne's recommendation that painters 'treat nature by the cylinder, the sphere, the cone'; Picasso's assertion that nature and art, being two different things, cannot be the same thing...Closer to our own day is the familiar tale about a couple of aspiring young painters from Washington, D.C., Kenneth Noland and Morris Louis, who early in 1953 visited the New York studio of an even younger Helen Frankenthaler and saw a remarkable picture that she had painted the previous fall, when she was twenty-three; they found that canvas, *Mountains and Sea* (1952), so stimulating that Louis later described Frankenthaler as 'the bridge between Pollock and what was possible'.
>
> Anyone interested in recent American art has heard this story more than once, and *Mountains and Sea,* with its luminous hues, diaphanous shapes and detached fragments of line, has become a kind of icon, regarded as the Urtext of stain painting because of the way Frankenthaler disembodied color by physically merging thinned-out pigment with the very fabric of the canvas.[8]

If the story of what *Mountains and Sea* made possible for ambitious American painting is a familiar one, what made possible the painting of *Mountains and Sea* itself has been thoroughly documented and analysed at the level of formal precedents and procedures. Barbara Rose and John Elderfield plot Frankenthaler's formation as a painter in detail in their respective monographs. They chart the artist's rigorous training in Cubist picture making with Paul Feeley at Bennington College and with Wallace Harrison in New York, the brief period of study with Hans Hofmann in Provincetown, her interest in Miró, Kandinsky, Gorky, and to a lesser extent Matisse, her introduction, through Clement Greenberg, to the work of the most significant painters of the Abstract Expressionist generation, her engagement with the work of de Kooning, and finally, her recognition that it was from the practice of Jackson Pollock that she could move in her own direction.[9]

In an interview with Henry Geldzahler conducted in 1965 for *Artforum*, Frankenthaler dates her first visit to an exhibition of work by Jackson Pollock to 1951. She says:

> The first Pollock show I saw was in 1951 at Betty Parson's gallery, early in the fall, probably September or October. It was staggering. I really felt surrounded. I went with Clement Greenberg who threw me into the room and seemed to say 'Swim.'[10]

Geldzahler then asks: 'Did it affect your work?' Frankenthaler answers:

> No, not immediately, within months. I went out to Springs and saw Pollock and his work, not only the shows. In 1951 I looked at de Kooning as much as Pollock. Earlier Kandinsky and Gorky had led me into what is now called

> 'Abstract Expressionist' painting; but these came after all the Cubist training and exercise. It all combined to push me on. Like Cubism which it came out of, painting in the de Kooning, Gorky idiom was first revealing, then inhibiting to me. I felt many more possibilities in Pollock's work. That is, I looked at and was influenced by both Pollock and de Kooning and eventually felt that there were many more possibilities for me out of the Pollock vocabulary. De Kooning made enclosed linear shapes and 'applied' the brush. Pollock used shoulder and ropes and ignored the edges and corners. I felt I could stretch more in the Pollock framework. I found that in Pollock I also responded to a certain Surreal element – the understated image that was really present: animals, thoughts, jungles, expressions. You could become a de Kooning disciple or satellite or mirror, but you could **depart** from Pollock. [11]

John Elderfield queries the accuracy of Frankenthaler's memory of the date she first saw Pollock's work in the gallery. If indeed it was in the fall of 1951, the exhibition at the Betty Parsons Gallery was of what the literature now refers to as Pollock's 'black and white' paintings, which ran through October and November. According to Elderfield, Frankenthaler was already visiting Pollock's East Hampton studio in the spring of 1951, and had seen some of the black and white works prior to the exhibition. He also argues that, given Frankenthaler's association with Clement Greenberg which began in May 1950, it is inconceivable that she did not see the 'most important and dramatic presentation' of Pollock's allover paintings, which included *Autumn Rhythm, Lavender Mist* and *One Number 31,* at Betty Parsons in November-December 1950.[12] Frankenthaler's remarks to Geldzahler about being 'staggered' and 'surrounded', and later to Rose of finding herself in a 'foreign country', certainly fitted better with an experience of the mural scale works in the 1950 show than with the black and white works of 1951.

Frankenthaler's conflation of the experience of the two exhibitions into the single year, 1951, in the Geldzahler interview, is surely the source of the emphasis placed on the connection between Pollock's black and white works and *Mountains and Sea* by all those who concern themselves with the genesis of the painting. But precisely how Frankenthaler arrived at the free floating, soak-stained colour of *Mountains and Sea* (albeit with residual charcoal drawn marks) from the linear drawing of Pollock's black and white paintings has never been convincingly demonstrated (fig. 4). The technical descriptions of the process are either unhelpfully abridged, or full but convoluted. Those that fall into the first category rely on re-quoting a small section of some remarks Frankenthaler made to Gene Baro published in an article in *Art International* in 1967, to the effect that Pollock's 'fluid calligraphy' enabled her to 'push the development of Cubism so that line *per se* disappeared, but...the memory or function of it remained'.[13] John Elderfield's treatment of the subject of Frankenthaler's debt to the black and white paintings from the chapter on *Mountains and Sea* in his monograph is the definitive extended technical analysis. It is necessary to quote at length to make my point:

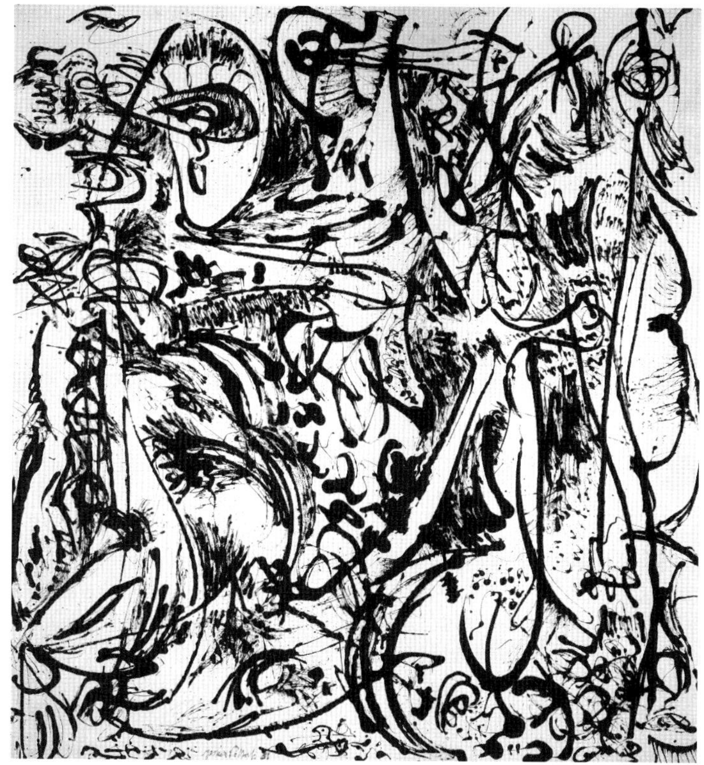

Fig. 4
Jackson Pollock, *Echo (Number 25)*, 1951, enamel on canvas, 91 7/8 x 86 in (233.4 x 218.4 cm) New York, Museum of Modern Art

It was only in rare instances (Number 3, 1951, is the classic example) that Pollock created a picture in which the configuration as a whole reads as being drawn – therefore satisfying his desire for a strong imagist presence – but the limits of that configuration do not because lines have literally been expanded into shapes – spread out as it were, from inside – and shapes, moreover, that thus created by expansion seem unbounded and unenclosed.

Except at their very edges, where they were softened by the capillary action of the contiguous area of untreated canvas, these new shaped lines still had the uniformity of tone and texture that drawn lines possess. Pollock seems consciously to have minimized the tactility and 'interest' of his paint in order to achieve, by minimal textural change from painted to unpainted areas of canvas, an effect of alloverness that offset the designed break in alloverness that tonal contrasts and imagery provided. Alternatively, because drawing is less local to the surface than Pollock's allover drawing, because of

> its tonal contrasts and its image character, the visibly continuous materiality of the canvas is needed to return it to the surface. This is precisely what Frankenthaler, even more than Pollock himself, realized. She also realized that densely uniform paint did not, in fact, allay but only accentuated value contrasts. She therefore thinned down her paint to a greater extent than Pollock's shiny enamel, which still seemed often to sit on top of the canvas. She avoided (almost entirely at first) black paint. And she usually gave painterly interest to the interior of shapes. As a result she was able to retain, indeed expand, Pollock's concern with imagery – but also to transform his draftsmanlike, and hence still tactile approach to imagery to the creation of a more purely painterly, visual art...she blended draftsmanship and the illusion of painterliness in a radically new way.[14]

This is an analysis published in 1989 in a monograph devoted to a survey of Frankenthaler's work into the 1980s. It is written with knowledge of later works, in particular a group of paintings made in the second half of the 1950s of which *Eden* (1956) is the best example. The technical procedures John Elderfield describes here more accurately apply to such later works than to what is actually in evidence as the material surface of *Mountains and Sea*. Just how Helen Frankenthaler arrived at the 'surface-matter' of *Mountains and Sea* on 26th October 1952 may be much more straightforward.[15]

Two events occurred in the spring and summer of 1952 just before the painting was made. The first one appears in all the literature. The second one does not appear at all. In the summer of 1952 Helen Frankenthaler went on holiday. She went on a motoring trip to Nova Scotia and Cape Breton where she 'did landscapes with folding easel equipment'.[16] This is the event that we all know about. The other one, which curiously, given the lengths to which Barbara Rose and John Elderfield both go in their monographs to detail the lead-up to *Mountains and Sea*, is never mentioned. In the spring of 1952 The Art Institute of Chicago and the Metropolitan Museum of Art, New York, collaborated to present an international loan exhibition of one hundred and twenty eight works by Paul Cézanne. It was installed in Chicago in February and March, and in New York in April and May. I want to speculate here upon a link between these two events and the appearance (in both the sense of its sudden arrival, and the way it looked) of *Mountains and Sea* in October.

Obviously there can be no disputing Frankenthaler's profound engagement with Jackson Pollock's painting practice at the beginning of the 1950s. As well as formal resources it offered the example of a life dedicated to art. At the level of anecdote, Larry Rivers recalled a visit he paid with Frankenthaler to Pollock's studio, probably sometime in 1951:

> While I may not have been a great admirer of Pollock, I think I admired the fact that he was an artist. I mean that he did this thing and did it all the time

> and was very serious. Had very large canvases. Had a barn in which he painted.
>
> I went out there with Helen Frankenthaler and we did one of these very youthful things. We walked to the sea, where we promised each other that we would really devote our lives to art.[17]

Undoubtedly *Mountains and Sea* was the first work in which Frankenthaler's engagement with 'the best painter of a whole generation' was fully registered at several levels.[18] By October 1952 when she painted *Mountains and Sea*, not only had Frankenthaler, to extend her own metaphor, learned the language of Pollock's foreign country, she also had significantly added to the vocabulary to describe aspects of the place of which Pollock was hardly aware. This, I want to argue, was substantially due to her arrival by another route: through Cézanne's Country.

An exhibition and three essays

Cézanne. Paintings, Watercolors, & Drawings: A Loan Exhibition presented by The Art Institute of Chicago in collaboration with The Metropolitan Museum of Art, New York, in 1952 was heralded by the January issue of *Art Digest* as 'the most important exhibition of the season'. Its installation in Chicago was marked by the same journal in its February issue, with an article called 'A Cézanne Exhibition: A Definition of Greatness', by James Fitzsimmons, in which he described the exhibition in the following terms:

> It adds up to the largest Cézanne exhibition we have had, and it might affect painting in this country to a considerable extent. For despite all that the expressionists, the fauves and the cubists have learned from Cézanne, much remains to be learned from his handling of color, from his use of line.[19]

An essay by Erle Loran himself, called 'Cézanne in 1952', came out in *The Chicago Art Institute Quarterly* also in February.[20] When the show reached New York in April, *Art News* for that month reproduced details from four Cézanne paintings on its cover, and printed an article by Theodore Rousseau Jr. called, 'Cézanne as an old master' which took the exhibition as an opportunity to consider Cézanne, 'in relation to the great tradition he revered'.[21] *The New Yorker* covered the show on April 12, and it was still being discussed in the September edition of American *Connoisseur*.[22] This was a well-publicised, major art world event in 1952. We also know that Clement Greenberg saw it.

In June 1952 the *American Mercury* published an article by Greenberg called 'Cézanne: Gateway to Contemporary Painting'. The final paragraph of the piece reads:

> Those fortunate enough to have visited the large international exhibition of Cézanne's oils, watercolors, and drawings that was installed through February

> and March of this year at the Art Institute of Chicago, and through April and much of May at the Metropolitan Museum of Art in New York, must surely have recognized the source of many things they had already seen in later painting. Some of the late landscapes – which I feel to be the culmination of Cézanne's art – are certainly as striking and as 'extreme' as a good deal of our best contemporary work.[23]

It is a well-documented fact that in 1951 and 1952 Helen Frankenthaler and Clement Greenberg spent a great deal of time in one another's company. They visited the studios of other artists, socialised on 'the scene' and went to exhibitions together. From John Elderfield's research we know for certain that Frankenthaler saw the Arshille Gorky retrospective at the Whitney Museum that ran through January of 1951, and the Henri Matisse exhibition at the Museum of Modern Art, installed from November 1951 to January 1952. To echo Elderfield's words on the subject of Frankenthaler's first visit to a Pollock exhibition, to me it is inconceivable that Frankenthaler did not see the 1952 Cézanne show at the Metropolitan Museum of Art, and more than likely that she saw it in the company of Clement Greenberg.

What is apparent, from the evidence of photographs alone, is that another way Frankenthaler and Greenberg spent their time, both together and separately, in the early 1950s was out of doors painting landscape. There is a photograph from 1950, reproduced in Mary Emma Harris's history of Black Mountains College, of Greenberg, Theodore Stamos and some female students on an outdoor painting excursion.[24] Greenberg taught on the summer school programme at the College that year and Frankenthaler joined him there for a week in August, where she made some watercolours and a small ink drawing on paper called *At Black Mountain*. According to John Elderfield Frankenthaler was already painting seriously outdoors in the landscape in July 1950 when she spent three weeks studying with Hans Hofmann at his summer school in Provincetown Massachusetts. He writes:

> The process of retracing the drawing and therefore the depths of Cubism but freeing herself from the Cubist style began at Provincetown. It began however, not in the studio and not in the specific context of 'modern art', but in nature and in the testing of 'modern art' ideas against the resistance afforded by direct confrontation with the natural world.[25]

In the chronology of her monograph Barbara Rose reproduces a photograph of Frankenthaler and Greenberg, with canvases propped against chairs, making landscape studies at David Smith's Terminal Ironworks at Bolton Landing.[26] Rose dates the photograph sometime in 1952. That summer Clement Greenberg accompanied Frankenthaler on the sketching trip to Nova Scotia.

John Elderfield's commentary on Frankenthaler's outdoor painting activities in Provincetown provides the cue for the introduction of the subject of the appearance of an interest in Cézanne in Greenberg's critical writing, an interest that runs roughly parallel with the landscape painting activities of painter and critic at the beginning of the 1950s. The quote brings together the ideas of 'modern art' and 'nature'. Elderfield's assessment of what Frankenthaler was doing at Provincetown in 1950: 'testing modern art ideas against the resistance afforded by direct confrontation with the natural world', glosses the argument of an essay by Greenberg called, 'The Role of Nature in Modern Painting', published in *Partisan Review* in January 1949. Greenberg states that his aim in this essay is to 'ascertain how Cubism...arrived at its characteristic form of purity and unity'.[27] He concludes that it was because the style maintained a reference to the structure of nature. In this the Cubist painters followed Cézanne who 'sought for the decisive structure of things that lay permanently under the accidents of momentary appearance'.[28] But because of their growing interest in the material nature of the picture plane itself it was only by:

> transposing the internal logic by which objects are organized in nature [that] aesthetic form could be given to the irreducible flatness which defined the picture plane in its inviolable quality as material object...Nature no longer offered appearances to imitate, but principles to parallel.[29]

If in 1949 Greenberg cites Cézanne only in passing as the origin of a modern abstract art whose coherence, substantiality and purity comes from the analogy between its formal structure and the structure of the natural world, by 1951 his work has become significant enough to warrant a whole essay devoted to it: 'Cézanne and The Unity of Modern Art.' By now Greenberg is writing of Cézanne as:

> The most copious source of what we know as modern art, the most abundant generator of ideas and the most enduring in newness. The modernity of his art, its very stylishness – more than a retroactive effect – continues.[30]

The essay opens with a defence of the diverse tendencies that make up modern art, against charges of proliferation as a symptom of its decline. Once the new manifestations of Surrealism have been 'consigned to the outer darkness of academicism in general, where they really belong – the scene', according to Greenberg, 'becomes more orderly'.[31] There are, he says, really only four or five different strands that can be detected in 'genuinely contemporary painting and sculpture' and these take up the 'loose threads' left untied by the instigators of the modern movement in the latter half of the nineteenth century.[32] He names Cézanne as the most abundant source of ideas yet to be followed through to their conclusions. For Greenberg, the 'unfading modernity' of Cézanne lies in what he sees as the paradox involved in his practice, that is, Cézanne's attempt to 'save the intrinsic principle of the Western tradition of painting: its concern with an ample and literal rendition of the illusion of the third dimension', without abandoning the 'independent abstractness of the formal facts', and the 'tangibility' of the medium of painting. The result of this was that:

> A new and powerful kind of pictorial tension was set up such as had not been seen in the West since the mosaic murals of fourth and fifth century Rome. The little overlapping rectangles of paint, laid on with no attempt to fuse their dividing edges, drew the depicted forms towards the surface while, at the same time, the modeling and contouring of these forms, as achieved by the paint dabs, pulled them back again into illusionistic depths. The result was a never-ending vibration from front to back and back to front.[33]

This pictorial tension is, for Greenberg, 'the emblem both of originality and mastery. It is present in all successful art, but is particularly, uniquely, perhaps more immediately, there in the works of Cézanne's old age.'[34]

By June 1952, and the essay 'Cézanne: Gateway to Contemporary Painting', the tension between spatial illusion and self sufficient surface has become an 'ambiguity' that Greenberg considers 'one of the largest sources of pleasure in art'.[35] In the final sentence of the essay he concludes that:

> For this and other reasons there is no better way for anyone who wants to learn to enjoy – not 'understand' – modern art than to apply himself to the pictures of the master from Aix.[36]

If evidence is needed for the mounting significance of Cézanne in Greenberg's thinking about the future direction of an American contemporary practice of painting, a glance at the evolution of the titles of the 1949, 1951 and 1952 essays should make it plain: 'The Role of Nature in Modern Painting', 'Cézanne and the Unity of Modern Art', 'Cézanne: Gateway to Contemporary Painting'.

In the context of Greenberg's critical foray into Cézanne's country, and the landscape painting activity of Frankenthaler and Greenberg in the country around New York, the Art Institute of Chicago/Metropolitan Museum of Art 1952 Cézanne exhibition was surely an event of considerable interest to them both. So let us speculate that they went to see it together. What did they see there? The one hundred and twenty eight works recorded in the exhibition catalogue come from all periods and represent most aspects of Cézanne's oeuvre, from 1860 to 1906.[37] Thirty-eight works were landscape studies in oil, watercolour and pencil from the late 1880s through to 1906.[38] There were five oil paintings and one drawing of L'Estaque made in the late 1880s; four of the oils were the views of the sea from L'Estaque (fig. 5). There was a study of the Lake of Annecy from 1896, and five oil paintings of Mont Sainte-Victoire. There were twelve watercolour landscape studies from around 1900, three of which had Mont Sainte-Victoire as their motif. From James Fitzsimmons's review of the exhibition

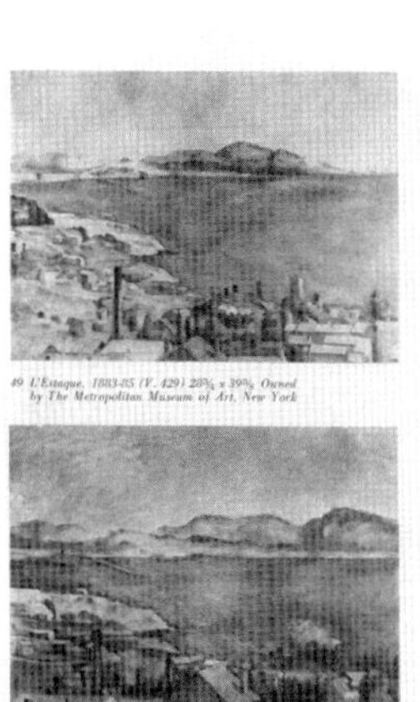

49 L'Estaque, 1883-85 (V. 429) 28¾ x 39⅝ Owned by The Metropolitan Museum of Art, New York

50 L'Estaque, 1886-90 (V. 493) 31½ x 38⅝ Owned by The Art Institute of Chicago

51 Gardanne, 1885-86 (V. 435) 24¾ x 35⅞ Presented to the United States Government in Memory of Charles A. Loeser. Lent by the United States Government. Gardanne is a small town near Aix.

Two versions of *L'Estaque (Nos. 49 & 50)* show how differently he approached the same spot. The first is a suavely balanced composition, the second a highly dramatic simplification. Round 1885-86 Cézanne became so geometric that his landscapes anticipate abstract painting by twenty years. "Treat nature by the cylinder, the sphere, the cone," he counseled Emile Bernard. "Lines parallel to the horizon give breadth . . . Lines perpendicular to this horizon give depth. But nature for us men is more depth than surface whence the need of introducing into our light vibrations, represented by reds and yellows, a sufficient amount of blue to give the impression of air." At the insignificant little village of Gardanne where he began to paint in 1886 such geometry and logic reach their height.

During the '80s, Cézanne often visited the aged Monticelli in Marseilles, grew friendly with Renoir who stayed with him at L'Estaque and who for a brief time came under Cézanne's influence. In 1882, one of Cézanne's portraits was slipped into the Salon through the intervention of a friend, Guillemet, who was a member of the Jury. In 1886, after years of bitter quarreling with his father over Hortense Fiquet, he married her in the presence of his parents.

Fig. 5
Paintings of *L' Estaque* by Paul Cézanne in the catalogue of
Cézanne: Paintings, Watercolors and Drawings: A Loan Exhibition, 1952

we know that all the watercolours and drawings were shown separately from the works in oil and filled two galleries. That would have been an impressive and rich concentration of work on paper. We know that at that time Frankenthaler was already keenly involved with the possibilities offered by working on paper. According to Karen Wilkin, who curated a show of Frankenthaler's works on paper from 1949-1984:

> Working on paper, in a wide variety of media, was extremely important to Frankenthaler at the start of her career...before *Mountains and Sea*, some of her most accomplished – and largest – early pictures were realized in gouache, watercolor, charcoal and crayon on photographer's backdrop paper.[39]

Both Wilkin and Elderfield also stress the importance to Frankenthaler of a watercolour made in 1951 called *Great Meadows* (pl. 2), which the artist regards as a harbinger of *Mountains and Sea*.[40]

At the end of the James Fitzsimmon's *Art Digest* review of the exhibition there is an interesting piece of information. Fitzsimmons writes that the last gallery of the show was given over to 'an ingenious and effective series of comparative photographs, color charts and other visual devices which analyze the characteristics of Cézanne's art'.[41] The photographs, not reproduced in the exhibition catalogue, but which it is fairly safe to speculate included images by Loran and Rewald, would

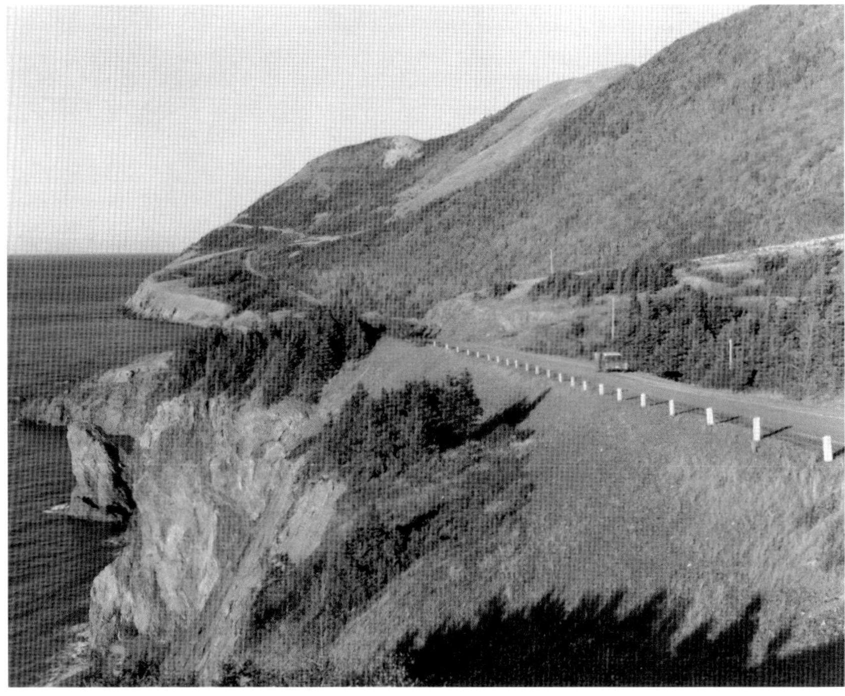

Fig. 6
Cap Rouge on the Cabot Trail, c.1956

have done something else as well: they would have brought to the attention of the exhibition visitor the characteristics of Cézanne's Country.

On holiday in Nova Scotia

I want now to present an imaginary scenario based on the kinds of things we have evidence young artists – and art historians do, like dashing off to Aix-en-Provence to see what Cézanne's Country looks like, and pledging their lives to painting on visits to artists they admire. It is a story about why Helen Frankenthaler and Clement Greenberg chose Nova Scotia as their holiday destination in the summer of 1952. It goes like this. With their current enthusiasm for Cézanne and painting landscapes out of doors, artist and critic visit the Cézanne exhibition at the Metropolitan Museum of Art in New York and see there the extraordinary collection of the artist's late landscape work. By comparison their attempts at painting in front of nature look pretty meagre. The problem, they decide, is that the studies they have been making are simply not ambitious enough, not hard won enough. The reason for this is that the settings of their own sketching trips, Bolton Landing, Provincetown, Black Mountain College, established artists' summer

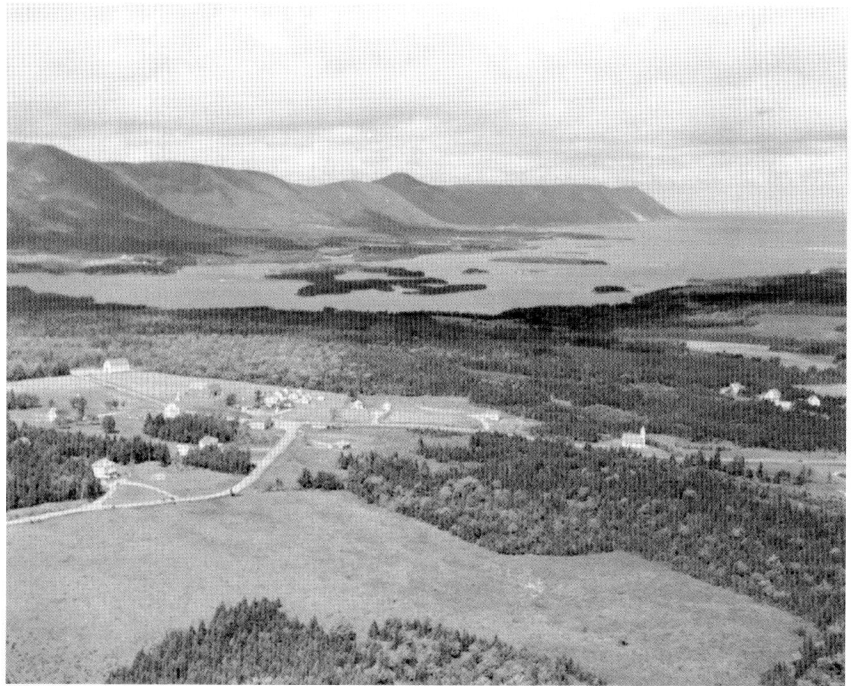

Fig. 7
Village of Cape North, c.1954

vacation spots and out of town studio locations, are, compared with the isolation and extremes of Cézanne's Provence in the 1890s, just too domesticated, not 'nature' enough. What they need is a confrontation with nature proper – and the closest piece of that is in Nova Scotia.

The photographs of Cape Breton Island and Pictou County, Nova Scotia taken between 1951 and 1959, supplied to me by the Graphic Materials Division of the Nova Scotia Public Archives, show the Cape Breton coast road, known as the Cabot Trail, winding through rugged mountainous terrain (fig. 6). In some photographs the mountains appear to run straight down to the open sea. In others they drop towards more sheltered stretches of water in long fjord-like channels which open out into inland lakes. There are spots where, from one side of the channel, it is possible to look across a stretch of water to mountains rising up behind it on the far side (fig. 7). The place names written underneath the photographs are mostly French – PresQu'ile, Cape Rouge, Isle Madame. In an interview Frankenthaler commented that, '…you find the combination of mountains and sea in few places here: in America only on the West Coast in the Big Sur area. It was that juxtaposition that struck me that summer in Nova Scotia.'[42] Striking the landscape might have been, but the combination of mountains and sea, was not, I would like to wager, a surprise (the quote itself seems structured as the answer to the question: where do you go in America to find the combination of mountains and sea?) I want to suggest that Nova Scotia was chosen as a summer destination precisely because it was a landscape in which that juxtaposition occurred: that the decision to travel there was prompted by the desire for a landscape that contained elements 'nature' enough, and 'Cézannian' enough to encourage a picking up of those 'loose threads' that Greenberg had been arguing in his essays were potentially a 'gateway' to new directions in contemporary painting.

Frankenthaler kept a journal during the Nova Scotia/Cape Breton trip. An entry for July 31 reads: 'NS (Nova Scotia) is clean and beautiful. Mountains and Sea ride to Picton extra special.'[43] Let us imagine this: as artist and critic drove along the curving coast roads (navigating perhaps, from a map full of French place-names) another landscape, we might call it a day-dreamed one, composed of still vivid images from the Metropolitan Museum exhibition, of *The Sea from L'Estaque*, *The Lake of Annecy* and various *Mont Sainte-Victoire* studies, unfurled before them across the actual landscape of Nova Scotia. The mountains and sea ride to Picton was 'extra special' because it in particular lent itself to a viewing through the memory of Cézanne's Mont Sainte-Victoire and L'Estaque studies. Back in the studio in New York, the double experience of the Metropolitan Museum Cézanne exhibition and sketching in the Nova Scotia landscape was registered on canvas as a single image: *Mountains and Sea.*

Without any reference to the 1952 Metropolitan Museum Cézanne exhibition, John Elderfield does, however, devote a long paragraph to the importance to Frankenthaler of the watercolours of both Cézanne and John Marin in the chapter on *Mountains and Sea* in his monograph, part of which reads as follows:

> The landscape subjects that Marin and Cézanne both used probably encouraged the making of lighter pictures for the brighter illumination that plein-air painting can provide tends to bunch together value contrasts at the lighter end of the color spectrum. Watercolor, however, expands the brightness and flatness of plein-air painting because it visibly reveals these qualities in the whiteness of its support, which always makes its presence felt due to the insubstantiality of its covering. Marin and Cézanne were important to Frankenthaler not only for their watercolors or for the lightness of their work, but, more importantly, because both of them had liberated their oil paintings by treating them like watercolors, which was what Frankenthaler began to do...In Cézanne's case this transposition of techniques also encouraged him to leave uncovered areas of white canvas between patches of thinned-down oil. This was especially interesting to Frankenthaler too.[44]

For many years now I have had pinned, side-by-side on the wall above my desk, a colour reproduction of *Mountains and Sea* and a colour reproduction of a Cézanne *Mont Sainte-Victoire* watercolour study, dated 1900-1906, from the collection of Mr and Mrs Henry Pearlman (pl. 3).[45] The affinity I saw between the two works was the starting point for the argument of this chapter. The use of unpainted areas of canvas is only one of several points of correspondence between *Mountains and Sea* and the late *Mont Sainte-Victoire* watercolour . The most striking similarity is not so much the unpainted areas of canvas as the colour of the painted ones. The blues and greens, ochre and pink are common to both. So is the overall triangular shape of the composition within the four sides of the picture. Admittedly, a comparison of the works in reproduction, with both reduced to roughly the same size when in actuality the Cézanne watercolour measures 12 ¼ x 18 ¾ in (31 x 47.6 cm) and *Mountains and Sea* 86 ⅝ x 117 ¼ in (220 x 297.8 cm), is a questionable one. Yet in the presence of *Mountains and Sea* in the space of the gallery the sense of the canvas as the sum of Frankenthaler's formation as a painter up to that moment, projected large through the small lens of a Cézanne watercolour, grows rather than diminishes.

Cézanne's Country in the studio

Frankenthaler's account of making *Mountains and Sea*, as reported by Gene Baro in his 1967 *Art International* article, captures all the excitement of a 'breakthrough'. I quote it in full here:

> I was then starting to use a concoction of housepaint enamel, turpentine and/or kerosene, and tube oil paints in varying amounts, mixed and spilled from empty coffee cans, both with and without the aid of wide brushes, on unsized cotton duck. Before I had always painted on sized and primed canvas – but my paint was becoming thinner and more fluid and cried out to be soaked, not resting. In 'Mountains and Sea', I put in the charcoal line gestures first, because I wanted to draw in with color and shape the totally abstract memory of landscape. I spilled on the drawing in paint from the coffee cans. The charcoal lines were original guideposts that eventually became unnecessary...I got up on a ladder after I made the picture, and looked down at it, and called to Friedel who was in his 'half' – we had a divider – to take a look. We were both sort of amazed and surprised and interested. Clem [Greenberg] and I...talked on the phone late afternoon to arrange evening plans and Friedel got on and ebulliently told him to come on over and look at the picture I'd just made. We all agreed that it was 'finished' and shouldn't be touched; that is complete and shouldn't be added to (I've often had temptations to dot the i and wreck the picture – only rear guard eyes need that spelling out.) In charcoal, I marked it 10/26/52, lower right. So Friedel helped me to staple it to the wall, and Clem encouraged me to go ahead and make more. I did in all kinds of combinations and possibilities; I couldn't try them out fast enough.[46]

The statement also indicates, however, that Frankenthaler did have a plan for the work before beginning: 'I wanted to draw in with color and shape the totally abstract memory of landscape.' One of the surprises of seeing the work for the first time in the gallery, (perhaps the result of years of exposure to various snippets of that much quoted heat of the moment account of its making) is how controlled the paint application actually is, and just how considered is each mark in relation to its neighbour, or neighbouring unpainted area. As well as 'spilled' paint there are two areas of the work where it is obvious that the paint has been in the one case manipulated with a brush after it has been spilled, and in the other not spilled at all but placed with a brush or something else (see pl.1). The first area is the blue horizontal band that runs off the right edge of the canvas where there are signs that liquid paint has been brushed into shape; the second is much more interesting. At the base of the canvas, and off-centre, a square blue mark abuts a leaf-shaped green one, they look like marks made with a large brush and their regular shape sets them apart from all the other marks on the canvas. John Elderfield makes reference to the leaf-green disc, 'placed at the very bottom' of the canvas, in his detailed analysis of the painting. In his opinion, 'On this spot the entire composition is balanced and suspended.'[47] I want to try something else: I want to suggest that the abutted blue and green marks are a sign of the work's dialogue with Cézanne. The shape, colour and relationship of the two marks resemble nothing so much as those used by Cézanne to build the foregrounds and middle-grounds of his late *Mont Sainte-Victoire* watercolour studies. And I want to go one step further to conjecture that the marks were either the first two placed on the canvas as a statement of Frankenthaler's intention to recall the landscape of Nova Scotia through the medium of a Cézanne watercolour, or that they were made at the completion of the painting as an acknowledgement of what she herself recognised only when she reached the top of her ladder. That was that the 'totally abstract memory' of the Nova Scotia landscape had appeared as a transformed Cézanne watercolour.

Perhaps this was a source of the excitement. The story Frankenthaler told Gene Baro about making the painting is a compelling 'breakthrough' narrative. It has all the ingredients: the young painter in the studio experimenting with the new techniques of the contemporary painter she most admires; the unprimed canvas on the floor, the thinned down paint, not dripped here but spilled, the revelation at the top of the ladder of something amazing, surprising and interesting enough to call over, right away, the foremost judge and supporter of ambitious American painting; the immediate dating of the work as a mark of its completion and significance. It is all there, all that is, except the slightest indication of what exactly it was about the painting they all found so amazing, surprising, and interesting.

In the essay 'Killing Men and Dying Women: A Woman's Touch in the Cold Zone of American Painting in the 1950s', Griselda Pollock discusses the problem of how to 'see' what artists who are women produce because:

> Their works come to us ready 'framed' by existing art historical discourses that define the meaning of the period and practices within which the artists worked. Such frames can make the work perfectly invisible, and worse, illegible except as something lacking in relation to what the dominant discourse produces as the canon. Art historical discourse already inscribes its own privileging of the masculine in art as the norm, leaving us feminists to fit the women in, against the grain of what has been validated as the centre of the artistic moment.[48]

Of course we cannot argue that *Mountains and Sea* is invisible in the formalist art historical discourse that has until recently defined the development of New York school painting in the 1950s: it has its place. My point is that the view of what the painting was on that exciting day in 1952 is obscured by what it became in May 1960 when, eight years after the event it made its first and last, brief appearance in Clement Greenberg's art criticism in an article in *Art International* about Morris Louis and Kenneth Noland: 'His first sight of the middle period Pollocks and of a large and extraordinary painting done in 1952 by Helen Frankenthaler, called *Mountains and Sea*, led Louis to change his direction abruptly.'[49] 'We were interested in Pollock but could gain no lead from him,' Kenneth Noland told a journalist a year later in 1961; 'Frankenthaler showed us a way – a way to think about, and use color.' Morris Louis summed it up, 'She was the bridge between Pollock and what was possible.'[50] According to Greenberg, staining as Louis developed it 'conveys a sense not only of color as somehow disembodied, and therefore more purely optical, but also of color as a thing which opens and expands the picture plane.'[51] As Anne Wagner has noted, the logic of painting, as Greenberg and Michael Fried perceived its development in the late 1950s and early 1960s towards the value of disembodied opticality, 'efficiently subordinates Frankenthaler's own artistic project to that logic'.[52] It persists in retrospective claims for *Mountains and Sea* as a direct development of Pollock's fluid black drawn line into expanding fields of stained colour.

It makes more sense to understand the treatment and disposition of colour in *Mountains and Sea* as the trace of Frankenthaler's renewed interest in Cézanne in 1952. The charcoal 'guideposts' may well have been 'Gorky-derived'[53] but they also recall the pencil skeleton of a Cézanne watercolour. Most Cézanne-like is the way the work organises itself spatially in an un-tethered relationship between painted and unpainted areas of canvas quite *unlike* Pollock's 1951 works in which the relationship between the 'black' and 'white' areas is one of either/or reversibility and mutual dependence: one defines itself against the other. The unpainted areas read either as solid figures, as in *Number 14*, 1951 (fig. 8) or, more rarely, as airy space that, in Frankenthaler's own description, 'goes on forever', as in *Echo: Number 25*, 1951.[54] In general the tendency in the 'black and white' works is to bind or shape the white areas (whether they read as figure or spacious ground) with the black lines, which often accumulate to form dense patches. Because of

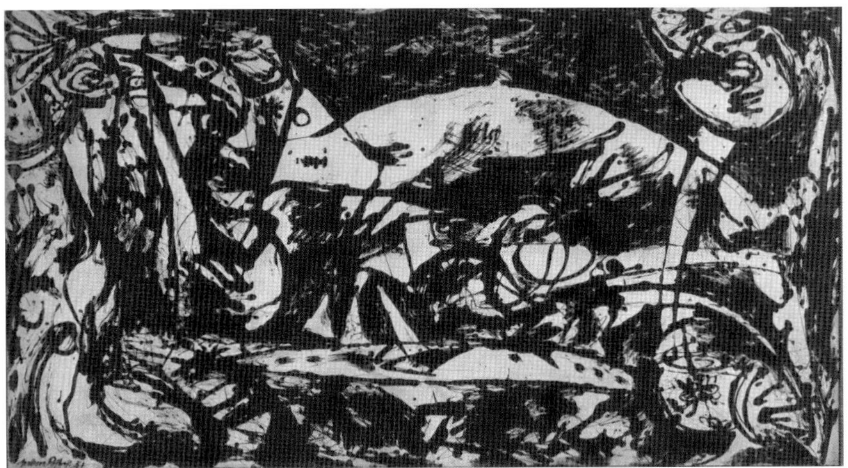

Fig. 8
Jackson Pollock, *Number 14*, 1951, enamel on canvas,
57 ⅝ x 107 in (146.4 x 271.8 cm) Tate Gallery, London

the tonally modulated washes in a late Cézanne watercolour the unpainted areas do not read as relying solely for their existence on the painted marks, nor are the marks shaped by the surrounding unpainted areas. In *Mountains and Sea* Pollock's 'white' areas are cut loose to float free of their defining 'black' mark, and vice versa. A legacy, I suggest, of Frankenthaler's timely exposure to a concentration of Cézanne's late watercolour studies in the Metropolitan Museum exhibition in the spring of 1952.

The scale of *Mountains and Sea*, the unprimed canvas, liquid paint, are all Pollock's: 'the understated image that was really present', landscape-like in the 'black and white' painting *Number 14* (1951) existed as an exhilarating, liberating precedent empowering Frankenthaler to risk the move of enlarging the function of colour and unmarked ground in a tiny Cézanne watercolour study to the massive scale of ambitious, contemporary New York painting. In the process new things happened, things that did not happen in a work either by Cézanne or by Pollock. But although they were new, it was tradition that had been mined for its unused resources to provide the material with which to take the developments of contemporary painting in a new direction. In this respect *Mountains and Sea* represented a profound example of the value of looking again at Cézanne as Greenberg had been advocating in 'Cézanne and The Unity of Modern Art', and 'Cézanne: Gateway to Contemporary Painting'. Or perhaps the initiative was as much Frankenthaler's?

It is not difficult to make a case to suggest that for the sections of close technical analysis of Cézanne's work, particularly in the 1951 essay, Greenberg drew on Frankenthaler's practical training and knowledge as a painter, and a visual education more thorough than his own. In the autumn of 1949 Frankenthaler attended a course in art history at Columbia University with Meyer Schapiro. In 1952, the year of the Cézanne exhibition and of *Mountains and Sea,* Abrams published Schapiro's book on Cézanne in the *Library of Great Painters* series, and also as a portfolio edition. The course Schapiro taught at Columbia University in the autumn of 1949 was called 'Modern Painting from 1848 -1900'. Although there is no record of the content of each lecture, the course must surely have included a study of Cézanne drawn from Schapiro's work for his book on the artist.[55]

Whatever the balance of interest and understanding of painter and critic in the work of Cézanne in the early 1950s, it is unimaginable that Greenberg did not recognise the achievement of Frankenthaler's engagement with its resources in *Mountains and Sea.* Yet he did not publicly acknowledge the significance of the painting when it was first shown in Frankenthaler's second solo exhibition at the Tibor de Nagy Gallery in February 1953, even though less than a month later he considered it important enough to invite Kenneth Noland and Morris Louis to travel from Washington to New York to examine it in Frankenthaler's studio.[56] He did not write about it when it was shown again in New York at the Stable Gallery in 1955.[57] The role of catalyst in which the influential critic eventually cast the painting has resulted in a critical blindness to how and what it meant in its own right at the time it was made. On 25 May 1960 *Mountains and Sea* entered the art historical canon as a 'bridge between Pollock and what was possible', but on 26th October 1952 it was an astonishing picture of what Cézanne's Country offered a young, ambitious, American painter who happened to be a woman profoundly involved in her own project to 'depart from Pollock'.[58]

2

1927: OTHER COUNTRIES, OTHER CÉZANNES

> How could one express in words these emotions of the body? Express that emptiness there?
>
> Virginia Woolf [1]

As difficult as a Cézanne

In April 1939 Virginia Woolf began the autobiographical essay 'A Sketch of the Past' as a break from work on her biography of the art critic and painter Roger Fry. Woolf opens the essay by stating her immediate problem: how to write a memoir. As a great reader of memoirs she knows the many ways in which it might be done. But it is not until she begins to write that a possible form emerges to: 'include the present – at least enough of the present to serve as a platform to stand upon'.[2] Thus, scenes of the past are written from the moment of Woolf's present life, the years 1939-1940, conveyed by recording daily events and fragments of conversation with friends. Not far into the essay she writes:

> May 15th 1939. The drudgery of making a coherent life of Roger has once more become intolerable, and so I turn for a few days' respite to May 1895. The little platform of present time on which I stand is, so far as the weather is concerned, damp and chilly. I look up at my skylight – over the litter of *Athenaeum* articles, Fry letters – all strewn with sand from the house that is being pulled down next door – I look up and see, as if reflecting it, a sky the colour of dirty water. And the inner landscape is much of a piece. Last night Mark Gertler dined here and denounced the vulgarity, the inferiority of what he called 'literature'; compared with the integrity of painting. 'For it always deals with Mr and Mrs Brown,' – he said – with the personal, the trivial, that is; a criticism which has its sting and its chill, like the May sky. Yet if one could give a sense of my mother's personality one would have to be an artist. It would be as difficult to do that, as it should be done, as to paint a Cézanne.[3]

This passage contains several chains of association, which intersect at the point where Woolf conjoins two things, the idea of giving a 'sense' of her mother's personality, and the image of a Cézanne painting. The concluding two sentences of this passage are an astonishing acknowledgement by Woolf, at the very beginning of a project deeply concerned with describing what she can remember of the presence and personality of her mother, Julia Stephen, and of the futility of attempting this through the act of writing. Why did she think it could only be done in painting? And why only in the particular kind of painting signified by the name Cézanne? What constitutes the difficulty involved in this kind of painting, and why does Woolf link it to the task of giving a 'sense' of her mother's personality? These are the questions I want to begin to pursue by tracking the associative links from which the conjunction of these two ideas emerges in a process of memoir writing conceived at its outset as a 'sketch'.[4]

Virginia Woolf first met Roger Fry in 1910, the year in which, at the invitation of the directors of the Grafton Gallery, he brought together the exhibition of modern French art, entitled *Manet and the Post-Impressionists*.[5] It opened to what Woolf describes in her biography of Fry as 'paroxysms of rage and laughter' from the public, and a violent division of opinion about the value of the work among the critics and contemporary British artists.[6] The exhibition ran from 8 November 1910 to 15 January 1911. Fourteen years later, on 18 May 1924, in a lecture delivered to the Cambridge Heretics Society called 'Character in Fiction', Woolf asserted that 'on or about December 1910 human character changed'.[7] The lecture re-works and expands an earlier essay on modern fiction written partly as a response to Arnold Bennett's review of her 1923 novel *Jacob's Room* in which he criticised her handling of character. At issue is the question of realism.[8] In the opinion of Arnold Bennett the novel can only succeed if the characters are 'real'. But what, asks Woolf is reality? In 'Character in Fiction' Woolf argues that the conventions of the Edwardian novel in which a character is built from minutely detailed descriptions of the material circumstances of her life are no longer adequate for the contemporary writer:

> I knew that if I began describing the cancer and the calico of my Mrs Brown, that vision to which I cling though I know of no way of imparting it to you, would have been dulled and tarnished forever.
>
> That is what I mean by saying that the Edwardian tools are the wrong ones for us to use. They have given us a house in the hope that we might be able to deduce the human beings who live there…But if you hold that novels are in the first place about people, and only second about the houses they live in, that is the wrong way to set about it. Therefore you see the Georgian writer had to begin by throwing away the method that was in use at the moment. He was left alone there facing Mrs Brown without any method of conveying her to the reader.[9]

In the preface to the catalogue of the second Post Impressionist Exhibition held in 1912 Roger Fry reviewed the English public's response to the first exhibition in 1910. He argued that the works exhibited there represented 'a reconsideration of the very purpose and aim as well as the methods of pictorial and plastic art'.[10] The sense of outrage felt by the public arose from a misunderstanding of what the artists set out to do:

> The difficulty springs from a deep-rooted conviction, due to long established custom, that the aim of painting is the descriptive imitation of natural forms. Now these artists do not seek to give what can, after all, be but a pale reflex of actual appearance, but to arouse the conviction of a new and definite reality. They do not seek to imitate form, but to create form; not to imitate life, but to find an equivalent for life...In fact, they aim not at illusion but at reality.[11]

Fry's arrival on the scene in 'Bloomsbury' at the beginning of 1910 shifted 'everyone's conversational attention' from philosophy to art.[12] Woolf's formal experiments in fiction, then, developed alongside the attempts of art critics, Clive Bell as well as Roger Fry, to interpret and explain new French painting and sculpture in the context of its first exposure in England. The essay 'Character in Fiction' registers the impact, signified as the unexplained reference to December 1910, of the lessons of *Manet and the Post-Impressionists.* Or perhaps we should say more accurately that it registers less the direct impact of the paintings themselves as Fry's interpretation of the formal innovation of the work as an attempt to find an 'equivalent to life', a 'new and definite reality'.[13] If Woolf's 'vision' of the reality of Mrs Brown was to be achieved, new 'tools', on the analogy with those developed in the field of visual art, had to be forged in the discipline of fiction writing. She pursued that vision in the formal experimentation that produced the novels *To the Lighthouse* and *The Waves.*

With this knowledge in mind it is not difficult to imagine the painful impact on Woolf of Mark Gertler's comment at dinner in 1939, so close, as we now know, to the end of her working life. When the painter aims at her his denunciation of literature as inferior compared to the 'integrity' of painting, he does so with deadly accuracy with his reference to 'Mr and Mrs Brown'. That Woolf took his comment as a judgement of the failure of her own efforts in literature we might take as signified by the image in which she registers its effect: 'a criticism which had its sting, and its chill, like the May sky'. In the passage immediately preceding the Gertler episode Woolf writes of her mother's death early in the morning of 5 May 1895:

> I leaned out of the nursery window the morning she died. It was about six, I suppose. I saw Dr Seton walk away up the street with his head bent and his hands clasped behind his back. I got a feeling of calm, sadness, and finality.

> It was a beautiful blue spring morning, and very still. That brings back the feeling that everything had come to an end.[14]

Here in this small section of 'A Sketch of the Past' a meditation on death, memory, the problems of writing a 'coherent' life, a sense of failure in the practice of art, but also the idea of art as a practice in which some sort of retrieval is attempted, ends with the invocation of the name Cézanne. Why might this be?

The straightforward explanation leads back to Woolf's association with Roger Fry and what in her biography of the critic she consistently describes as Fry's 'excitement' about Cézanne. In the essay 'Retrospect', Fry writes about his belated discovery of Cézanne who had, to his mind, worked out the problem of how to use the 'modern vision' of the Impressionists, which for Fry lacked structural organisation, 'with the constructive design of the old masters'. The extent to which his enthusiasm for Cézanne permeated Bloomsbury can be gauged from an entry Woolf made in her diary for 18 April 1918. She records a visit to the home of John Maynard Keynes (a friend and member of her intellectual circle) made in the company of Fry and her sister Vanessa Bell, to look at a still life by Cézanne recently purchased by Keynes.

> [S]o to Gordon Sqre; where first the new Delacroix & then the Cézanne were produced. There are 6 apples in the Cézanne picture. What can 6 apples *not* be? I began to wonder. There's their relationship to each other, & their colour, & their solidity. To Roger & Nessa, moreover, it was a far more intricate question than this. It was a question of pure paint or mixed; if pure which colour: emerald or veridian; & then the laying on of the paint; & the time he'd spent, and how he'd altered it and why, & when he'd painted it – we carried it into the next room, & Lord! How it showed up the pictures there, as if you put a real stone among sham ones; the canvas of the others seemed scraped with a thin layer of rather cheap paint. The apples positively got redder & rounder and greener.[15]

In Woolf's slightly irritable account of the two painters' professional scrutiny of the detail of the work's material surface, an event from which no doubt she felt excluded, nonetheless we have evidence of the writer's exposure to an explication of the nature of the technical procedures entailed in making such a painting: a description, that is, at a strictly material level, of its difficulty.

In her essay, '"Inevitable relations": aesthetic revelations from Cézanne to Woolf' Rebecca Stott rightly argues that while the lecture, 'Character in Fiction' was as near as Virginia Woolf ever came to an aesthetic manifesto,[16] it is in the novel *To the Lighthouse* that she 'dramatises many of the aesthetic problems which she had discussed in that lecture'.[17] In the exchange between Lily Briscoe and William Banks on the lawn in front of Lily Briscoe's painting, for example, Stott hears in Lily's faltering explanation of why she makes 'no attempt at likeness', an echo of Fry's argument for anti-illusionistic, anti-mimetic realism in painting. Her rejection of the 'pale, elegant, semi-transparent' style of the 'Paunceforte' school as inadequate in the face of the scene that presents itself to her to be painted: the 'bright violet' of the jacmanna, the 'staring' white of the wall, and the shape beneath the colour, recalls Fry's critique of Impressionism: 'They, or rather some of them, reduced the artistic vision to a continuous patchwork or mosaic of coloured patches without architectural framework or structural coherence.'[18]

Woolf has Lily Briscoe express her frustration with the progress of her painting in images close to Fry's in that passage from 'Art and Life':

> She could have wept. It was bad, it was infinitely bad! She could have done it differently of course; the colour could have been thinned down and faded; the shapes etherealized; that was how Paunceforte would have seen it. But then she did not see it like that. She saw the colour burning on a framework of steel; the light of a butterfly's wing lying upon the arches of a cathedral.[19]

Woolf's abiding fear about her experiments with narrative structure in her search to write the reality of character as a succession of 'moments of being', was that the novels would read as 'pale', 'semi-transparent'.[20] If the modern novelist was best advised to look to technical developments in contemporary European painting as a source for the discovery of new linguistic tools with which to forge the modern novel, Fry's architectonic conception of the work of Cézanne appealed to Woolf's concerns about structure in her own novel writing. But which aspects of 'Cézanne's Country' in particular offered Woolf possibilities in this struggle in the middle years of the 1920s? A closer examination of the writer's description of what Lily Briscoe's painting looks like, and her conception of what it is 'of' will help us to determine this.

Lily Briscoe begins a painting out of doors. She is on holiday. She sets up her easel at the edge of the lawn of a house on a cliff-top overlooking the sea. She looks towards the house. The scene she faces involves the figure of the woman of whom she is a guest, Mrs Ramsay, sitting in a window with her son James. But the painting is not a portrait in the conventional sense, as Lily attempts to explain to her holiday companion the scientist William Banks:

> What did she wish to indicate by the triangular purple shape, 'just there?' he asked.
>
> It was Mrs Ramsay reading to James, she said. She knew his objection – that no one could tell it for a human shape. But she had made no attempt at likeness, she said. For what reason had she introduced them then? he asked. Why indeed? – except that if there, in that corner, it was bright, here, in this, she felt the need of darkness. Simple, obvious, commonplace, as it was, Mr Banks was interested. Mother and child then – objects of universal veneration, and in this case the mother was famous for her beauty – might be reduced, he pondered, to a purple shadow without irreverence.

> But the picture was not of them, she said. Or not in his sense. There were other senses too, in which one might reverence them. By a shadow here and a light there, for instance. Her tribute took that form, if, as she vaguely supposed, a picture must be a tribute. A mother and child might be reduced to a shadow without irreverence. A light here required a shadow there.[21]

Not concerned to accomplish a likeness, Lily describes her practice of painting as a response to the power of something she had once seen clearly. She names it the power of the vision of her picture, which now she must 'grope for amongst hedges and houses, and mothers and children'. At the close of Lily's conversation with William Banks Woolf describes the painting as 'a few random marks scrawled upon the canvas', which her fictional painter, in desperation, judges 'infinitely bad'. This first painting is eventually abandoned. The second painting, which Lily begins at the opening of the third section of the novel, is described only twice: once as a collection of 'brown running nervous lines', the painting's starting point – its 'guide-posts' – and then again in the final paragraph of the novel immediately before the painter draws the famous line in the centre of the composition and declares it finished: 'There it was – her picture. Yes, with all its green and blues, its lines running up and across, its attempt at something.'[22]

Gone now is the purple triangular shape of the first work, the allusion to Raphael's compositional structure in his treatment of the theme of Madonna and Child, and art history's paradigm of all mother and child pictures. Lily's attempt at something in painting that crucially involves Mrs Ramsay as its subject ends up closer to the genre of landscape than it does to that of portraiture. Put more directly, the picture Lily Briscoe finally paints is not a Cézanne portrait but a Cézanne landscape, 'with all its greens and blues, its lines running up and across'. In the physical absence of Mrs Ramsay in the second half of the novel Lily is quite literally left with only hedges and houses amongst which to grope for her 'something' in paint.

But what is this 'something'? What, in more precise terms, is the nature of the thing Lily struggles for? What does Woolf understand as the subject matter of the painting, and what bearing does her exposure to the work of Cézanne have on that understanding? At the moment Lily Briscoe picks up her brush to begin the painting, Woolf introduces an image followed immediately by an idea. The image is of birth:

> She could see it all so clearly, so commandingly, when she looked: it was when she took her brush in hand that the whole thing changed. It was in that moment's flight between the picture and her canvas that the demons set on her who often brought her to the verge of tears and made this passage from conception to work as dreadful as any down a dark passage for a child. Such she often felt herself – struggling against terrific odds to maintain her courage; to say: 'But this is what I see: this is what I see,' and so to clasp some miserable remnant of her vision to her breast, which a thousand forces did their best to pluck from her.[23]

The idea is about the nature and the naming of love:

> And it was then too, in that chill and windy way, as she began to paint, that there forced themselves upon her other things, her own inadequacy, her insignificance, keeping house for her father off the Brompton Road, and had much ado to control her impulse to fling herself (thank Heaven she had always resisted so far) at Mrs Ramsay's knee and say to her – but what could one say to her? 'I'm in love with you'? No, that was not true. 'I'm in love with this all', waving her hand at the hedge, at the house, at the children? It was absurd, it was impossible. One could not say what one meant.[24]

At the novel's outset, then, Woolf figures the activity of painting as bound up with some sort of beginning and some sort of love. At its close a painting finally emerges as a response to 'emptiness' impossible to express in words (by Lily to a different companion on the lawn whose profession is the crafting of words, the poet, Mr Carmichael). All three experiences as they arise in the activity of painting substantially involve what Lily Brisoe calls 'these emotions of the body'. What are we to make of this description?

The painter and psychoanalysis

In 'A Sketch of the Past' Woolf writes of the genesis of *To the Lighthouse* as follows:

> It is perfectly true that she obsessed me, in spite of the fact that she died when I was thirteen, until I was forty-four. Then one day walking around Tavistock Square I made up, as I sometimes make up my books, *To the Lighthouse;* in a great, apparently involuntary, rush. One thing burst into another. Blowing bubbles out of a pipe gives the feeling of the rapid crowd of ideas and scenes which blew out of my mind, so that my lips seemed syllabling of their own accord as I walked. What blew the bubbles? Why then? I have no notion. But I wrote the book very quickly; and when it was written, I ceased to be obsessed by my mother. I no longer hear her voice; I do not see her.
>
> I suppose I did for myself what psycho-analysts do for their patients. I expressed some very long felt and deeply felt emotion. And in expressing it I explained it and then laid it to rest. But what is the meaning of 'explained' it?[25]

If the 1924 essay 'Character in Fiction' signals Woolf's engagement with the emergence in her circle of an aesthetic discourse around developments in early twentieth-century French visual art, her description in 1939 of the sudden eruption of *To the Lighthouse* alerts us to the other culturally significant discourse to which she was historically and personally so close: psychoanalytic thought and its development and promotion in London in the 1920s. Interest in psychoanalysis took firm root in London's literary world in the early years of the 1920s. For Woolf it was especially close to home. Her brother and sister-in-law, Adrian and Karin

Stephen, trained as psychoanalysts in the mid 1920s, and in 1922 James Strachey, brother of Leonard and Virginia Woolf's close friend Lytton Strachey, persuaded them to take over publication of the International Psycho-Analytical Library at the Hogarth Press. Yet in spite of her proximity to the debates within Bloomsbury around the effect of psychoanalytic thinking on aesthetic practices, and regardless of her physical proximity to Freud's texts, packing them for distribution in the basement at the Hogarth Press, Woolf claims to have avoided reading Freud until 1939.[26] She did, though, register her reservations about the infiltration of psychoanalysis into the field of fiction writing in a 1920 article called *Freudian Fiction,* in which she reviewed a novel by J.D. Beresford called *An Imperfect Mother.* Woolf's primary objection to the novel was the writer's transformation of 'characters' into 'cases' through the application of a 'patent key that opens every door, that simplifies rather than complicates, detracts rather than enriches'.[27]

In the essay *The Artist and Psycho-Analysis* Roger Fry mounted a far weightier challenge to what he saw as the uniformed colonisation of visual art by Freudian psychoanalysis and its offshoots. The paper, initially presented to the British Psychological Society, was published by the Hogarth Press as one of their *Hogarth Essays* series in 1924, the year Woolf delivered her 'Character in Fiction' lecture at Cambridge. The fundamental argument of Fry's paper is that the psychologists are ignorant of the distinctive practice that characterises a work of art as such. He believes that confusion has arisen because two distinct types of activity have been classed together under the single category of 'art'. The first, according to Freud's analysis of the artist's engagement with fantasy life, aims to create 'a fantasy-world in which the fulfilment of wishes is realised':

> There is, in fact, a path from phantasy back again to reality, and that is – art. The artist has also an introverted disposition and has not far to go to become neurotic. He is one who is urged on by instinctive needs which are too clamorous; he longs to attain to honour, power, riches, fame, and the love of women; but he lacks the means of achieving these gratifications. So, like any other with an unsatisfied longing, he turns away from reality and transfers all his interest, and all his libido too, on to the creation of his wishes in life.[28]

In Fry's characterisation, the second type of artistic activity is concerned with the contemplation of formal relations:

> I believe this latter activity to be as much detached from the instinctive life as any human activity that we know; to be in that respect on a par with science. I consider this latter the distinctive esthetic activity. I admit to some extent the two aims may both appear in any given work of art but I believe them to be fundamentally different, if not in their origins, at least in their functions.[29]

Art whose subject matter (as opposed to its system of formal relations) bears a direct relation to wishes unattainable in everyday life is, according to Fry, available for interpretation in gross 'psycho-biographic' terms.[30] His example is a case study from Oskar Pfister's work on art and psychoanalysis, in which he writes, 'Everything was present…except the faintest glimmer of any artistic feeling.'[31]

For Fry 'artistic feeling' is a sensitiveness to purely formal relations when the artist's 'whole attention is directed towards establishing the completest relationship of all the parts within the system of the work of art'. In the viewer the contemplation of the results of such an attention on the part of the artist gives rise to: 'a special emotion which does not depend upon the association of the form with anything else whatever':

> [N]o one who has a real understanding of the art of painting attaches any importance to what we call the subject of a picture – what is represented. To one who feels the language of pictorial form all depends on *how* it is presented, *nothing* on what.'[32]

Fry chooses to illustrate his point with the example of Cézanne: 'Cézanne, who most of us believe to be the greatest artist of modern times, expressed some of his grandest conceptions in pictures of fruit and crockery on a kitchen table.'[33]

Nevertheless an interesting question does arise for Fry from his consideration of relations between art and psychoanalysis. 'What,' he wonders, 'is the psychological meaning of this emotion about forms, (which I will call the passion for beauty)…?' He is willing to concede that the love of abstract beauty might ultimately derive from the libido. The question then is: 'What is the source of the affective quality of certain systems of formal design…?'[34] He follows the question with a speculation:

> Now, from our definition of this pure beauty, the emotional tone is not due to any recognizable reminiscence or suggestion of the emotional experiences of life; but I sometimes wonder if it nevertheless does not get its force from arousing some very deep, very vague, and immensely generalized reminiscences. It looks as though art had got access to the substratum of all the emotional colours of life, to something which underlies all the particular and specialized emotions of actual life. It seems to derive an emotional energy from the very conditions of our existence by its revelation of an emotional significance in time and space. Or it may be that art really calls up, as it were, the residual traces left on the spirit by the different emotions of life, without ever recalling the actual experiences, so that we get an echo of the emotion without the limitation and particular direction which it had in experience.[35]

Fry concludes the essay by calling upon the psychoanalysts to step in and investigate his wild amateur speculations with their 'precise technique' and 'methodical control'. I want to argue that such an investigation was in fact undertaken and appeared in print not long after Fry delivered the challenge in his paper: but not in the field of psychoanalysis. It appeared in 1927 in the exercise of another kind of 'precise technique' and 'methodical control' dedicated to the re-invention of character in fiction. It is to the text of *To the Lighthouse* that we must turn for a dramatic conceptualisation of links at a *structural* level between psychic processes and formal relations in painting, the existence of which Fry can only intuit in *The Artist and Psycho-analysis.* It is by way of Woolf's novel that we can really begin to plot a move from painting as a system of disinterested formal relations to its connection to 'very deep, very vague, and immensely generalised reminiscences' inscribed semiotically at the level of technical procedures/embodied processes.

***Studland Beach*, or the painting Lily Briscoe does not make**

If the activity of Woolf's fictional painter, and the way her painting looks in her 1927 novel, does indeed register at some level the impact in her cultural environment of *Manet and the Post-Impressionists,* its effect was somewhat delayed. The impression the exhibition made on an actual painter, Woolf's sister Vanessa Bell, was immediate and direct. I want to compare the description Woolf provides of Lily's fictional painting with two real studies of a single theme made by Bell: *The Beach, Studland* (pl. 4), and *Studland Beach* (pl. 5). Recall that Fry's exhibition *Manet and Post-Impressionists* opened in November 1910 and closed in January 1911. *The Beach, Studland,* an oil study on board, dates from around September 1911, and its development on canvas, *Studland Beach,* is dated 1912-13, by which time Fry had mounted his second Post-Impressionist show. In her essay 'Vanessa Bell: *Studland Beach,* Domesticity, and "Significant Form"', Lisa Tickner complicates Richard Shone's assessment of *Studland Beach* (1912-13) as: 'in its move towards abstraction …one of the most radical works of the time in England'.[36] For sure, writes Tickner, as a radically simplified image it can be understood in terms of Clive Bell's idea of 'significant form': 'an aesthetic purged of narrative sentiment, or circumstantial detail'.[37] But she argues the painting is not fully accountable in terms of Bell's aesthetic theory. If *To the Lighthouse* is, by Virginia Woolf's own admission, a working through of 'some very long felt and deeply felt emotion' connected with her mother, Tickner argues that Vanessa Bell's Studland Beach studies are also haunted by the figure of Julia Stephen.

Reversing the historical chronology of the production of the two works Tickner writes: '*Studland Beach* is Vanessa's *To the Lighthouse.*' [38] Like Woolf's novel it recalls the beach of the sisters' childhood summers in St Ives. Tickner speculates that holidays at Studland with her own children, Julian and Quentin, revived for Vanessa memories of her mother, and of St Ives as a place of childhood bliss cut short too soon by the death of Julia Stephen. The beach, then, is the site of at once the memory of maternal presence and of maternal absence. For Lisa Tickner the central theme of *Studland Beach* is motherhood. In a passage about the psychic dimension of childbirth and maternity in relation to two events close to the making of the Studland beach paintings, the birth of Quentin Bell in 1910 and the miscarriage suffered by Vanessa in 1911, she writes:

> Most women, in giving birth, renew psychic contact with their mothers, or, more technically, with the internal unconscious representations that make up their maternal imagos. Most women also experience at some point a kind of matrophobia, described by the poet Adrienne Rich as 'a womanly splitting of the self, in the desire to become purged once and for all of our mother's bondage, to become individuated and free'. Even – or especially – at moments of liberation or transgression, there is often 'a deep fear of destroying one's mother or child by separating'.[39]

It is motherhood as the site precisely of this 'very modern ambivalence and loss' that Tickner sees inscribed in Vanessa Bell's painting.[40] As she shows in the substance of her argument, however, it is a theme evident only marginally at the level of 'significant form'. Rather it is to be found in the picture's mis-en-scène: the beach motif, and the placement and associative work of the undeniably massively simplified, but still clearly figurative elements, and in references to works of art of the past. That is to say fundamentally at the level of subject matter.

If *Studland Beach* is Vanessa Bell's *To the Lighthouse,* returning paintings and novel to the actual historical chronology of their production there is a compelling argument to be made for *To the Lighthouse* as Virginia Woolf's *Studland Beach.* The two Studland beach studies have their fictional counterparts in two scenes in part three of *To the Lighthouse.* One occurs as a memory, the other as its day-dreamed reconfiguration when Lily Briscoe works on her second canvas, ten years after beginning the first, when Mrs Ramsay is no longer alive. As she begins to paint Lily remembers 'a windy morning. They had all gone to the beach'.[41] Mrs Ramsay sits beside a rock writing letters. Occasionally she raises her bespectacled eyes to watch Lily and the young, academic Charles Tansley standing at the water's edge skimming pebbles. Lily breaks off from painting to stand on the edge of the lawn to look for the Ramsays' boat on its voyage across the bay to the lighthouse. When she returns to work on the canvas she thinks again of Mrs Ramsay on the beach, a memory of intense clarity 'ringed round, lit up, visible to the last detail, with all before it blank and all after it blank, for miles and miles'.[42] But now Lily's place in the scene has altered and she is sitting beside Mrs Ramsay on the beach.

Both Vanessa Bell's Studland Beach paintings can be considered as composed of two parts, the left-hand side with the dune/rock-like form and the two seated figures in the foreground, separated by a space from the right-hand side of the picture with the figures grouped around the bathing tent. To support Lisa Tickner's speculations about the psychological effect of holidays at Studland on Vanessa Bell, the composition suggests to me a reading of the paintings as figuring simultaneously two different temporal modes. Childhood in the left side, adulthood in the right, separated by the central vertical band of incident-less space. It is as if in her novel Woolf has zoomed in to concentrate on just the left-hand side of the compositions. In the 1911 painting, *The Beach, Studland* the smaller seated figure is less defined than in *Studland Beach*, it almost merges with the form against which it is drawn. The seated figures in *The Beach, Studland* look toward something at the water's edge at the extreme left of the canvas. Lisa Tickner describes it as 'a local incident of rocks and waves in the middle distance'.[43] Woolf remodels it in the novel to resemble Charles Tansley and Lily Briscoe skimming their stones at the water's edge. In the 1912-13 painting, *Studland Beach,* these shapes have gone. The smaller seated figure is as defined as its companion now, and they sit separately but side by side facing the sea like Lily and Mrs Ramsay in Lily's day-dreamed revision of her first beach memory. In terms of form and facture the 1912-13 picture is a simplification, a flattening out of the 1911 study, a more dream-like image. Woolf's description of Lily's second fantasmatic scene: 'ringed round, lit up, visible to the last detail, with all before it blank and all after it blank, for miles and miles', captures the picture's quality.

We might speculate that Vanessa's Studland beach paintings were memorable and significant to her sister Virginia as the site of a shared memory both of childhood well-being, and the pain of loss connected with the death of their mother. Woolf draws on their figurative, narrative content for her description of the images Lily thinks about as she paints. But, significantly, they are not models in terms of motif, process or appearance for the painting Lily actually makes. In the manner of their simplification of form and colour, neither *Studland Beach* painting owes much to Cézanne.[44]

By 1927 and *To the Lighthouse* Woolf's interest in painting was not at the level of subject matter. Lily Briscoe understands its *modus operandi* at the most fundamental structural level.

> Where to begin? – that was the question; at what point to make the first mark? One line placed on the canvas committed her to innumerable risks, to frequent and irrevocable decisions.[45]

The passage contains two ideas. The first is of difficulty, the difficulty of beginning, and once begun of making 'frequent and irrevocable' decisions. Now, nowhere in the field of the new French art that constituted such a vital part of Woolf's cultural environment in the years between 1910 and the writing of *To the Lighthouse* is the agony of decision making, about how and where to place one mark in relation to the next, more remarked upon than in the critical discourse around the work of Cézanne. Emile Bernard's interpretation of Cézanne's own comments about his work, *Souvenirs sur Paul Cézanne et lettres,* was published in Paris in 1912. Joachim Gasquet's book *Cézanne* appeared in 1921. Fry had reviewed Ambrose Vollard's *Cézanne* (Paris 1914) for the *Burlington Magazine* in 1917. In 1926 Fry published in *L'Amour de l'art* the text that was to become, in expanded form, *Cézanne: A Study of his Development* published by Leonard and Virginia Woolf at the Hogarth Press in

1927, the same year as *To the Lighthouse.* Given Woolf's interest in Fry's intellectual projects, together with her exposure to the discussions of the painters in her circle engaged with Post-Impressionism on the canvas, it is reasonable to speculate that accounts of Cézanne's difficulty translating his perceptual sensations into the material of paint would have been familiar to Woolf.

The second idea is about figure/ground relations: 'Where to begin…at what point to make the first mark,' worries Lily. Not just in this passage but throughout the novel Lily's struggle is with painting described by Woolf as pared down to its most basic structural elements: figure/ground. Nowhere is the problem of the articulation of pictorial space more utterly and evidently a question of fundamental structural relations between mark and unmarked ground than in the landscape watercolour studies of Cézanne's last years. Theodore Reff notes that Fry was the first to appreciate some distinctive quality in Cézanne's late works. Fry writes in his book on Cézanne, '[F]or certain intelligences among posterity, the completest revelation of his spirit may be found in these latest creations.'[46] Perhaps now we have a partial answer to our question why in 'A Sketch of the Past', Cézanne represented for Woolf the essential difficulty of painting. But what was it, we might ask, that triggered the move in Woolf's thinking to make this particular kind of painting activity an accompaniment to the story of Lily's attachment to and (never quite) loss of Mrs Ramsay in *To the Lighthouse*? Furthermore why did this connection not emerge until the middle of the 1920s? After all, Woolf had been around Fry and his enthusiasm for Cézanne since 1911.

To take the last question first. We know that Woolf read the proofs of Fry's essay *The Artist and Psycho-Analysis* before publication by the Hogarth Press. In a letter to him dated 22 September 1924 she wrote:

> [S]o I must write off at once and say how it fills me with admiration and stirs up in me, as you alone do, all sorts of bats and tadpoles – ideas, I mean, which have clung to my roof and lodged in my mind, and now I'm all alive with pleasure.[47]

The bats and tadpoles, I would like to wager, were stirred up by Fry's question about the source of the emotion about forms. In May, just four months earlier, in her 'Character in Fiction' lecture, Woolf could only make passing reference to the first Post-Impressionist exhibition. She was familiar with the technical procedures underlying formal innovations in new French painting from her years of conversation with Fry and the other painters of her circle. But at that time she had no clear idea how these tools for the signification of 'a new and definite reality' in the visual arts might be translated for use in the field of fiction. How could they be mobilised to construct the reality of character as she experienced and imagined it as a woman writing novels in the mid 1920s? *The Artist and Psycho-Analysis* signalled a way. In *To the Lighthouse* Woolf imaginatively concretises Fry's generalised speculations; she links an account of the 'distinctive esthetic activity' of painting, exemplified by Cézanne, with a story of human emotions experienced in response to specific events in life. I want to consider the nature of the events around which the novel is structured in relation to another text that appeared on the horizon of Woolf's intellectual landscape in the early 1920s.

Yet if one could give a sense of my mother's personality one would have to be an artist

As we have seen, Fry's characterisation of art as wish fulfilment in *The Artist and Psycho-Analysis* was based upon Freud's passing remarks about the artist's relation to fantasy life from the very end of lecture XIII, 'Symptom Formation', in the 'Introductory Lectures in Psychoanalysis'. The 'Introductory Lectures' were published in the first English edition, translated by Joan Rivière, in London in 1922. The same year saw the first publication in English of another text by Freud, which contains an idea about the psychic roots of artistic activity at precisely the structural level Fry demands in *The Artist and Psycho-Analysis*. The essay in question is 'Beyond the Pleasure Principle', published by the Hogarth Press in October 1922 as volume one of the *International Psycho-Analytical Library*. While the implications of Freud's observations in 'Beyond the Pleasure Principle' for art making are absent from Fry's paper, there is an extraordinary parallel between the psychic material Freud works with in his essay and the themes Woolf explores in *To the Lighthouse*.

Freud's theoretical speculations in 'Beyond the Pleasure Principle' were written as a response to the phenomenon of traumatic neurosis in soldiers returning from active service in the First World War. The condition was manifest symptomatically as the repetition in dreams of the situation of the trauma-inducing incident. In thinking about the function of repetition in relation to inaccessible or repressed traumatic material Freud moves by way of the chance observation of an instance of repetitious behaviour in normal waking life. He notices the activity of his eighteen-month old grandson Ernst during periods when his mother is absent.

> The child had a wooden reel with a piece of string tied round it ...What he did was to hold the reel by the string and very skilfully throw it over the edge of his curtained cot, so that it disappeared into it, at the same time uttering his expressive cry 'o-o-o-o'.[48]

Freud and the child's mother interpret this sound as a representation of the German word '*fort*' ('gone').

> He then pulled the reel out of the cot again by the string and hailed its reappearance with a joyful '*da*' ['there'].This, then, was the complete game – disappearance and return.[49]

In a footnote Freud records a subsequent observation of a variation on the game. On his mother's return the child greets her with the vocalisation 'Baby o-o-o-o!

In her absence, Freud tells us, Ernst had discovered his reflection in a full-length mirror that did not quite reach the ground so that by crouching down he could make his own reflection disappear: he could make himself '*fort*'/'gone'.

Freud makes three different speculations about the meaning of this activity. The first is in relation to the pleasure principle, that is, the hypothesis in psychoanalysis that human mental mechanisms are automatically directed towards lowering unpleasurable tension arising both from external and internal stimulation:

> It was related to the child's cultural achievement – the instinctual renunciation (that is, the renunciation of instinctual satisfaction) which he had made in allowing his mother to go away without protesting. He compensated himself for this, as it were, by himself staging the disappearance and return of the objects within his reach...The child cannot possibly have felt his mother's departure as something agreeable or even indifferent. How then does his repetition of this distressing game fit in with the pleasure principle? It may perhaps be said in reply that her departure had to be enacted as a necessary preliminary to her joyful return, and that it was in the latter that lay the true purpose of the game.[50]

The second interpretation is that the activity of the child is an attempt to transform the passive experience of being overwhelmed by loss into one in which he takes an active part and masters the situation by repeating it, however unpleasurable, as a game. Freud's third interpretation is that the game is an attempt to satisfy an impulse suppressed in the child's actual life and that throwing away the toy is an act of revenge on his mother for leaving him. This is another form of mastery in which the child makes himself responsible for sending the mother away and the repetition of the activity yields pleasure, but of a different sort. At the end of his analysis of Ernst's game Freud makes the following observation:

> Finally a reminder may be added that the artistic play and artistic imitation carried out by adults, which unlike children's, are aimed at an audience, do not spare the spectators (for instance, in tragedy) the most painful experiences and yet can be felt by them as highly enjoyable. This is convincing proof that, even under the dominance of the pleasure principle, there are ways and means enough of making what is in itself unpleasurable into a subject to be recollected and worked over in the mind.[51]

Here we see a link made in the field of psychoanalysis between the repetitious play of children and the 'cultural achievement' of instinctual renunciation that such play continued into adulthood, and intended for public exposure as artistic activity, represents. Freud's final comment on the subject is of particular significance for my argument:

> The consideration of these cases and situations, which have a yield of pleasure as their final outcome, should be undertaken by some system of aesthetics with an economic approach to its subject matter.[52]

This reads like the reverse side of Fry's challenge to the psychoanalysts to scientifically investigate the psychic structures underpinning the source of satisfaction derived from the contemplation of certain systems of formal design.

To my mind, what we have in 1927 with *To the Lighthouse* is a site where the two systems, aesthetic and psychoanalytic at their most basic structural level can be seen to co-emerge. The narrative of Lily Briscoe figures the economic nature of an aesthetic system at its simplest and clearest, the binary mark/unmarked-ground relation of the painting process as a structure linked to psychic yields of unpleasure and pleasure related to experiences of the unavailability/absence of the mother. Lily in effect plays the adult, artistic game of *fort/da* as a response to the unavailability as desired object in life/actual loss in death of Mrs Ramsay. She finally achieves the fabrication of a cultural object, the painting, by 'instinctual renunciation'/actual loss of the pleasure afforded by the material presence of the mother's body. Lily's motor action of moving to make marks/holding back from making them with her brush is, like little Ernst's game with the reel and string, accompanied by verbal activity, represented in the novel as interior monologue. Image and word, it is important to stress, have no illustrative connection: Lily Briscoe does not paint a version of *Studland Beach.* Lily's work on the canvas has the status of what Fry defined in *The Artist and Psycho-Analysis,* as 'distinctive esthetic activity'. Let us return to Fry's paper for a moment: in summation his fundamental criticism of psychoanalysts when they speak about art is imprecision in the use of the concept of wish-fulfilment: 'Freud uses wish of a desire which has been repressed from consciousness and remains active in the unconscious. The true Freudian wish is incapable of direct satisfaction.' [53] Yet in 'The Introductory Lectures on Psycho-Analysis' Freud himself does not strictly adhere to his own definition, when he speaks of the artist urged on by the instinctive needs for 'power, riches, fame and the love of women'. These are not, argues Fry, repressed wishes because they are allowed into consciousness and therefore capable of direct fulfilment. It is the psychoanalyst's habit of 'passing from the strict sense of wish to the ordinary sense' that is misleading in the domain of art.[54] The concept we need to be able to theorise Fry's intuition about the roots of formal configurations in painting – represented as the double structure of Lily's activity in Woolf's novel – is that which had its roots in Freud's work as early as 1895 in the 'Project for a Scientific Psychology', namely the thing-presentation/word-presentation relation. Freud's first topography of the psychical apparatus is differentiated as the unconscious, preconscious and conscious systems. He uses the terms thing-presentation and word-presentation to distinguish between two types of traces of activity in the preconscious and unconscious systems. The first type, derived from things, is essentially visual, the second, essentially auditory, is derived from words. The preconscious system is characterised by the fact that in it thing-presentations are bound to word-presentations, whereas in the unconscious only thing-presentations are found.[55]

Can we, then, theorise Woolf's representation of what happens when Lily Briscoe paints in terms of Freud's first topography as activity fundamentally connected to the preconscious domain where there is a relation between thing-presentation and word-presentation in which we might equate the essentially visual and unconsciously rooted thing-presentation with the associated pressure Lily refers to as 'these emotions of the body': the pressure of pre-verbal affective material below the level of full consciousness? This is a subject to which I will return in chapter four. For now suffice it to say that in general Woolf's narrative appears to parallel Freud's observation that it is the absence of the maternal body that motivates the activity of symbolic substitution, in terms both of object symbols – the painting, and language – the fantasy scenarios that accompany the activity. But if Woolf did know something of Freud's ideas in 'Beyond the Pleasure Principle' (even if not from actually reading it herself) and explores them in fiction through the character of Lily Briscoe, she has already made a significant transposition from a masculine to a feminine player. Does this difference make any difference?

Let us now look more carefully at Woolf's description of Lily Briscoe's painting process and start by returning to the two passages that seem to link painting with the ideas of beginnings, and of 'love'. Lily stands on the lawn concentrating on her *motif*:

> She could see it all so clearly, so commandingly, when she looked: it was when she took her brush in hand that the whole thing changed. It was in that moment's flight between the picture and her canvas that the demons set on her who often brought her to the verge of tears and made this passage from conception to work as dreadful as any down a dark passage for a child. Such she often felt herself – struggling against terrific odds to maintain her courage; to say: 'But this is what I see: this is what I see,' and so to clasp some miserable remnant of her vision to her breast, which a thousand forces did their best to pluck from her.[56]

Lily is faced with a new, unmarked canvas, for the painter the space of unlimited possibilities and, simultaneously, a field always already complete. The first mark quite literally shatters the integrity of the canvas: terrifyingly. It is as Lily moves to paint that the second thought, the one about love, arises:

> And it was then too, in that chill and windy way, as she began to paint, that there forced themselves upon her other things, her own inadequacy, her insignificance, keeping house for her father off the Brompton Road, and had much ado to control her impulse to fling herself (thank Heaven she had always resisted so far) at Mrs Ramsay's knee and say to her – but what could

> one say to her? 'I'm in love with you'? No, that was not true. 'I'm in love with this all,' waving her hand at the hedge, at the house, at the children? It was absurd, it was impossible. One could not say what one meant.[57]

If the first mark divides an always already unified field, each subsequent one has to be a move towards remaking that original state. With the images Woolf chooses as the thoughts to accompany Lily's start on her painting she unequivocally equates unmarked canvas with the body of the mother generally in the birth metaphor, and specifically with the character of Mrs Ramsay as the mother figure in the novel's narrative. As Lily makes her first mark the idea of her subjectivity as separate and different from Mrs Ramsay enters Lily's mind as a categorical inadequacy at the juncture of gender and social class: her status as spinster, and the location of her dwelling. Desiring complete knowledge of her difference, Lily wants to be in the space of Mrs Ramsay, to be, in the act of painting, emerged (re-emerged) in 'this all', hedge, house, children, that carries with it a quality of emotion impossible to convey in words, for which the word 'love' stands only as an inadequate approximation. But her beginning turns out, by her own judgement, to be 'infinitely bad' and the memory that accompanies her despair at what she sees on the canvas carries the psychic material underpinning the perceived formal failure. The setting is Lily's bedroom late at night, the event the arrival of Mrs Ramsay and a moment of physical intimacy between the two women:

> Sitting on the floor with her arms around Mrs Ramsay's knees, close as she could get, smiling to think that Mrs Ramsay would never know the reason for that pressure, she imagined how in the chambers of the mind and heart of the woman who was, physically, touching her, were stood, like the treasures in the tombs of kings, tablets bearing sacred inscriptions, which if one could spell them out would teach one everything, but they would never be offered openly, never made public. What art was there, known to love or cunning, by which one pressed through into those secret chambers? What device for becoming, like waters poured into one jar, inextricably the same, one with the object one adored? Could the body achieve it, or the mind, subtly mingling in the intricate passages of the brain? or the heart? Could loving, as people called it, make her and Mrs Ramsay one? For it was not knowledge but unity she desired, not inscriptions on tablets, nothing that could be written in any language known to men, but intimacy itself, which is knowledge, she had thought, leaning her head on Mrs Ramsay's knee.
>
> Nothing happened. Nothing! Nothing! as she leant her head against Mrs Ramsay's knee.[58]

This is a richly condensed passage full of ideas. Two are significant for the present argument. First, there is the link made between knowledge and its linguistic symbolisation. The body of Mrs Ramsay is likened to a tomb concealing tablets bearing sacred writings, laws, or a system that reveals, but also strictly defines the rules and limits of knowledge. But like the tombs of Egyptian kings this chamber must be broken open for its secrets to be revealed. Echoes here of the revenge-mastery dimension of Freud's *fort/da* game: language acquisition as symbolic violence towards the mother. But it is not knowledge of this kind that Lily desires, 'nothing that could be written in any language known to men', and Woolf's locution here is explicitly gendered; she writes known to 'men' and not 'man', as universal signifier of all human kind. There is knowledge, she intuits, connected specifically to women. But obviously it cannot be found in achieving unity, in a complete merging of mind/body, of self and other 'like waters poured into one jar'. And physical intimacy, which Lily 'had' thought of as knowledge, fails utterly: 'And yet, she knew knowledge and wisdom were stored in Mrs Ramsay's heart.'[59]

On the canvas Lily's problem is, unsurprisingly, 'how to connect this mass on the right hand with that on the left'. She considers two solutions: 'she might do it by bringing the line of the branch across so; or break the vacancy in the foreground with an object (James perhaps) so.' Her reason for rejecting both these options is, on the face of it, a little more surprising: 'But the danger was that by doing that the unity of the whole might be broken.'[60] From the bedroom scene we know that 'nothing had happened' in terms of accessing what Mrs Ramsay knew in unity as physical proximity – one reason why the mass on the right is separated by a space from the other on the left. But in this state the painting already has, we are told, a unity that would be broken by doing something about an empty space in the foreground. So why does anything else *have* to be done, why is it that Lily cannot call it finished there and then? Because, I suggest, the 'unity' she is thinking of here is the cultural definition of wholeness as a system of two differently constituted (the house and the hedge) but complementary unities, (Mrs Ramsay's subject of conversation during her nocturnal visit is the advocacy of the 'universal' laws of marriage against Lily's defence of remaining single). This translates into an idea of compositional 'wholeness' as a set of culturally valorized conventions in painting, a formal system 'known to men' against which Lily measures the look of her picture. It already has a variety of that, but she is compelled to go on, she knows there is another knowledge to be conveyed. But to go on is to go on to make something that is not recognisable as wholeness in painting, but rather looks like the confirmation of Charles Tansley's whispered words in her ear, 'Women can't paint, women can't write.' The profound doubt that this produces in Lily stops her continuing with the work altogether for the remainder of the first part of the novel. Viewed from the perspective of Freud's *fort/da* game transposed into the field of painting, the unity of Lily's picture as a culturally recognisable 'whole' object depends entirely on the vacancy, in psychoanalytical terms the repression of the maternal body, at its centre; in material terms unmarked canvas, the ground against which the individual unity of each 'mass', i.e. masculine and feminine subject position, is defined as such. But for Lily Briscoe this is not the whole of wholeness.

When she takes up again the problem posed by this painting it is ten years later, a period marked (interestingly in terms of the context in which Freud wrote 'Beyond the Pleasure Principle') by the devastation wrought by the First World War, and by the death of Mrs Ramsay. Trying to manage feelings stirred up by her return to the Ramsays' summer residence Lily remembers her picture and decides to begin it again. She sets up her easel on the edge of the lawn in the same spot as before, facing the steps and French window, now empty, and its framing 'masses' of wall and hedge. As Mr Ramsay leaves with his son James and daughter Cam, on the long awaited, but no longer desired, boat trip across the bay to the lighthouse, Lily starts work on a new canvas. She experiences once more the terror of the first mark, its double nature as traumatic and promising represented not metaphorically this time, but directly and explicitly as 'a painful but exciting ecstasy'. Woolf's description of Lily's activity more obviously now suggests a parallel with little Ernst's game:

> With a curious physical sensation, as if she were urged forward and at the same time must hold herself back, she made her first quick decisive stroke. The brush descended. It flickered brown over the white canvas; it left a running mark. A second time she did it – a third time. And so pausing and so flickering, she attained a dancing rhythmical movement, as if pauses were one part of the rhythm and the strokes another, and all were related; and so, lightly and swiftly pausing, striking, she scored her canvas with brown running nervous lines which had no sooner settled there than they enclosed (she felt it looming out at her) a space.[61]

If Lily's motor responses bring to mind *fort/da,* her description of the production of space recalls what can be deduced of Cézanne's practice from the late works. Geneviève Monnier in her essay on the late watercolours remarks that Roger Fry was the first critic to observe that in some of the oil studies, notably the *Mont Saint-Victoire* series of 1902-1906 where patches of canvas are left unpainted, Cézanne used the medium like watercolour, heavily diluting the oil-bound pigment with turpentine.[62]

Lily's idea about the nature of the space that looms out at her is narrated as follows:

> For what could be more formidable than that space? Here she was again, she thought, stepping back to look at it, drawn out of gossip, out of living, out of community with people into the presence of this formidable ancient enemy of hers – this other thing, this truth, this reality, which suddenly laid hands on her, emerged stark at the back of appearances and commanded her attention.[63]

Here at the level of her symbolic object, her painting, Lily experiences an anxiety figured as absence threatening to overwhelm by the pressure of its presence. How does she proceed, what form does her attempt at controlling the anxiety take? She begins to model the 'hideously difficult white space' with 'greens and blues' and as she does so the first scene on the beach with Mrs Ramsay comes into her mind:

> They chose little flat stones and sent them skipping over the waves...What they said she could not remember, but only she and Charles throwing stones and Mrs Ramsay watching them. She was highly conscious of that...When she thought of herself and Charles Tansley throwing ducks and drakes and of the whole scene on the beach, it seemed to depend somehow upon Mrs Ramsay sitting under the rock with a pad on her knee, writing letters...That woman sitting there, writing under the rock resolved everything into simplicity; made these angers and irritations fall off like old rags; she brought together this and that and then this, and so made out of that miserable silliness and spite (she and Charles Tansley squabbling, sparring, had been silly and spiteful) something – this scene on the beach for example, this moment of friendship and liking – which survived, after all these years, complete, so that she dipped into it to refashion her memory of him, and it stayed in the mind almost like a work of art.[64]

Almost like the work of art she abandons in part one of the novel in fact, the composition that depended for its wholeness on the complementariness of the individual 'masses' of wall and hedge determined by the 'vacancy in the foreground'.

But rather than its being a problem, an unwanted space, here rearticulated and figured at the level of the fantasy scenario, Lily recognises its presence as a crucial structural function. The beach memory ends as follows:

> What was the meaning of life? That was all – a simple question; one that tended to close in on one with years. The great revelation had never come. The great revelation perhaps never did come. Instead there were little daily miracles, illuminations, matches struck in the dark; here was one. This, that, and the other; herself and Charles Tansley and the breaking wave...Mrs Ramsay making of the moment something permanent (as in the other sphere Lily herself tried to make of the moment something permanent) – this was of the nature of a revelation.[65]

Lily as maker identifies with Mrs Ramsay as a symbolic figure, representing a creative structuring force in the cultural sphere. But this only comes into view for the woman who is *not* her biological daughter – at the moment Mrs Ramsay is involved in her own creative activity (letter writing) outside the framework of the family where all is subordinated to the demands of Mr Ramsay as creative intelligence. Again Lily stops work, this time not out of doubt but curiosity; she walks to the edge of the lawn to watch the Ramsays' boat set sail out across the bay. When she returns to her canvas there is a significant change in her response to the problem of white space: 'Heaven be praised for it, the problem of space remained, she thought taking up her brush again. It glared at her. The whole mass of the picture was poised upon that weight.'[66] There follows a very Fry-on-Cézanne-like statement of her intentions to make what sounds more like a watercolour than an oil study:

> Beautiful and bright it should be on the surface, feathery and evanescent, one colour melting into another like colours on a butterfly's wing; but beneath the fabric must be clamped together with bolts of iron. It was to be a thing you could ruffle with your breath; and a thing you could not dislodge with a team of horses.[67]

As she begins to paint Lily's mind 'throws up' once more the scene on the beach, but now she sees herself not with Charles Tansley under Mrs Ramsay's gaze at some distance from her, but sitting beside the older woman who looks out to sea in silence. The failure of touch to satisfy Lily's desire to become 'one with the object one adored' (and this is a noticeably Freudian articulation of the desire in terms of Woolf's use of the word 'object' rather than 'person') and the failure of intimacy as knowledge marks the nocturnal bedroom scene with Mrs Ramsay. Sight (or more precisely a looking in silence, the condition of the activity of painting) is the sense connected with her acceptance of 'the extreme obscurity of human relationships'. Lily does not search the face of Mrs Ramsay for what she wants. To imagine desired oneness as a meeting or entwining of gazes would be to repeat the failure of the attempt at a tactile merging. But neither does sight here signify total separation – Lily speaks of 'the extreme obscurity of human relations', not their complete unknowability.[68] Sight and obscurity are directly linked in this scene. Mrs Ramsay has put on her spectacles in an attempt to identify an object floating in the sea. 'Is it a boat? Is it a cask?' she asks. The two women sit beside one another looking out to sea in silence and the question remains unanswered. Yet rather than the frustration and disappointment experienced in the failure to fully know the 'object one adored' in the bedroom scene, for Lily here 'The moment at least seemed extra-ordinarily fertile.'[69]

And yet it is not before an enormous struggle with a painful sensation of emptiness that Lily completes her painting as she looks at the place in her *motif* where the figure of Mrs Ramsay once was. This is focused in an extra-ordinary passage that reads like a dramatic condensation of theoretical speculations in 'Beyond the Pleasure Principle':

> The physical sensations that went with the bare look of the steps had become suddenly extremely unpleasant. To want and not to have, sent all up her body a hardness, a hollowness, a strain. And then to want and not to have – to want and want – how that wrung the heart, and wrung it again and again! Oh Mrs Ramsay! she called out silently, to that essence which sat by the boat,

> that abstract one made of her, that woman in grey, as if to abuse her for having gone, and then having gone, come back again. It had seemed so safe, thinking of her. Ghost, air, nothingness, a thing you could play with easily and safely at any time of day or night, she had been that, and then suddenly she put her hand out and wrung the heart thus.[70]

Yet the solution to her painting seems connected more to the imagined scene in which Lily sits beside Mrs Ramsay with something between them that is obscure but fertile, and less to the fantasy mastery of the pain produced by her absence implied in the passage above. In the final paragraph of the novel Lily looks at her canvas and draws 'a line there, in the centre' and decides that it is finished. But where does the line go? Is it a horizontal or a vertical line? We do not know; Woolf does not make it clear. Like the object that bobs in the sea it is ambiguous, oscillating between two possibilities boat/cask, horizontal/vertical. The problem in Lily's first painting is with a 'vacancy' in the foreground associated, as I have argued, with Mrs Ramsay. The second painting is Lily's attempt at some resolution to this problem and the line marks the moment of the painting's completion. How, then, does it work according to the logic of painting as a displaced site of *fort/da* that I have set up and followed through Lily's narrative? The line breaks a vacancy described now not as the 'foreground' but as the 'centre'. Given the position of the boat/cask in the water in the beach scene, I want to suggest that this is a centre in depth rather than width; that we think formally of the problem as one of the middle distance rather than foreground. The composition seems now no longer to depend on the structuring presence as absence of unmarked ground/maternal body, but hinges on a visually ambiguous, oscillating element that disturbs the clear distinction between background/foreground, figure/ground.

At the level of the fantasy scenario, knowledge of Mrs Ramsay for Lily is neither complete nor incomplete. Her presence as a tactile, material body is *almost* felt – they sit beside one another but without touching. To see is not a matter of getting a clear picture of one another; they gaze together but out to sea, their point of mutual concentration an unclear and shifting field. We might elaborate from the perspective of 'Beyond the Pleasure Principle' to say that in the narrative of Lily Briscoe Woolf represents something, in her own non-psychoanalytic formulation, 'a sense of my mother's personality', that interrupts, and only momentarily (not the 'great revelation' but 'the little daily miracles') while residing within the logic of, *fort/da* as cultural symbolic substitution conditional upon maternal absence. In Lily Briscoe's second painting a different psychic-corporeal substructure achieves borderline visibility in the space of what is in formal terms 'Cézanne's Country'. When Vanessa Bell first read *To the Lighthouse* she wrote her sister a letter and in it she said: 'By the way surely Lily Briscoe must have been rather a good painter – before her time perhaps, but with great gifts really?'[71]

3

A SPATIAL FEELING CONNECTED WITH LANDSCAPES[1]

Changing vistas, motion caught

From the very earliest to the most recent published statements, two interrelated themes consistently arise when Helen Frankenthaler speaks about her painting practice. One is spatial ambiguity and the other is landscape. The earliest substantial statement, and still one of the clearest accounts of Frankenthaler's concerns and working processes, appeared in 1958 in the catalogue of an exhibition mounted by the Whitney Museum of American Art called *Nature in Abstraction: The Relation of Abstract Painting and Sculpture to Nature in Twentieth Century American Art.*[2] In addition to an introductory essay by John I. H. Baur, the catalogue features artists' statements made in response to a question put to them by the Whitney: 'Do you feel that nature has any serious relation to your work?' Frankenthaler answers: 'The relation of nature to my pictures changes in degree from picture to picture, and takes different forms.' She states unequivocally, however, that, 'I see most of my paintings as landscapes or vistas, changing views, motion caught. I get some ideas from making studies outdoors or just noticing the designs and complications in nature.'[3] Further into the statement the relation between, not specifically landscape but a more general 'nature', gets more complex:

> In the last couple of years I have made paintings in which an animal shape or a nose and mouth, numbers, apples, etc., appears as part of an otherwise totally abstract picture. These images are not put down to be recognized for what they are, nor are they surrealist. They seem to be spontaneous and necessary points of departure, often disappearing completely, on and off, before the picture is finished. As I say I am puzzled because I don't have a fixed *idea* about this, and I seem to find myself in something new in terms of

> nature. I think that, instead of nature or image, it has to do with spirit or sensation that can be related by a kind of abstract projection.[4]

'Nature' in painting is equated with spatialisation of a particular kind:

> Thus in looking at pictures (mine or others'), after the initial impact of the painting proper, I usually find or project nature into the pictures I particularly like. I think this is involved with my feeling that a 'successful' abstract painting plays with space on all different levels, at different speeds, with different perspectives, and at the same time remains flat.[5]

At the end of the interview spatial ambiguity and the idea of beauty are linked.

> Painters are no longer trying to create a false view or distance, but instead can make shapes, lines, colors, blottings, etc., work for them – a certain area of the canvas can seem one hundred miles back in the picture and also appear smack-flat next to the area beside it, and not merely because of the reality that the canvas *is* flat. On this level I think abstract painters are still working in terms of illusion. For me the most beautiful pictures of any age have this ambiguity.[6]

There is a lot going on here. I want to begin with the section of the statement in which Frankenthaler speaks specifically of landscape: 'I see most of my paintings as landscapes or vistas, changing views, motion caught. I get some ideas from making studies outdoors or just noticing the designs and complications in nature.' A more familiar reference to the practice of making studies in landscape appears in Frankenthaler's much quoted description of the process of making *Mountains and Sea,* published thirteen years after the event in 1965 as part of the *Art Forum* interview with Henry Geldzahler:

> In 1952 on a trip to Nova Scotia I did landscapes with folding easel equipment. I came back and did the 'Mountains and Sea' painting and I know the landscapes were in my arms as I did it.[7]

'I know the landscapes were in my arms as I did it.' This is a striking assertion, in its lack of restraint, outright corporeality: erotic charge even. These are 'landscapes', not *the landscape* note, held in the present of making *Mountains and Sea* in the studio, close to the body like a child or a lover. It is striking for its conviction. Frankenthaler's locution is sure and precise: 'I know the landscapes were in my arms as I did it,' not, it was as if the landscapes were in my arms as I did it. The literalness of the statement functions to destabilise its status as a figure of speech. What are we to make of it?

Let us start by turning our attention to the outcome of another working holiday in Cézanne's Country. In July and August of 1960 the French philosopher Maurice Merleau-Ponty stayed in Aix-en-Provence at Le Tholonet, a village not far from the studio Cézanne built at Les Lauves, where he wrote the essay published the following year in the journal *Art de France* under the title 'Eye and Mind'. The essay was a response to what worried Merleau-Ponty – the potential dominance of 'operational thinking' in science, seen most clearly in the ideology of cybernetics.[8] In it he argues for a mode of thinking located at the site of the body as it is lived in association with things in the world and other human bodies. It is important to define precisely what Merleau-Ponty means by the body. It is not the physical body that is the object of biology, but rather the location of a complex set of correspondences in the field of perception, or, to put it more precisely, the structure of the perceptual field *is* the coexistence of subject and phenomena as lived interrelatedness; neither can exist independently of the other in its own terms. In Cathryn Vasseleu's useful formulation: 'The lived body is a cultural identity produced within the perceptions that dawn through it.' While biology 'treats "the body" as a thematisable object moving towards an already abstract meaning', for Merleau-Ponty the body is a 'living substance or existence which must be assumed contingently as the condition for the expression of a point of view'.[9]

The epigraph to 'Eye and Mind' is a statement by Paul Cézanne as recorded by Joachim Gasquet:

> What I am trying to convey to you is more mysterious; it is entwined in the very roots of being, in the impalpable source of sensations.[10]

The centrality of the activity of painting to Merleau-Ponty's ontological formulations in the essay is introduced with a quotation from the poet Paul Valéry to the effect that the painter 'takes his body with him' in his work:

> Indeed we cannot imagine how a *mind* could paint. It is by lending his body to the world that the artist changes the world into paintings. To understand these transubstantiations we must go back to the working, actual body – not the body as a chunk of space or a bundle of functions but that body which is an intertwining of vision and movement.[11]

The epigraph to 'Eye and Mind' leads back to 1945 and 'Cézanne's Doubt', the essay Merleau-Ponty devoted entirely to the study of the painter's work. Two quotations from Emile Bernard's *Souvenirs de Paul Cézanne* of remarks attributed to the painter are surely the keys to the significance of Cézanne for Merleau-Ponty's thought as it develops fifteen years later in 'Eye and Mind', most important: 'The landscape thinks itself in me and I am its consciousness.'[12] Secondly:

> 'We have to develop an optics, by which I mean a logical vision – that is, one with no element of the absurd.' 'Are you speaking of our nature?' asked

> Bernard. Cézanne: 'It has to do with both.' 'But aren't nature and art different?' 'I want to make them the same. Art is a personal apperception, which I embody in sensations and which I ask the understanding to organize into a painting.'[13]

Movement, or more accurately a 'motor project', exemplified by the kind of activity Cézanne describes, is not just prompted by visual stimuli, it is the extension and end point of vision itself.[14] The painting is not a *representation* of the world but a material extension of it, a trace of body/consciousness/world in a continual process of coming-into-existence in the perceptual field. While the structure of subject and object relations is conceived as an intertwining, a circuit of outside/vision to inside/movement, simultaneously embodied vision produces distance/difference. Lived perception is by definition a relation of reversibility. Enveloped in the visual field we are positioned, at once, as seers in a subjective reality, and as objects seen by others. At the same time, as seers, we are divergent even within ourselves. This is because the same body that looks at things can also see parts of itself; it is in a reversible position as both subject and object for itself. '*Écart*' is Merleau-Ponty's term for this condition, variously rendered in English translation as 'deflection', 'divergence', 'spread', 'deviation' and *'dehiscence'* (a bursting, or an opening by divergence of parts). He writes:

> The enigma derives from the fact that my body simultaneously sees and is seen. That which looks at all things can also look at itself and recognize, in what it sees, the 'other side' of its power of looking. It sees itself seeing; touches itself touching; it is visible and sensitive for itself. It is not a self by transparency, like thought, which never thinks anything except by assimilating it, constituting it, transforming it into thought – but a self by confusion, narcissism, inherence of the see-er in the seen, the toucher in the touched, the feeler in the felt – a self then that is caught up in things, having a front and a back, a past and a future...[15]

In this account of subject-object relations there never is total split or separation but consciousness in divergence and deflection, self-world a seemingly paradoxical structure of unity at a distance and difference within the same. This is the 'synergistic' system of correspondences that Merleau-Ponty calls 'flesh'. Cathryn Vasseleu explains that '[t]he *body* is a term within flesh – it participates in so far as it becomes perceivable *only through its structuration as perceiving/perceived*.'[16]

Cézanne's late landscape pictures, in particular the watercolour studies, provide Merleau-Ponty with an example of lived light and space, as opposed to its conceptualisation in Cartesian thought, where it is understood by comparison, by means of measurement; in other words according to an idea that precedes and is outside the lived experience of the phenomena. In the Cartesian system:

> …it is best to think of light as an action by contact – not unlike the action of things upon the blind man's cane. The blind, says Descartes, 'see with their hands'. The Cartesian model of vision is modelled after the sense of touch.[17]

Perspectival projection is an example of a model of 'blind' vision constructed according to the pre-existing system of geometry. In corporeally-based perception space is '…reckoned starting from me as the null point or degree zero of spatiality. I do not see it according to its exterior envelope; I live it from the inside; I am immersed in it.'[18] It no longer is 'a matter of speaking about space and light, but of making space and light, which are *there*, speak to us'.[19] If space and light are already *there* then the painter is working within the field of the vision of things at the same time s/he looks at them. The world makes the painter visible in its sight as the painter makes the visible world in her/his by painting; their roles are reversible. 'That is why,' writes Merleau-Ponty, 'so many painters have said that things look at them.'[20] It is complete fascination with the maddening ambiguity of the lived perception of voluminosity, with the how and where of the depth of the world/self, the confusing narcissistic space of existing 'caught up in things' that, according to Merleau-Ponty, 'animates' the painter. Not just any painter, a painter like Cézanne who was driven to attempt to 'unveil' the visible means by which the world comes to be before our eyes in its visibility. In so doing painting 'gives visible existence to what profane vision believes to be invisible'.[21] What painting reveals is the normally invisible ground of the visibility of things as we see them in our everyday lives. This is not a function of light that illuminates things from the outside but of *lighting* as a relation. *Lighting* is not detachable from the things we see and is entirely dependent on our situation as seers in the perceptual field. Merleau-Ponty sets out this distinction in a crucial passage in 'Eye and Mind'. It opens with an indirect reference to Cézanne:

> What exactly does he ask of it? To unveil the means, visible and not otherwise, by which it makes itself mountain before our eyes. Light, lighting, shadows, reflections, color, all these objects of his quest are not altogether real objects; like ghosts they have only visual existence. In fact they exist *only at the threshold of profane vision*; they are not ordinarily seen. [Italics mine]. The painter's gaze asks them what they do to suddenly cause something to be, and to be *this* thing, what they do to compose this talisman of a world, to make us see the visible.[22]

A brilliant example of space as a function of *dehiscence* comes not from a painting by Cézanne but rather from Rembrandt's *The Nightwatch.*

> The hand pointing towards us in *The Nightwatch* is truly there only when we see that its shadow on the captain's body presents it simultaneously in profile. The spatiality of the captain lies at the intersection of the two perspectives which are incompatible and yet together. [23]

Lighting, manifest here as shadow, is the medium of visibility. It comes into view in painting as the normally invisible 'lining' of the visibility of the things as we see them in the world. Secondly lighting attains visibility as *depth*. The spatiality of the captain in *The Night Watch*, the voluminosity of which he is a part, is created as a thickness, rather than the void dividing solid objects in Cartesian space, *between* one view of the object, the hand, and another in the immaterial shadow it casts. But lighting attains only borderline visibility. Depth, which is the visibility of lighting, always has the quality of ambiguity because its structure is one of an oscillating reversibility between its own visibility and those things it makes visible. Visibility and invisibility coexist in their difference and painting is the place we catch sight of divergence as the structure of lived subject/object relations in the field of perception. Merleau-Ponty goes so far as to say that, in effect, paintings are never paintings of anything other than that structure:

> The painter's vision is not a view upon the *outside*, a merely 'physical-optical' relation with the world. The world no longer stands before him through representation; rather it is the painter to whom the things of the world give birth by a sort of concentration or coming-to-itself of the visible. Ultimately the painting relates to nothing at all amongst experienced things unless it is first of all 'autofigurative'. It is a spectacle of something only by being a 'spectacle of nothing', by breaking the 'skin of things' to show how things become things, how the world becomes world.[24]

The idea of lighting becomes clearer in the example of corporeally located perception of colour. Merleau-Ponty quotes Paul Klee quoting Cézanne's statement that colour is the 'place where our brain and the universe meet':

> Thus the question is not of colors, 'simulacra of the colors of nature'. The question rather concerns the dimension of color, that dimension which creates – from itself to itself – identities, differences, a texture, a materiality, a something...[25]

Colour is the example *par excellence* of those 'not altogether' objects the painter seeks that have only visual existence; furthermore the visual existence of colour as any particular colour is relational and highly unstable. In lived perception the colour of an object does not remain identical in any context. There is no 'true' colour that can be abstracted from the specific perception of a thing in its relation to other things. In painting the invisible 'flesh' of the everyday visibility of things finds its most profound manifestation as a shifting depth, never determinable in its extent, produced by colour modulation. Bridget Riley, a painter herself deeply engaged with the practice of Cézanne, and with a long-standing interest in the work of Merleau-Ponty, puts it like this:

> I…did not realize for a very long time to what a profound extent the basis of colour is instability…one never sees colour isolated, so you never know exactly what any particular colour is. On a canvas, true, it is physical paint, but a colour is not material. Each shade gives off a different light, and these interact according to what is next to what…[26]

> Colour is the proper means for what I want to do because it is prone to inflections and inductions existing only through relationship: malleable yet tough and resilient. I do not select single colours but rather pairs, triads or groups of colour which taken together act as generators of what can be seen through or via the painting.[27]

Merleau-Ponty quotes Giacometti's view that 'Cézanne was seeking depth all his life'.[28]

> [I]n the watercolors of Cézanne's last years, space (which had been taken to be self-evidence itself and of which it was believed that the question of *where* was to be asked) radiates around planes that cannot be assigned to any place at all: 'a superimposing of transparent surfaces,' 'a flowing movement of planes of color which overlap, advance and retreat.' [29]

Here Merleau-Ponty's argument for painting as ontology paradoxically hinges upon an account of the figure ground relation as a metaphor for lived subject/object relations in the perceptual field. He describes a work that, in its rhetorical articulation of unmarked paper that is as unstable in its status as ground as the planes of colour that fail to definitively cohere as figure, provides representational support for a lived perception experienced as the ambiguous, shifting space of a divergent world/self 'by confusion, narcissism, inherence of the see-er in the seen'. This is more semiotics than ontology, more translation than 'transubstantiation'. Yet a series of paint marks at the same time is the material residue of particular moments of the painter's immersion in the perceptual world, of a moving eye as '*that which* has been moved by some impact of the world, which it then restores to the visible through the traces of the hand'.[30]

It is a sense of a corporeally defined perception, the idea of the painter 'lending' her body to the world that I hear lodged in Frankenthaler's sentence 'I know the landscapes were in my arms as I did it.' In the catalogue for the *Nature in Abstraction* exhibition at the Whitney Museum the painter defines landscape, we remember, as 'changing views', 'motion caught'. There is no trace of the Nova Scotia sketches in the Frankenthaler literature. There are no reproductions of works on paper directly attributed to that holiday trip in the summer of 1952.[31] But in a Merleau-Pontian sense, their actual existence is neither here nor there, either then or now. In Frankenthaler's statement it is not the sketches that were in her arms but the landscapes. If we re-cast her words in the light of Merleau-Ponty's thinking in 'Eye and Mind', they read something like this. The painting body back in New York poised over the bolt of raw cotton duck tacked to the studio floor was itself constituted *as* the changing views, the movement of light and colour across the Nova Scotia landscape intertwined in each movement of the painter's eye and hand, whose trajectory ended in the painted marks of the sketches made *in situ*. It is not that Frankenthaler brought the sketches home to work *from*, but rather that the process entailed in their making constituted the painting body that back in the studio had there, with diluted pigment and canvas on the floor, to relocate and re-articulate itself now in relation to the contingencies of Pollock's Country.

To experience perception's corporeally defined reality as Merleau-Ponty proposes it, of course, does not mean that we ever rid ourselves of the *thought* of seeing. Vision is always doubled, there is the thought of seeing, *and* vision as it actually occurs as body, what Merleau-Ponty calls 'vision in act', or 'action at a distance', thought 'occasioned' by what happens in the body. Obviously any painter who turns to landscape as the starting point for a painting always already sees it through the filter of other paintings, how could it be otherwise? They are her/his resources, providing a vocabulary, sets of rhetorical devices determined in different historical and social formations to be worked with and through. Indeed, for the painter other paintings can well be described using Merleau-Ponty's formulation as structures of 'vision as an operation of thought'. Cézanne, no less than any other painter, was exempt from seeing Provence filtered through Poussin and the Venetians he loved, looked at and copied in the Louvre on his visits to Paris. From 1893 onwards he had a reproduction of Poussin's second version of the *Arcadian Shepherds* (1638) pinned to the wall of the studio he built at Les Lauves as his base for that solitary work in landscape from which the last works emerged.

What captivates Merleau-Ponty about Cézanne's practice in relation to his own philosophical project is the compulsion, manifest in the paintings and the texts recording Cézanne's approach to his work, to dispel existing cultural screens between the act of painting and what he saw through direct exposure to 'some impact of the world'. Put another way, and inflected with Greenberg's concerns as art critic in the early 1950s: Cézanne describes his sensations in front of nature as something like a seismic reverberation through the body acting to shatter existing mental images and dislodge internalised cultural conventions for visually organising the world in painting.

Fundamentally the practice signified by the name 'Cézanne' functions in the work of both Merleau-Ponty and Greenberg (though differently) as a myth of beginnings and renewals. The re-appearance of the Mont Sainte-Victoire motif in *Mountains and Sea* signals Frankenthaler's involvement in a particular moment in the culture of advanced New York painting as it was being defined in the criticism of Clement Greenberg in relation to his conception of the figure of Cézanne. I want to argue, though, that the primary value of Cézanne for Frankenthaler was that she recognised, inscribed in the late watercolours, something like Merleau-Ponty's notion of a contingent process of corporeally defined perception as a non-binary structure of subject-world as unity at a distance and difference within the same.

Indeed unity at a distance and difference within the same is not a bad description of the relation between pigment and support arising as a result of the technical 'innovation' of soak-stain for which *Mountains and Sea* is noted. It is difficult to determine the location of the weave of the canvas (its tooth) in relation to the patches of coloured pigment: is it sitting behind or is it breaking the surface of the chromatic element? Oscillation between the two possible positions produces the shallowest depth-as-blur, the effect is most intense in the central vertical section of the canvas.[32] Julia Brown has written that in *Mountains and Sea* 'background and foreground coexist'.[33] This is only the case, however, in the middle vertical third of the painting where colours do not overlap but stack up with unmarked areas of canvas equal in their relative values to produce a single plane. Indeed we might read the depth-as-blur, the thickness of the central third of *Mountains and Sea*, as an effect of *dehiscence,* a bursting which constitutes the painting's composition. In the left vertical third of the painting, unmarked canvas, with some light lemon, billows forward barely anchored by six stains of colour combining to create a diagonal movement from bottom right to top left. In the right-hand third of the painting a green hill/boat-like shape overlaps a horizontal blue band producing the illusion of recession. If we look at reproductions both of the Pearlman collection *Sainte-Victoire* watercolour and *Mountains and Sea* (see pls. 1 & 3) it is as if in *Mountains and Sea* the Cézanne watercolour has burst open from the top down the centre like a seed pod, the two halves held fast together at the base precisely by the overt signifiers of Cézanne in the painting: the abutted square blue mark and leaf-shaped green one fundamental building blocks of his late watercolours. It is as if immersed in the visual field of the tiny Cézanne watercolour, working within its gaze, Frankenthaler discovered its 'flesh' as *Mountains and Sea.*

To describe *Mountains and Sea* in these terms is to shift Merleau-Ponty's notion of painting as an ontological process from its operation in nature to the artwork as cultural site or place. In 'Eye and Mind' Merleau-Ponty has this to say about the historical life of works of art:

> As for the history of art works, in any case, if they are great, the sense we give to them later on has issued from them. It is the work itself that has opened the perspective from which it appears in another light. It transforms *itself* and *becomes* what follows; the interminable interpretations to which it is *legitimately* susceptible change it only into itself.[34]

Merleau-Ponty calls this an 'active manner of being' for art works made in the past as phenomenological, material objects continually in the process of being made *in the present.* In this passage he manages to articulate a sense of artworks in the mode they exist for painters. Not as formalist art history would have them as stylistic 'influences', and not only as the sites of a multiplicity of pre-existing rhetorical, historical, social, psychic and political meanings. For painters they also exist as present, phenomenological worlds, perceptual fields within whose vision the painter comes to exist as painter. But their visibility, their lighting as the invisible dimension of their worlds, no less than those of the natural one, must be found in the act of painting. If the tiny eye of a Cézanne watercolour caught Frankenthaler in its gaze, her exposure to the perceptual field of Jackson Pollock was quite literally by a total, corporeal immersion in its materiality: the vast expanse of unprimed canvas, the partial visibility resulting from its position flat on the floor, the unpredictability of fluid paint.

In January and February 1978, the André Emmerich Gallery in New York hosted a touring exhibition called *Helen Frankenthaler: a Selection of Small Scale Paintings 1949-1977*, organised by the U.S. Information Agency.[35] Footage of the painter supervising the hang of the exhibition is included in *Frankenthaler: Toward a New Climate*, Perry Miller Adato's film about Frankenthaler and her work made in the same year.[36] In medium close-up directly to the camera Frankenthaler informs us, 'This is a show of work I've never shown before, it dates from 1949 until now. Making small pictures is a necessity and a real part of me, but it wasn't where I really lived.' The present tense of the beginning of the sentence suggests that making small pictures still is part of Frankenthaler's practice in 1978. The switch to the past tense at the end of the sentence coincides with Frankenthaler's walking up close to a tiny painting called *New Jersey Landscape*. She says of the work, 'This I have great sentiment and nostalgic feelings for because I made it in '52': the year of *Mountains and Sea*. Making small pictures in landscape as an engagement with another set of small pictures made in landscape, Cézanne's watercolours, was, I suggest, crucial to Frankenthaler in 1952, even though by then Pollock's 'foreign country' on the studio floor was where she 'really lived'. Time and again, in the Frankenthaler literature, the artist associates the activities both of making and looking at painting with the idea of place, of habitation. 'I seem to find myself *in* something new in terms of nature,' Frankenthaler says in the *Nature in Abstraction* catalogue interview, looking back at her own paintings made during the previous two years. She is loath to fix whatever it is she finds herself 'in' as an idea, a concept, but offers a description of what happens in the making process. Recall the passage I quoted at the beginning of this chapter:

> In the last couple of years I have made paintings in which an animal shape or a nose and mouth, numbers, apples, etc., appears as part of an otherwise totally abstract picture. These images are not put down to be recognized for what they are, nor are they surrealist. They seem to be spontaneous and necessary points of departure, often disappearing completely, on and off, before the picture is finished.[37]

Perhaps what is registered in this description is the process of painting as the production of embodied knowledge of other paintings as perceptual fields, as, in fact, a number of 'places'. The *Nature in Abstraction* interview appeared in 1958.

The apples and numbers to which Frankenthaler refers in this passage about something new in terms of nature appear as elements in a specific painting made during the previous two years. The painting is *Eden* of 1956, a significant reworking of the pastoral genre. I offer a reading of *Eden* in the final chapter of this study. In 1952 the relation of *Mountains and Sea* to nature is already complex: a nesting of Cézanne's Country (culture) in Nova Scotia (an actual landscape) in Pollock's material world of painting on the studio floor, which he had declared *was* nature.[38]

These emotions of the body

I have argued that Virginia Woolf's *To the Lighthouse*, a novel concerned with finding 'new tools' for the representation of character in fiction, parallels in significant ways Freud's theorisation of subject formation in the psychic domain. I have argued that in the narrative of Lily Briscoe's struggle to make her painting Woolf imagines a possibility beyond Freud's proposition in 'Beyond the Pleasure Principle' that the activity of symbolic substitution and language acquisition is a response to the absence of the maternal body. In the final remembered/daydreamed scene of Lily Briscoe and Mrs Ramsay on the beach Woolf imagines a structure of subjectivity that does not involve either loss or mastery of the maternal body. I have argued that this psychic configuration is inscribed as spatial ambiguity, a blurring of the distinction between figure and ground in the painting Lily Briscoe finally makes. In an article written in 1995, titled '"These Emotions of the Body": Intercorporeal Narrative in *To the Lighthouse*' Laura Doyle, working with the feminist problematic in the discipline of literary criticism, reads *To the Lighthouse* in association with Merleau-Ponty's phenomenology, drawing attention to points of intersection between the two bodies of thought.[39] Just as I have argued that the Lily Briscoe narrative functions to supplement the Freudian Oedipal account of psychic subject formation with a different, maternal imaginary, in Doyle's reading of the novel it inflects Merleau-Ponty's neutral, universal philosophical discourse with the question of sexual difference.

For Doyle, *To the Lighthouse* is an example of a resistance to what she describes as 'Western logocentrism's "absent centre" as the effaced materiality of history'.[40] It is precisely through Lily Briscoe's painter's consciousness of the materiality of things and other human beings in the physical world that the spaces 'rendered empty by patriarchal culture and thought' are 'reincarnated'. Doyle suggests that with the character of Lily Briscoe the writer creates 'a site of hitherto uncoded embodiment' which transgresses the patriarchal framing of corporeally defined experience within which the traditional mother, represented by Mrs Ramsay in the novel, is both caught and complicit.[41] Doyle's argument hinges upon the emphasis Woolf places on the difference between Mr and Mrs Ramsay's relation to the physical world in part one of the novel. Mr Ramsay blindly rampages alone through its garden *mise-en-scène* locked in his mental world of acts of heroism, of individual error and death's confirmation of the irreducible separateness of each human subject in life. By contrast, Mrs Ramsay is rarely free from the demands and material needs of family and guests. When she does have a moment to herself she articulates a different sense of what it means to be alone:

> It was odd, she thought, how if one was alone, one leant to things, inanimate things; trees, streams, flowers; felt like they expressed one; felt they became one, in a sense were one; felt an irrational tenderness thus…as for oneself. [42]

Doyle argues, however, that Mrs Ramsay's relation with the material world is coded by her 'heterosexual orientation' in it.[43] A *leaning towards* inanimate things is channelled by the conventions of Victorian patriarchal heterosexuality, enshrined in the institution of middle-class marriage, into a total submission to, and identification with, them. Organising the material necessities and providing the material texture of the life that both supports and grounds Mr Ramsay's flights of abstract philosophical thought literally wears Mrs Ramsay out, as Lily Briscoe observes. Yet it is Mrs Ramsay's swing in the other direction that marks the end of her narrative and prefigures the end of her life. In the short paragraph that brings the first section of the novel to its conclusion, Mrs Ramsay relinquishes altogether her way of knowing the world as a corporeally defined reality. She acquiesces in her husband's insistence that the weather will not be fine enough to make the trip to the lighthouse the following day. Mr Ramsay responds to his wife's lived experience of nature's signs: that the wind often changed, for example, with fury at 'the folly of women's minds'.[44] Mrs Ramsay submits to the abstract proof of the barometer and Mr Ramsay's brutal pursuit of 'truth'. His mind, like 'a hand raised shadowing her own', in the end obliterates it altogether.[45]

In her role as a woman who engages in an activity of representation Lily Briscoe upsets the patriarchal conventions of the Ramsays' world. Her mode of existence is not a complete fusion with inanimate things; they do not 'express her' as they do Mrs Ramsay. Her painting mediates. The activity of painting *leans* on the existence of material things but simultaneously, as representation, it functions to produce a measure of distance from them. Yet it is never a complete separation; painting is a material process. Furthermore, the formal language of Lily's painting does not tip over into a totally abstract system of mark and colour, it retains a reference to the motif, walls, hedges, tree branches. As such the activity of painting figures in the novel as resistance to the dematerialising and disembodied mode of philosophical and scientific thought, represented by the character of Mr Ramsay, which proves fatal to Mrs Ramsay's embodied knowledge. Socially, Lily Briscoe's rejection of the institution of marriage, which she links to her dedication to painting, marks her transgression of the heterosexual economy, which determines the either/or choices Mrs Ramsay must make in relation to the human and non-human world. While Mrs Ramsay either mutely lives her embodied relation with the material world, or must relinquish it under the pressure of objective, universal 'law' in the form of her husband, the unmarried artist manages to represent a different mode of embodied knowledge in painting.

For Doyle, Merleau-Ponty's idea of the reversibility of seer and seen in the field of perception as 'dehiscence', an opening onto one another at a distance as a kind of fleshing out of the space between, implies that the non-human world is recognised as a source of continuity between past and future. Inanimate things 'endure beyond the temporality of individual humans' who have nevertheless inhabited 'the same orders of temporality and spatiality'.[46] This interpretation enables Doyle to argue that although Mrs Ramsay's life comes to a shockingly abrupt end in the central section of the novel, her status in the remainder of it is not entirely defined in terms of absence. Some residue, some texture, of Mrs Ramsay subsists as consciousness/knowledge in the inanimate world that 'expressed' her in life and endures beyond her death. This is the same inanimate world with which Lily engages in the process of painting. From this perspective Lily's painting is indeed not, as she herself insists, 'of' Mrs Ramsay. It does not *represent* Mrs Ramsay but rather is her 'transubstantiation' as the flesh of the world.

While Lily often comments on the power of distance in her narrative, space is never empty. It is never a void entirely separating here and there, one thing from another, but is akin to the element Merleau-Ponty names 'flesh'. Again and again space is corporealised in Lily's narrative. Having set up her easel on the edge of the lawn as Mr Ramsay, Cam and James set off on their trip to the lighthouse, Lily immediately turns from facing her new canvas to look out across the bay. Woolf describes her condition:

> She felt curiously divided, as if one part of her were drawn out there – it was a still day, hazy; the lighthouse looked this morning at an immense distance; the other had fixed itself doggedly, solidly, here on the lawn.[47]

Not only is some part of Lily Briscoe 'drawn out' across the space of the bay, it is also drawn into it to mingle with the vaporous density Woolf gives that space. The day is hazy and the space has a texture that tips sight into the zone of tactility creating a very Merleau-Pontian sense of corporealised vision. As Lily struggles at close range with the formal and technical elements of painting to articulate space on her canvas, she returns to the view of the bay, 'moved as she was by some instinctive need of distance and blue'.[48]

> So much depends then, thought Lily Briscoe, looking at the sea which had scarcely a stain on it, which was so soft that the sails and the clouds seemed set in its blue, so much depends, she thought, upon distance: whether people are near us or far from us; for her feeling for Mr Ramsay changed as he sailed further and further across the bay. It seemed to be elongated, stretched out…[49]

Again the space across which Lily gazes is not empty but filled with material 'feeling', 'emotions of the body' stretched out through elements of landscape described so as to evoke memories of tactile sensation in the reader. Sails and clouds are embedded in a 'soft sea', and by the end of the passage Lily herself feels immersed, to a point that restricts speech, in an element made up of 'all sorts of waifs and strays' of inanimate things into which many human lives had spilled:

> One need not speak at all. One glided, one shook one's sails (there was a good deal of movement in the bay, boats were starting off) between things, beyond things. Empty it was not, but full to the brim. She seemed to be standing up to the lips in some substance...[50]

The most striking image of all in terms of Merleau-Ponty's insights in 'Eye and Mind' is of Lily Briscoe pacing the space between her easel and the view of the bay. Her process of painting involves not solely a movement of the eyes from the canvas on the easel to the motif in front of it. The activity also includes a movement of the whole body across the lawn through morning light between the close materiality of paint and the distant view of the lighthouse. It is an image that concretises Merleau-Ponty's idea of the painter's body as the site of that intertwining of vision and movement, subject/world he calls 'flesh', becoming 'transubstantiated' as painting. The problematic space between the forms in Lily's painting (the wall and the hedge of the motif she looks at) finds its resolution in corporeal terms. Woolf's narrative displaces the space between the two forms *on* the canvas onto the distance between two viewpoints *off* the canvas that Lily literally fills with her body as she moves through it between her picture/motif and the bay. Initially, Lily describes the problem with her picture in lateral terms: the need to connect the mass on the right with that on the left involving a 'vacancy' in the foreground. Yet the introduction of some object, some form, into that space is not the answer. The solution is figured off the canvas not as an object but as a *movement* between the poles of proximity (the canvas) and distance (the edge of the lawn and the view across the bay) in the visual field. A space between them, a measure of distance, of depth, is at once opened up and filled by a body moving through it. The process of moving and painting, an 'intertwining of vision and movement', has the effect of provoking for a brief moment the return of Mrs Ramsay to her place in the window *between* the 'masses' of wall and the hedge.[51]

For Doyle the character of Lily Briscoe functions to extend the intercorporeality of persons and things beyond the realm and life of the mother, breaking up the tradition that burdens the mother with full responsibility for it.'[52] This is necessarily an extension beyond the realm of the family with which the mother is synonymous. Neither Mrs Ramsay's daughter, nor the same social class as the Ramsay family, Lily Briscoe breaks the closed family and social circuit. Momentarily she opens up a space, dramatised in the second phantasmatic beach scene, for not simply the one way transmission Doyle theorises, that of some of the burden of Mrs Ramsay's intercorporeal knowledge to Lily Briscoe, but also in the other direction, from Lily to Mrs Ramsay, the necessity of providing embodied knowledge with representational support. We could read Mrs Ramsay's activity of letter writing on the beach as a signifier of transmission in this direction. Doyle's Mereau-Pontian reading of the beach scene can be pushed further. Lily Briscoe functions as a figure of *écart* deflecting the conventions of heterosexual patriarchy that produce for Mrs. Ramsay in the first part of the novel the either/or options of merging with, or complete separation from, the material world of objects and other human beings. In the remembered/daydreamed beach scene Lily Briscoe functions in perfect accord with her profession as a painter. Momentarily she spatialises (as the movement of *dehiscence*) Mrs Ramsay's relation with the world.

4

SOMETHING NEW IN TERMS OF NATURE

> There is perhaps a good reason why we should re-examine the archaic form of the pastoral, re-examine a certain return to nature or the hope invested in a nature that you shouldn't imagine our ancestors thought of in simpler terms than we do.
>
> Jacques Lacan[1]

The matrixial gaze

In her feminist readings in the history of philosophy collected under the title *An Ethics of Sexual Difference*, Luce Irigaray performs a reading of the 'The Intertwining – The Chiasm' section of Merleau-Ponty's *The Visible and the Invisible.*[2] From the outset Irigaray articulates what Merleau-Ponty cannot say, indeed what cannot be said in the discipline of philosophy because the latter is a discourse determined by patriarchal social order and a phallocentric psychic economy indifferent to sexual difference.

> M-P.
> *'The visible about us seems to rest in itself. It is as though our vision were formed in the heart of the visible, or as though there were between it and us an intimacy as close as between the sea and the strand.'* (pp.130-31)
> I.
> If it were not the visible that was in question, it would be possible to believe that Merleau-Ponty is alluding here to intra-uterine life. Moreover, he uses 'images' of the sea and the strand. Of immersion and emergence? And he speaks of the risk of the disappearance of the seer and the visible. Which corresponds doubly to a reality in intrauterine nesting: one who is still in this

> night does not see and remains without a visible (as far as we know); but the other seer cannot see him. The other does not see him, he is not visible for the other, who nevertheless sees the world, but without him.[3]

In her reading of 'The Intertwining – The Chiasm' Irigaray makes explicit that which Laura Doyle only implies with her juxtaposition of Woolf's *To the Lighthouse* and Merleau-Ponty's philosophical speculations in *The Visible and the Invisible.* Irigaray specifies Merleau-Ponty's metaphoric use of maternity in his ontology of flesh, its unacknowledged debt to the 'maternal-feminine'.[4] Yet missing from both Irigaray's and Doyle's work with Merleau-Ponty is Woolf's crucial insight in *To the Lighthouse* about painting as the exemplary site of the inscription of a subjectivising process in a different relation to the maternal-feminine, albeit inscribed within the inescapably phallic structure of the practice.[5]

Through her particular interpretation of the processes and technical procedures of painting, to which she was exposed through her intimacy with painters and critics of painting, Woolf brings a different difference into language in *To the Lighthouse.* Lily Briscoe paints and offers a commentary on what she discovers through painting. Furthermore in *To the Lighthouse* painting functions on the border between the phenomenological and the psychic worlds of Lily Briscoe: in terms of the theoretical tools I have thus far brought to bear on the Lily Broscoe narrative, between Freud and Merleau-Ponty.

In 1995 Bracha Lichtenberg Ettinger, an Israeli painter and psychoanalyst working in Paris, published *The Matrixial Gaze* under the imprint of the Feminist Arts and Histories Network Press.[6] In *The Matrixial Gaze* discoveries made in an actual practice of painting are pursued theoretically in the field of Freudian and Lacanian psychoanalytical thought about the function of aesthetic activity. Lichtenberg Ettinger's thinking is also informed by Merleau-Ponty's work on the ontological status of aesthetic practice.[7] In her preface to *The Matrixial Gaze* Griselda Pollock locates Lichtenberg Ettinger's work as part of 'the re-consideration of the politics of visual representation associated with French intellectual and political traditions since *Psychoanalyse et Politique*, the publishing venture *des femmes*, and the writings of Julia Kristeva, Hélèn Cixous, Annie Leclerc and Luce Irigaray.'[8] From work across these several discourses and practices emerged the possibility of proposing the late pre-natal, intra-uterine environment as a model for expanding the Lacanian concept of a monistic, phallic Symbolic to include another signifier for the psychic processes by which human subjectivity is formed. As a symbolic concept the *Matrix* raises to the level of signification traces gleaned from an archaic pre-natal space of encounter with the 'invisible specificity of the female body'.[9] The *Matrix* is a subjectivising 'stratum' of spatial negotiation and adjustment between '*I*' and the unknown '*non I*' in which there is a recognition of difference but where each neither rejects nor assimilates the other.[10]

Woolf's Lily Briscoe narrative offers us an imaginative purchase on the concept of the *Matrix* and its aesthetic mode of trans-scription, *metramorphosis.* The 1927 novel imaginatively pre-figures the work of Bracha Lichtenberg Ettinger in the 1990s. Yet it can only be identified as a pre-figuration precisely through the frame of Lichtenberg Ettinger's 1990s theorisation of a signifier, 'in and from the feminine', that allows us to name the final beach scene in *To the Lighthouse* in the field of a different, *sub*-symbolic as a *matrixial* configuration.[11] *The Matrixial Gaze* allows us to name the moment between Mrs Ramsay and Lily Briscoe on the beach, which, in 1927, Woolf can only have Lily Briscoe describe in terms of its affect as, 'extraordinarily fertile'. It also enables us to theorise a psychic terrain that I want to argue is inscribed in *Mountains and Sea* to a significant degree.

As did Virginia Woolf, Helen Frankenthaler publicly dissociates her work from the discourse of psychoanalysis, perhaps like Woolf fearing the closure of vulgar, pop-psychological reductive interpretation. Nonetheless, while in 1951 Greenberg was critically consigning Surrealism, the movement that explicitly engaged with Freud's discoveries, to the 'outer darkness of academicism'; Frankenthaler responded to 'a certain surreal element' in Pollock's black and white paintings shown the same year. Frankenthaler described the attraction as 'the understated image that was really present: animals, thoughts, jungles, expressions'.[12] It is not in terms of 'image', however, but at the level of Frankenthaler's endless fascination with painting's fundamental spatialising capacity that I want to consider *Mountains and Sea* in relation to the fundamental *subjectivising structures* elaborated in the discourse of psychoanalysis. I want to consider *Mountains and Sea* in conjunction with Lichtenberg Ettinger's propositions in *The Matrixial Gaze,* a specifically feminist intervention into the Freudian/Lacanian elaboration of 'some system of aesthetics with an economic approach to its subject matter'.[13]

As the title indicates *The Matrixial Gaze* involves an engagement with Jacques Lacan's theory of the gaze as *objet a* in the scopic field. This is elaborated in Seminar XI, *The Four Fundamental Concepts of Psychoanalysis,* and it is indebted to the work of Merleau-Ponty and his thinking about how painting functions in the perceptual field. But for Lacan Freud's thought precisely represents, to borrow Frankenthaler's words, 'something new in terms of nature'. In his seminar *The Ethics of Psychoanalysis,* delivered in Paris between 1959 and 1960, Lacan argues that Freudian psychoanalysis signalled the end of that 'dream of a total, complete, epidermic contact between one's body and a world that was itself open and quivering', characteristic of the 'exercise of poetic lyricism'.[14] Lacan's example is the poetry of Walt Whitman. Delivered as Merleau-Ponty began work on 'Eye and Mind' in Cézanne's Country at Le Tholonet, *The Ethics of Psychoanalysis* critically pre-empts the philosophical propositions Merleau-Ponty was to offer in a text itself both poetic and lyrical.

'The Freudian project has caused the whole world to re-enter us, has definitely put it back in its place, that is to say, in our body and nowhere else,' writes Lacan.[15] While there is a significant difference between Whitman's dream of a complete epidermic contact between the body and the world and Merleau-Ponty's notion of 'flesh', as a *chiasmic* consciousness producing relation between human subject and world, Merleau-Ponty's concept retains the sense of a generalised all-over relation. By contrast, in the Freudian account of subject formation, the points of contact between the body and the world are specifically located as the actual openings of the body, the oral, anal and genital zones which, from birth, constitute the pathways of the child's exchange with its external surroundings. They are the regions of the body that solicit the most attention and care, and consequently stimulation, from the mother (or child's first care giver) and are thus 'predestined' as sites of sexual excitation and sources of the sexual drive (*triebe*). In 'Three Essays on the Theory of Sexuality' (1905) Freud defines them as the 'erotogenic zones'. He identifies four relational aspects that define the structure of the drive namely, pressure, source, object and aim. Pressure is the charge of energy that directs the organism towards its aim. The aim of the organism is to be rid of the state of tension existing at the source of the drive, and it is through the object that the drive can achieve its aim.

In the early stages of infancy the sexual 'instincts' are attached to the functions of the body concerned with self-preservation – hunger being the prototypical one. The pleasure the infant derives from sucking at the breast is associated in the first instance with the satisfaction of hunger. The breast is the object of the satisfaction of its need. But the pleasure is not solely derived from the satisfaction of hunger but also in some degree from the stimulation of the mucous membrane of the mouth in the action of sucking. The breast as the object of the satisfaction of that pleasure becomes detached from its function as provider of nourishment. Only when the breast has to be abandoned and is lost as object does the sexual drive become independent of its initiating movement in need. It then functions in auto-erotic mode when the infant takes part of itself for its object, as in the example of thumb sucking, or else it takes some other external object as substitute, a blanket, a toy. A 'component instinct' of sexuality is associated with each of the somatic sources of excitation located at the openings of the body. It is the attainment of satisfaction of the sexual drive, by a process of detachment from a direct tie with the particular somatic apparatus providing the material for self-preservation (its original object), along a chain of symbolically representative objects that characterises the sexual drive. The crucial outcome of this process is that this split becomes the point of emergence of fantasy activity that involves elements often far removed in character from the original corporeal object.[16]

The drive has its source in bodily stimulus, but in 'Instincts and Their Vicissitudes' Freud writes that, 'Although instincts are wholly determined by their origin in a somatic source, in mental life we know them only by their aims.'[17] He characterises the drive as 'lying on the frontier between the mental and the physical', and it is the mental dimension of sexual instinct he defines with the term 'libido'.[18]

Libido involves the idea of a 'psychical representative', the mechanism by which the somatic is inscribed in the psyche. It is inscribed there in two ways, as a quantity of affect and as an 'ideational representative' registered in the unconscious. According to Laplanche and Pontalis an 'ideational representative' ('*Vorstellungsreprasentanz*') should be understood to mean, 'a delegate (in this instance, a delegate of the instinct) in the sphere of ideas'.[19] Ideational representatives are not only registered in the unconscious but are for Freud the very material of which the unconscious system is constituted, in the first instance in the mechanism of 'primal repression':

> We have reason to believe that there is a *primal repression*, a first phase of repression, which consists in the psychical (ideational) representative of the instincts being denied entrance into the conscious. With this a fixation is established; the representative in question persists unaltered from then onwards and the instinct remains attached to it.[20]

Freud speculated that the mechanism of primal repression was probably set in motion by very intense archaic experiences.

In Merleau-Ponty's phenomenology consciousness is called into being – is *drawn out* – by 'some impact' of the perceptual world. In Lacan's reading of Freud's account of beginnings the traumatic violence of the impact of our earliest world forces it completely inwards/into words. Nonetheless, it is Merleau-Ponty's account of the primacy of visual perception that provides the context for Lacan's theorisation of the gaze in seminar XI. *The Visible and The Invisible,* left unfinished when Merleau-Ponty died in 1961, was published posthumously in 1964, the year Lacan delivered seminar XI, and he makes direct reference to the event in the seminar.[21] 1964 also saw the re-publication by Gallimard of 'Eye and Mind' as a separate monograph. Lacan's unacknowledged debt to 'Eye and Mind' in seminar XI takes the form of the central role he gives painting in his elaboration of the gaze as *objet a* in the scopic field.

The implication for painting of Lacan's reading of the Freudian project is that henceforth the relation between the painter and 'nature' can only ever be phantasmatic. From Merleau-Ponty's perspective painting is the material trace, the end point of an external movement, a 'motor project', in and of the phenomenal world, a 'transubstantiation' of corporeally defined perception. In terms of the libidinal economy painting is the end point of an internal, unconscious movement no longer directly attached to its corporeal prototype but inscribed with residues of corporeality at the ideational level.

For Merleau-Ponty painting is a manifestation and extension of the intertwining of subject/world in a relation of unity at a distance and difference within the same. Painting is 'fleshly' consciousness materialised. For Lacan, on the other hand, painting as a function of the gaze is an indicator of something missing in any visual representation of the subject/world relation.

> In our relation to things, in so far as this relation is constituted by the way of vision, and ordered in the figures of representation, something slips, something passes, is transmitted, from stage to stage, and is always to some degree eluded in it – that is what we call the gaze.[22]

For Merleau-Ponty painting is bound up with the texture and density of being *between* seer and things seen, and seer as both subject and object for itself in the field of perception as *écart* and *dehiscence*, an opening up/onto and divergence. In the Lacanian psychic domain painting connects with the opposite, a lack in being. It connects with the psychic residues of primal repression, occasioned by the split of the subject from its archaic modes of experience linked to the Other (mother), felt as the traumatic and painful presence of an absence, a no-thing, which is, in psychoanalytical terms, a psychic object, a psychic *thing*. This is Lacan's *objet a*, whose pressure in the visual field is felt as the gaze, which is invisible and hidden from us, but by which we unendingly long to be seen.

Lacan takes up Merleau-Ponty's proposition of the pre-existence of space and light in the world, so that the painter is already working within the field of the vision of things at the same time as s/he looks at them. But for Lacan while we are 'beings who are looked at in the spectacle of the world', the world does not reveal this fact to us in the field of perception.[23] For Merleau-Ponty the invisible 'lining' of the visibility of the world is materialised in the process of painting as *lighting*, the connective depth and spacing of subject/world. For Lacan light in its 'natural' relation to the eye functions in the opposite direction, to obscure, flatten and separate the seeing eye from the point of the world's vision. He indirectly references, and concurs with, Merleau-Ponty's critique of the Cartesian model of light in 'Eye and Mind' as the disembodied, constructed relation of perspectival systems:

> The essence of the relation between appearance and being, which the philosopher, conquering the field of vision, so easily masters, lies elsewhere. It is not in the straight line, but in the point of light – the point of irradiation, the play of light, fire, the source from which reflections pour forth. Light may travel in a straight line, but it is refracted, diffused, it floods, it fills – the eye is a sort of bowl – it flows over, too, it necessitates, around the ocular bowl, a whole series of organs, mechanisms, defences.[24]

It is the play of light in 'its pulsatile, dazzling and spread out function' which Lacan calls 'the gaze as such', or the *objet a*.[25] Taking Merleau-Ponty's idea of *lighting* as a pre-existing, corporeally defined spatiality in which we are immersed whose structure, invisible in everyday life, the painter can reveal, Lacan reconceptualises light in the Freudian domain locating its function as connected to the eye as one of the body's libidinised openings onto the world. Lacan makes of light in the natural world an 'eye beam' whose field of illumination is eroticised:[26]

> That which is light looks at me, and by means of that light in the depths of my eye, something is painted, something that is not simply a constructed relation, the object on which the philosopher lingers but something that is an impression, the shimmering of a surface that is not, in advance, situated for me in its distance. This is something that introduces what was elided in the

> geometral relation – depth of field, with all its ambiguity and variability, which is in no way mastered by me. It is rather it that grasps me, solicits me at every moment, and makes of landscape something other than perspective, something other than what I have called the picture. [Bracha Lichtenberg Ettinger's correction of Alan Sheridan's translation].[27]

Diffuse light, as manifestation of the gaze, spreads out as an opaque screen separating the eye from the unseen point from whence it comes – the unseen viewpoint of the gaze. The 'eyes' the world turns towards us as patterns of coloured shape in the perceptual field are blind imitations. Lacan uses the example of *ocelli,* eye-like markings such as those on a butterfly's wing.[28] The eye is both captivated and deceived by light as a pulsating stained screen resisting access to the point of view of the gaze. Just as we are immersed in space and light which pre-exist us in Merleau-Ponty's theorisation, so we are surrounded by the Lacanian gaze, located as subjects who are also objects for others and for ourselves. We actively look, and at the same time are situated as a stain (amongst stains) on the opaque screen to be looked at. In the phallic, scopic dimension the subject is analogous to *ocelli*:

> From the outset, we see, in the dialectic of the eye and the gaze, that there is no coincidence, but, on the contrary, a lure. When, in love, I solicit a look, what is profoundly unsatisfying and always missing is that – *You never look at me from the place from which I see you.*
>
> Conversely, *what I look at is never what I wish to see.*[29]

For Lacan painting is a manifestation of the gaze in its function as deceptive lure, a screen in the field of culture as the play of light is a screen in the realm of nature. He takes the example of *trompe-l'oeil* painting as representative of the function of painting *per se.* The status of *trompe-l'oeil* painting is not that it competes with appearance, its fascination for us arises in the moment when, caught in its thrall, we realise that it is a representation: 'the picture is the appearance that says it is that which gives the appearance.' [30] Painting is a dialogue with that which is beyond appearance. It draws attention to the lacking something *beyond* the visual field precisely by screening it with a deceptive illusion *in* the visual field.

It is in the register of the split between the eye and the gaze that, according to Lacan, we are to understand 'the taming, civilising and fascinating power of the function of the picture'. Painting provides food for the eye desperate in its hunger for the gaze. It stays the subject's search for the gaze, appeases for a while its desire to be looked at by the gaze. It suspends momentarily the eye/gaze relation organised according to the Oedipus complex by engaging the subject's (including the painter's own) narcissistic fantasies. This, according to Lacan, 'is the pacifying, Apollonian effect of painting'.[31] In the other direction he cites the expressionism of painters such as Munch and Ensor as making a direct appeal to the gaze in the field of the Other. Presumably this is because such painting in the agitated and overt display of its parts *as* painting makes a spectacle of itself in an attempt to catch the attention of the gaze.[32]

In the passage from Merleau-Ponty's conception of painting in 'Eye and Mind', to Lacan's re-working of it in *The Four Fundamental Concepts of Psychoanalysis*, its status changes. It moves from an activity involved with the emergence of the hidden, contingent, spatial organisation of world/subject in the field of conscious perception as occasioned at the site of the body in movement through the phenomenal world, to one in dialogue with a dimension *for ever* beyond appearance. The eye desires the lost archaic gaze for ever hidden from it by the flat mimetic screen of the perceptual field. What is lost to painting in its transition from the philosophical discourse of Merleau-Ponty to the psychoanalytic discourse of Lacan is its *lived* spatialising function. Space is collapsed at the site of a subject phallically constituted in two dimensions by the opposition one/Other manifest in the scopic zone as appearance/beyond appearance, visibility/invisibility.

Bracha Lichtenberg Ettinger's intervention into the field of Lacan's theorisation of the function of painting in relation to the gaze has its starting point in implications left undeveloped by Freud in his 1919 essay 'Das Unheimliche', ('The "Uncanny"'). Interested in 'feelings of repulsion and distress' that can be a component of the aesthetic experience, Freud takes as object of his analysis E.T. A. Hoffmann's *The Sand-Man*, a story in which sight is the central motif.[33] Freud locates the source of the frightening atmosphere of the tale in anxiety about damaged eyes, experienced most acutely in childhood and recurring in adult life. From the study of mythology, and his analysis of the dreams and fantasies of neurotic patients, Freud concludes that the fear of blindness is often a substitute for the dread of castration, the eye being a substitute for the male sexual organ. 'The self-blinding of the mythical criminal Oedipus,' Freud writes, 'was simply a mitigated form of the punishment of castration.'[34]

In his opening analysis of the linguistic usage of the German word 'unheimlich' (literally 'unhomely', or unfamiliar) Freud finds that its opposite, 'heimlich', has amongst its many shades of meaning, 'one which is identical with its opposite… what is *heimlich* thus comes to be "*unheimlich*"'.[35] Thinking psychoanalytically about this instance of linguistic usage Freud makes the following proposition:

> In the first place if psycho-analytic theory is correct in maintaining that every affect belonging to an emotional impulse, whatever its kind, is transformed, if it is repressed, into anxiety, then amongst instances of frightening things there must be one class in which the frightening element can be shown to be something repressed which *recurs*. This class of frightening things would then constitute the uncanny; and it must be a matter of indifference whether what is uncanny was itself originally frightening or whether it carried some *other* affect. In the second place, if this is indeed the secret nature of the uncanny, we can understand why linguistic usage has extended *das Heimliche* ['homely'] into its opposite, *das Unheimlich*…for this uncanny is in reality nothing new or

> alien, but something which is familiar and old-established in the mind and which has become alienated from it only through the process of repression.[36]

In his discussion of the relation between the experience of uncanniness and the repressed infantile castration complex Freud makes the passing observation that for some people the idea of being buried alive is the most uncanny thing of all:

> And yet psycho-analysis has taught us that this terrifying phantasy is only a transformation of another phantasy which had originally nothing terrifying about it at all, but was qualified by a certain lasciviousness – the phantasy I mean, of intra-uterine existence.[37]

Calling upon an instance from clinical experience to support his thesis, Freud makes a direct analogy between dreams of a place or country and the maternal body:

> There is a joke saying that 'Love is home-sickness'; and whenever a man dreams of a place or a country and says to himself, while he is still dreaming: 'this place is familiar to me, I've been here before,' we may interpret the place as being his mother's genitals or her body.[1] In this case too, then, the *unheimlich* is what was once *heimlich*, familiar; the prefix '*un*' ['un-'] is the token of repression.[38]

Close reading these passages Bracha Lichtenberg Ettinger finds a possibility left open by Freud for proposing another unconscious subjectifying dimension in addition to castration anxiety. Even if Freud writes that 'it must be a matter of indifference whether what is uncanny was itself originally frightening or whether it carried some *other* affect', in so saying he is making a distinction between two possibilities. The fear of being buried alive, a transformation of a fantasy of intra-uterine existence, is not originally frightening but carried 'some *other* affect Freud calls "a certain lasciviousness"'. Bracha Lichtenberg Ettinger argues that, unlike Lacan in his re-reading of Freud, Freud himself does not subjugate the intra-uterine fantasy retroactively to the fantasy of castration. This leads her to begin to conceive of the co-existence with the castration complex a subjectivising function linked to feminine 'corpo-reality'. It leaves its trace in symbolic representation but has hitherto been un-speakable in a representational order governed by the phallus as exclusive signifier. If the *matrix* is a *symbolic* filter some level of (almost) repression must be involved to constitute it as such, so it is important to note that Freud suggests that womb fantasies and the fantasy of castration have a different relation to repression. Womb fantasies become frightening *only by force of repression*, whereas the experience from which the fantasy of castration arises is *originally* frightening *before* it is repressed:

> These two complexes being mounted on two different 'tracks', a matrixial phantasy cannot be dissolved into a castration phantasy, and so, the *Unheimlich* arises not only 'from proximity to the castration complex' but also from proximity to the matrixial complex of phantasy that is linked to sexual difference 'viewed in a *female's* way', to the feminine/prenatal encounter in the Real that touches its *several* partners and not only the woman.[39]

It follows then that the matrixial complex of fantasy co-emerges *with* the castration fantasy; neither excludes the other. This point is important for the argument to follow about the function of colour in *Mountains and Sea.*

To recapitulate: the Freudian account of the formation of human subjectivity as a process of individuation entails the detachment of the drives from their need-propelled connection to bodily orifices, which as a result are constituted as erotogenic zones. Traces of the repressed experience of these archaic separations 'return' in fantasmatic configurations through the processes of condensation and displacement, and they achieve symbolic articulation in Freudian/Lacanian analytic discourse as the rhetorical figures of metaphor and metonymy. To propose the *matrix* as a relational trans-subjectivising zone prior to archaic separations entails imagining a different pathway by means of which *almost* repressed traces of the matrixial encounter come to be inscribed in the symbolic register.

To my mind one of the most difficult aspects of the *matrix* to think and to write about is its character as a subjectivising space of several – more than one, but not an infinite number – of co-emerging and co-fading *partial* subjects and *partial* objects. If the *matrix* transports into signification traces gleaned from archaic experience prior to splitting there are obvious implications for its relation to the *objet a.* If the *objet a,* delegate of the *thing,* arises in the split from archaic experience connected with orifices of the body which are thus constituted as libidinalised sites of fantasy, there are two obvious implications for the *matrix.* In a zone of continual spatial adjustment (which by definition can never be a total separation) between *I* and *non I* – an 'encounter between the most intimate and the most distanced unknown' (modelled on the late intra-uterine relation) there never arises a *thing* as a whole *thing,* that is to say, the psychoanalytic object in the *matrix* is a partial object, felt as an almost painful/almost pleasurable, almost presence of an almost absence. The 'almost' in this linguistic attempt at catching a sense of the matrixial *objet a,* its never quite rhetorical figure, is a *movement,* the process of co-emerging-co-fading Lichtenberg Ettinger calls *metramorphosis.* In the *matrix,* then, libidinal investment is different. Not determined as specific erogenous zones connected with the body's actual openings into the world, it functions as 'erotized aerials of the psyche'.[40] With this image Lichtenberg Ettinger catches the sense of the libido as both an extension out from and a between, a relational and all-over subjectivising, that is to say *signifying,* erotic affect of the most intimate exteriority. As *matrixial fantasy,* Frankenthaler's statement about making *Mountains and Sea,* 'I *know* the landscapes were in my arms as I did it' quite literally makes *sense.*

Difficult to think and difficult to write, I have absolutely no problem understanding the concept of the *matrix* and its operational mode *metramorphosis* from experience with the materials and processes of painting. I have argued that the technical procedures and processes of painting are inextricably caught up in the binary logic of *fort/da*. That is to say, painting can only proceed as a temporal/spatial play of the material there/not thereness, mark/no mark, form/no form, of the figure/ground relation. Yet also fundamental to painting as the articulation of material substance is its instability. At the most obvious level there is the capacity of paint and canvas to flip between a presence as material, and material by means of which an image of something in the world, or from the imagination, is transmitted. Colour, because it functions as a relation, is the most unstable of all elements of painting, and thus has the capacity for spatial negotiation and adjustment of the utmost subtlety. To which Frankenthaler introduces another level of ambiguity when she soaks colour into the weave of unprimed canvas further blurring the distinction between figure and ground.

Bracha Lichtenberg Ettinger defines *metramorphosis*, the process of continuous investment of each partial subject and partial object in the common space of the *matrix*, as follows:

> *Metramorphosis* is a creative principle. *Relations-without-relating* with the other – based on attuning of *distance-in-proximity* (and not on *either* fusion *or* repulsion) – reflecting and creating *differentiation-in-co-emergence* and accompanied by shared diffused and minimal pleasure/displeasure *matrixial affects* of silent alertness, open an *within/with-out* space. They induce instances of co-emergence of meaning.[41]

I suggest that traces of the *matrixial* subjectivising strata, a *matrixial* knowledge, are inscribed in *Mountains and Sea* at every level of the painting and that is why it is so difficult to '*see*' from the perspective of dominant, phallically determined art-critical knowledge. And I mean difficult to see not only, indeed not even, in the sense of the painting's literal quality of not-quite-focused visuality. The painting is difficult to 'read' semiotically from within the frame of the conventions of dominant art critical knowledge in its specific manifestation in 1952, precisely because the *affect* of the *matrixial objet a* inscribed in the painting troubles the terms upon which the 'clarity' of that discourse depends.

I indicated earlier that a concern with emphasising the material flatness of the picture-plane in the central vertical third of the painting co-exists with perspectival projection from front to back from the left to the right vertical sections of the canvas. Yet within the 'flat' central section the soaked colour produces a shallow space as the illusion of a continuous oscillation between figure and ground (as it does throughout the whole of the painting). Pollock had already breached the traditional distinction between line and colour, drawing and modelling with his dripped skeins of liquid pigment. But in *Mountains and Sea* Frankenthaler moves between a) colour as drawing b) colour as reference to the external world of landscape suggested in the right section of the canvas; and c) colour as specific and unmistakable reference to a historical precedent and resource, as in the blue and green Cézannian watercolour brushmarks enlarged at the base of the canvas. In some parts of the painting 'space' (in the sense of unmarked ground as Merleau-Ponty uses it in his description of a Cézanne watercolour) 'radiates around planes that cannot be assigned to any place at all', in others, notably in the left-hand section, it reads securely as background. Finally, *Mountains and Sea* touches in the most intimate way on art criticism itself. In a painting practice maintained in the presence of Greenberg's influential critical advocacy of a painting rid of any reference beyond its own means, *Mountains and Sea* embraces a fascination with 'the understated image that was really present'.

While *metramorphosis* as an aesthetic, signifying process is not exclusive to painting, I propose that painting is its privileged site, just as language is the privileged site for the operation of metaphor and metonymy as rhetorical devices. But consistent with Lichtenberg Ettinger's theorisation of the matrix as an expansion of (not a replacement for) the Lacanian phallic Symbolic, *metramorphosis* occurs *within/swerves across* the binary, phallic procedures of painting. There is no better fictional dramatisation of the co-existence of these spatio/temporal structures than Woolf's story of Lily Briscoe in *To the Lighthouse.* There exists, however, a representation of Helen Frankenthaler's working process in which the 'climate' of *metramorphosis* is palpable.

Helen Frankenthaler paints a picture

At the end of Perry M. Adato's 1978 film *Frankenthaler: Toward a New Climate,* Helen Frankenthaler paints a picture. I deliberately echo, here, the title of the series of articles run in *Art News* in the 1950s that documented artists at work in their studios.[42] Adato's film is a direct descendant of that series. But the animated image reveals a dimension of the working process invisible in photographs. Let us call it a certain kind of attention. The most striking example of what I mean occurs at the moment painting begins. Frankenthaler, in a white house painter's overall, walks towards a rectangular stretched canvas, head down, thoughtfully stirring paint in a can. Stopping at its short edge she looks up and across it then kneels with one knee on the canvas, brush in can, poised to make the first mark. At the precise moment she leans forward to do so, her movement is curtailed, she hesitates. She straightens up and glances diagonally across to the opposite corner of the canvas. It is as if she has heard a sound from there indicating something happening to which she must attend before moving decisively to brush on a wide sweep of mulberry coloured liquid pigment close to the centre of the canvas. She swiftly follows through by pouring the colour from the can in a liquid trail on top of the brush mark. The flood begins to take its own course out into the surrounding canvas. The artist intervenes with a brushed response. The painting sequence is cut with annoying frequency (36 edits in 5 minutes 45 seconds) so that the real-time rhythm of work is continually interrupted and manipulated. It is clear enough, though, that a sense of timing is crucial to the process. Timing implies a relation, a finely tuned sense of when to come in. With that slight hesitation signifying acute attention Frankenthaler enters her painting like a vocalist in a song whose instrumental line has already begun. It is difficult to say with any certainty, then, whether the first mark is an initiation or a response. For certain, the painter chooses to act with colour in a fluid state (for the most part) and in so doing encourages the extended duration of the active life of the material. She accepts the consequences for her intentions of its prolonged instability, allows it to guide her next move.

Andrew Forge, curator of the touring exhibition of Frankenthaler's small paintings organised by the U.S. Information Agency in 1978, wrote an article for *Art International* in which he employs the idea of 'collaboration' in a discussion of the artist's process.[43] The article appeared in the April-May 1978 issue of the journal, a month after *Toward a New Climate* was broadcast by WNET/Channel thirteen, New York. When Forge uses the conceit of speaking as if he were Frankenthaler describing the process of painting, I suspect he builds upon what he saw in Adato's film:

> As I work, I attend so closely to the face of the painting in front of me that I lose sight of the boundaries between me and it. When I see something that I have done to it, it is like a clue to further things I must do – it amplifies my attention. Trains of thought and feeling are set in motion which I have to complete, or at least explore, and the impulse to do so is such that I cannot distinguish between what is interior to me and what is out there on the canvas. Naturally I attribute these desires to the painting rather than to myself, for it is only in the painting that they have concrete or stable existence and the painting is the only means I have of either being aware of them or acting upon them.[44]

Is, then, what we witness in *Toward a New Climate*, albeit truncated and manipulated by the temporal demands of the film, evidence of a *metramorphics* of femininity?

We can proceed by comparison. Indeed to play, as I have, on T.J. Clark's description of Pollock's painting activity as a 'metaphorics of masculinity' already signals an engagement with the best known comparison of the two working processes in the history of feminism's consideration of post World War II American painting.

In the essay 'Killing Men and Dying Women: A Woman's Touch in the Cold Zone of American Painting in the 1950s' Griselda Pol…But it is impossible – ridiculous at this point – to try and sustain the 'Griselda Pollock writes' mode of 'objective' scholarly citation. We've sat around and talked about this stuff for too many years now, as student and supervisor, lately as colleagues in the university, on trains, planes, in galleries, restaurants as friends. I'm less and less inclined to carve out from the body of your work the chunks I need to support 'my' argument, determine and contain with quotation marks the otherness of 'your' text, a device that simultaneously authorises its incorporation into mine. Legitimate academic practice is structurally Oedipal.

In 'Killing Men and Dying Women' you refer to T.J. Clark's description of Jackson Pollock's painting practice as 'metaphorics of masculinity' when you return, for a third time in your work, to a comparison of photographs of Frankenthaler and Pollock at theirs.[45] I have a special interest in 'Killing Men and Dying Women', an essay in which you explore murderous, Oedipal creativity in several registers. You acknowledge your debt to our conversations about painting in the essay, and footnote my forthcoming work on Frankenthaler.[46] To add support to your argument in 'Killing Men and Dying Women' that creative daughters are no less susceptible to the 'anxiety of influence' than creative sons, I should say here that what you did write about Frankenthaler there almost stopped my forthcoming work coming at all. I thought then that there was little else I could contribute to the subject.[47] *

Your analysis of Pollock's 'metaphorics of masculinity' in 'Killing Men and Dying Women' is perhaps the last word on the subject of his technique analysed from the perspective of psychic fantasy structured according to the phallic logic of *fort/da*.

> Any painting that results from such a staging of the encounter of artist and canvas as a field, as a territory of the (m)Other, is the product of risk, experienced in that procedure, that what the painter threw from his stick, was also part of himself, and that what he covered, was his own absence/nonsense. At the same time there is the equal possibility that what he covered was the m(O)ther, what he mastered was her absence, and what he distanced was her engulfing presence, separation from which is the necessary condition of the would-be-subject's existence as a subject.[49]

---

*This abrupt and tetchy direct address to Griselda Pollock in the context of an academic text may come as a shock, or even an affront to some readers who may feel alienated or embarrassed by exposure to the violent energy of a private struggle. Pressure to reject or assimilate the feminist 'mother'/feminist 'daughter' is, however, a reality, and the integrity of this particular work of feminist scholarship, which engages with a founding feminist analysis of the potentially deadly effects of the Oedipal psychic structure on art making and the formation of art historical canons, would be seriously undermined if its own Oedipal dimension were not acknowledged when it was recognised. I decided to monitor by performing in the text the effect of destructive forces that at this point threatened to stall it. An ongoing 'conversation' with Griselda Pollock surfaces now and again throughout the rest of the book. It developed as rhetorical strategy designed to register certain trans-subjectivising events from which knowledge co-emerged during the course of researching and writing the text that became this book. My purpose is to acknowledge not only the unavoidable 'familial' Oedipal tensions involved in a feminist intellectual genealogy in process, at close quarters, but as well to catch accompanying movements of a matrixial subjectivising psychic stratum that promises a future for feminist work relations *in difference* that will inevitably affect dominant proprietorial structures of cultural knowledge production, circulation and reception.[48]

In the famous film of Pollock painting made in 1951 by Hans Namuth and Paul Falkenberg, we do not see how he moves to begin work.[50] They film the preliminaries: he swaps a pair of good shoes for paint spattered boots, mixes paint in a can with a stick, lights a cigarette, then there is a cut to painting already in progress. After Frankenthaler's measured activity what strikes me now watching Pollock in action is that once he starts he does not stop. His movement is continuous but for one moment when he has to remove the burning cigarette-butt from his mouth and tosses it to one side. The act breaks the rhythm of his movement and from his body's reaction to the split second falter the idea suggests itself that the source of his 'focused fury of creation' is actually panic – he *must* not stop.[51] He needs to keep response-time to a minimum. The speed and manner of paint application (the two inextricably linked) function to blind him to all aspects of the independent action of each skein he throws – save one: its position in his immediate field of vision.

Following the logic of your analysis I can add that Pollock collapses the time of response to, and reflection upon, the movement of the 'm(O)ther', upon which I have argued, from the evidence of her actions in *Toward a New Climate,* Frankenthaler's practice depends to a significant extent. In his terror of 'm(O)ther' time Pollock evacuates space. The Namuth film makes explicit in terms of process what we experienced as its result in the Jackson Pollock retrospective at the Tate Gallery: a deadly airlessness, the oppressive pressure of impacted paint matter. Mostly the paintings extend laterally, very rarely in depth.

Centre stage at the conference on Jackson Pollock at the Tate Gallery in April 1999, T.J. Clark argued that cancelling out the 'virtuality' of middle space created in the play between size and scale, where most painting had operated until then, is precisely what makes Pollock's paintings absolutely of their time.[52] 'True scale – true elation and terror and endlessness (the scale of experience in 1950) – is reached through the medium of true size.' [53] Clark focused on Pollock's small paintings of the 1950s in his talk. This is what he had to say about *Number 6, 1950*:

> It wanted to create the illusion of molecular compression, of course on the verge of turning into its opposite – explosive, destructive force (not exploding, but reaching critical mass)...Serge Guilbaut was right to intuit in them a truly horrifying, truly horrified sense of fusion and fission, small and large, nucleus and particle scatter. What was new to the cold war sense of space was the notion – a commonplace notion, leaking uncontrollably from Los Alamos to *The New Yorker* – of small and large as instantly convertible, as terrible immediate transforms of each other.[54]

Confirming one thread of your argument in 'Killing Men and Dying Women' about the deadly effects of phallocentric culture, by disavowing the gendered implications of what (and indeed how) he argued, Clark performed the other, that a phallically determined art history is no less murderous.

Never never land

In 1998, in the course of a brief conversation over coffee in a bar a few blocks away from her Manhattan studio, I asked Helen Frankenthaler what she was currently working on. She replied,

> I'm not making work at the moment, it doesn't seem so important – I no longer feel like dying for the sake of the work in the way I used to. And I think it's the wrong time for painting. History goes in cycles and this is not the time for painting. The end of painting was with Noland's final chevrons.[55]

At the time I was surprised and irritated by what I interpreted as Frankenthaler's masochistic loyalty to this cliché of the Greenbergian formalist end-game of avant-garde painting, according to whose linear, progressive logic her own practice never had quite qualified as painting anyway.

There is no denying the extent of Frankenthaler's social and psychic investment in the Father. *Toward a New Climate* is an interesting document in this respect. In an uncharacteristic gesture for one usually so reticent about revealing the psychic dynamics of her life, Frankenthaler provides some information about her childhood and the roots of her life as a painter in Adato's film.

> My father thought I was special from the day I was born and as a result I guess I felt special and somehow became what he projected onto me which was special. I was a very wilful child, I mean if I wanted to do something I wanted it my way. My father used to give in and feel this is what she wants, leave her alone, and my mother would say 'but she can't, she can't stay up that late, she can't go to the theatre, she should not be at the horse races,' and he would say 'why not, let her sleep in the afternoon, skip school, it's more important that she be exposed to this' – and I got spoiled.[56]

Frankenthaler's narration runs over a sequence of black and white images. First the announcement in the *Daily Mirror* of her birth to *Justice A. Frankenthaler and his wife Martha*. A photograph shows a nurse holding the tiny baby with the caption *Proud father? You Judge*. Next, a montage from a series of home movies beginning with a sequence of the infant Helen in white tennis dress and shoes shaking hands with her father over the net at the end of a match. A slightly older Helen holding a container imperiously demanding her father's immediate presence at the spout of a large pump she is managing to operate with vigour disproportionate to her size: Helen on a pony, then laughing with other children beside a huge car with a white dog at the window, sequences of the family on outings and holidays. Hers was clearly a privileged childhood with Alfred Frankenthaler at its centre.[57]

'When my father died everything changed,' explains Frankenthaler over the image of a page from the *New York Times* dated Monday 8 January (year out of frame). *Frankenthaler dies at 58*, reads the caption under his photograph. 'I was alone with a widowed mother in wartime New York,' continues Frankenthaler, 'and I was frightened. Bennington really saved my life; they took me seriously, anything you wanted to try, if you were serious and imaginative and a risk taker, was possible.'[58] Frankenthaler was twelve years old when her father died at the beginning of 1940. She entered Bennington College in 1946.

Weighed down by the grief and fear of private loss during those years, reports from Europe appearing in the American media must have made Frankenthaler acutely aware that affluence and social position were no guarantees against persecution and systematic murder in the public sphere. Surveys taken in America between 1940 and 1946 show that Jews were consistently seen as a greater menace to the welfare of the United States than were any other national, religious, or racial group.[59] A special little girl loses the man who constituted her as such, a loss whose terrors are magnified in the field of social and historical events in which she is situated. Bennington, a progressive liberal arts college for women (without female faculty members at that time) saved Frankenthaler's life because it stood in for her father. Like her father it took her wilfulness and ambition seriously. Perhaps as importantly, Bennington offered Frankenthaler refuge and protection from the manifestations of her mother's grief. We do not know: Frankenthaler has little to say about her mother in *Toward a New Climate* or anywhere else in the literature about her art.

In 'Killing Men and Dying Women' you write that sharing in the project of ambitious American painting in the 40s and 50s where sexual difference was 'publicly disavowed in the name of transcendent truths', women who were artists took a considerable risk. They had to negotiate the terms of their own interventions in the Oedipal game of 'reference, deference, and difference'. Those interventions would necessarily result from 'the whole complex of who each one of them was', which inevitably included 'dimensions of social, cultural psychic and even corporeal experience that is unacknowledged by a phallocentric culture'. At the same time they had endlessly to dodge 'the curatorial sniffing out of what would be deadly to their desires for recognition, the contaminating signs of a disqualifying "femininity"'.[60]

Evidence that Frankenthaler was quick to master the language of her field of activity comes in *Toward a New Climate* from the mouth of the painter Friedel Dzubas, with whom Frankenthaler shared a studio in 1952. 'You came out of a kind of never-never land with these paintings,' he reminisces to Frankenthaler. To camera he continues, 'These little paintings of hers, they had a kind of maturity that we all tried for, a kind of relaxed authority.'[61]

So exactly how is Frankenthaler positioned in the 'doubled field' you diagnose? You see I don't think she concerned herself that much with dodging 'the contaminating signs of femininity' in her work. Compared with Joan Mitchell, Nell Blaine, Grace Hartigan and Jane Wilson, contemporaries in whose company she appeared in the famous 1957 *Life* magazine photo-feature article, 'Women Artists in Ascendance', Frankenthaler's work is literally awash with elements that might be culturally construed as feminine.[62] Perhaps financial security, social position, a privileged education, and the confidence that she was special all took the edge off the necessity to dodge. What you write in 'To Inscribe in the Feminine: A Kristevan Impossibility? Or Femininity, Melancholy and Sublimation', however, read in tandem with the memory of a childhood as daddy's special little girl Frankenthaler chooses to make public in *Toward a New Climate,* does help to illuminate her position at the psychic level:

> According to a Kristevan analysis, the cultural terms on offer for the production of art have been structurally shaped by history in the possibilities and difficulties of the mother/son axis. The parallel for the feminine subject would have then to be a father/daughter axis which is the basis of so much of mediaeval feminine mysticism: a kind of holy incest practised by women mystics like Hildegard of Bingen, who called herself 'a feather on the breath of God'. That axis involves the identification of the daughter with the Father and with order, law, the symbolic, in relation to which 'she', the submissive daughter, smuggles in her feminine *Jouissance* as mystic masochism. In modern times this option has not been available for perverse negotiation.[63]

Bizarre as it may sound stated as baldly as this, I detect latent in the art historical/critical accounts of the genesis of *Mountains and Sea* the residue of the idea of holy incest. It comes into view as an effect of the anachronistic 'success' of Frankenthaler's identification with the Father. Let me show you what I mean.

In dominant art historical/critical analysis of the development of Frankenthaler as a painter between 1950 and 1952 in the lead up to *Mountains and Sea,* emphasis consistently falls on the relation between her practice and Pollock's. This does not mean to say that other factors are not taken into account, but that Pollock was the seminal figure in the creation of *Mountains and Sea* is axiomatic in the literature. The emphasis on the relation between the two bodies of work is produced in the repetitious practice of lifting from their original contexts and reworking, replies to questions asked of Frankenthaler about her encounters with the paintings of Jackson Pollock in exhibitions in 1950 and 1951. The sources for the quotes are the two earliest substantial articles on Frankenthaler's work, Henry Geldzhaler's 1965 *Artforum* interview with the artist, and Gene Baro's article for *Art International* published in 1968, in which he included extracts from correspondence with Frankenthaler.[64] However, to my mind, at the root of this critical practice is Morris Louis's much quoted statement that for fellow painter Kenneth Noland and himself Frankenthaler's *Mountains and Sea* was 'a bridge between Pollock and what was possible'.

I suggest that this statement can be read as the symptom of a repression. The Frankenthaler literature never disguises the power of the daughter's identification with the painter father; it was impossible to ignore. It was incandescent. Frankenthaler's brilliant understanding and utilisation of Pollock's painterly resources was overwhelming: in *Toward a New Climate* Dzubas recounts his amazement at the young Frankenthaler's intelligence and facility. Louis and Noland were famously stunned. Yet Louis's statement is a particularly revealing example of your point about the unavailability of the daughter/father psychic axis in the twentieth century. You point to a historical moment, in the mediaeval social order, when feminine *jouissance* could lean for representational support on a tradition of ecstatic religious experience generated in masochistic ascetic and penitential practices.

The absence of a symbolic site for 'perverse' negotiation of the daughter/father axis in modern times is registered in Louis's statement in which *Mountains and Sea* is characterised precisely as a painting which is not one. It falls between one thing, the work of Pollock, and another, i.e. what was possible for other men in a son/father relay – what you call 'reference, deference, difference'.[65] Louis's statement registers symptomatically the repressed scandal of *Mountains and Sea.* Undeniably present in its power, *Mountains and Sea* did not count as painting precisely because it was the illegitimate outcome of the practice of an *unholy*, that is to say a secular, incest culturally forbidden between brilliant young women and canonical artist fathers. Dzubas's expression 'never never land' registers as a spatio-temporal paradox the impossibility of naming the place in which Frankenthaler's 'little paintings' gained 'maturity' and 'relaxed authority'.

Frankenthaler's joy?

> Now again, moved as she was by some instinctive need of distance and of blue, she looked at the bay beneath her…
>
> Virginia Woolf [66]

In the story of beginnings and endings that characterises the authorized version of moves in post WWII American avant-garde painting, the innovation of stained colour in *Mountains and Sea* is both a beginning – Frankenthaler's opening gambit in the game as you would say – and also the beginning of the end of the game itself. Though implicated in the death of painting, administering a shot of liquid pigment to ease the labour of its last gasp in the work of Louis and Noland, Frankenthaler side-stepped its demise in her own work by what she described in the 1968 *Artforum* interview with Henry Geldzhaler as a tendency to 'side-develop':

> …one can look so pure that the result is emptiness – many readings of a work of art are eliminated and you are left with one note that may be real and pure but it's only that – one shaft…Often what I seem to fight is the idea that I'm on to something and going to drive it into the ground. I tend to side-develop, not to hang on, but in seeming to side-develop that's the way I really show my mark and continuity.[67]

The implication of 'side-development', however, is precisely registered in the other way in which Frankenthaler linked painting and death in her remark to me in 1998, when she said, 'I no longer feel like dying for the work in the way I used to.' I want to explore these two 'deaths', that of painting, and that of the ability to sustain a creative energy connected with 'side-development', specifically in relation to the question of colour in and beyond *Mountains and Sea*.

Supervising the hanging of the exhibition of her small works in *Toward a New Climate* Frankenthaler pauses to talk about a small painting called *With Blue* (1953). She describes the work (pl. 6) as 'a demonstration of what I was really about on a much larger scale around the post *Mountains and Sea* period':

> I was very involved in the whole problem of ambiguity. This blue is essentially the same blue in the same shape in the same part of this canvas, but each stroke and each bleed acts very differently and each one is necessary and they are all the same and doing the same job but they are totally different and not the same at all.[68]

Her linguistic formulation of the function of blue in the picture itself seems caught up with her involvement in ambiguity. I will return to its apparent lack of clarity in due course.

The productive problematic of Julia Kristeva's essay *Giotto's Joy* is precisely the difficulty of situating colour 'both within the *formal system* of painting and within painting considered as a practice'.[69] In a study of Giotto's Arena Chapel frescoes at Padua Kristeva locates the situation of colour and space in relation to the function of narrative and representation in the cycle of paintings. Narrative and representation are the level at which the 'theological norm' of the historical period is signified in the work.[70] Through distinctive articulation, particularly the striking effect of blue in the Arena Chapel, colour and space draw attention to themselves as elements of the *vehicle* of narrative and representation. That is to say, colour and space come into view as signifiers of the narrative as *painting*. They carry affective values independent of those, social and ideological, signified by narrative and representation. The fundamental argument of Kristeva's essay is, however, that colour and space appear independent precisely *because of* the 'everpresent norm' of narrative and representation – 'It tears itself from the norm, bypasses it, turns away from it, absorbs it, goes beyond it, does something else – always in relation to it.'[71]

For Kristeva colour and spatial organisation in Giotto's painting is the sign of a movement towards 'relative independence from a signifying practice patterned on verbal communication'.[72] That is to say away from painting in which meaning primarily resides at the level of narrative and representation. At the beginning and at the end of the essay Kristeva situates her interest in the work of Giotto. In the summation of her argument in the final paragraph she writes, 'I have made use of certain elements in Giotto's painting in order to present several problems relevant to painting as signifying practice.' The object of her reflections on Giotto's work has been, she writes, 'to encourage a return to the ("formal" and ideological) history of painting's subject within its contemporary production; to present the avant-garde with a genetic-dialectical reflection on what produced it and/or that from which it sets itself apart'.[73] In this project Kristeva takes her cue from Walter Benjamin:

> It is not a question of presenting works [...] in correlation to their own times, but rather, within the framework of the time of their birth, to present the time that knows them, that is, our own. [74]

'Giotto's Joy' first appeared in *Peinture* in January 1972. In 1965 something of the 'dialectical necessity and difficulty' of re-thinking the efficacy of avant-garde painting as a signifying practice is already registered in Frankenthaler's remarks to Henry Geldzhaler about the pursuit of purity turning to emptiness:

> Many readings of a work of art are eliminated and you are left with only one note that may be real and pure but it's only that, one shaft. For example, the best Mondrians, Newmans, Nolands, or Louis are deep and beautiful and get better and better. But I think many of the camp followers were empty.[75]

In Kristevan terms, what we have in the last work of Louis, in *Delta Theta (3-19)* of 1961, for example, and in Noland's 'final' chevrons, the diamond-shaped canvases of 1966, is colour totally independent of narrative and representation (fig. 9). Leaving aside for now questions about the withdrawal of the pictorial signified as *the norm* of painting by the mid 1960s, here let us approach Frankenthaler's comment about Noland and the death of painting from her own formalist perspective.

Louis and Noland took from *Mountains and Sea* the extreme condensation of the two signifiers of *painting as painting,* colour and space, resulting from the soak-stain technique, and pursued its possibilities *exclusively.* To extend Frankenthaler's suggestively phallic metaphor, in their hands it became one 'shaft', with a very limited life. Removed from its situation in *Mountains and Sea* relative to those elements of narrative and representation still functioning in the painting: the presence of Cézanne as a signifier of origins and renewals in the image of *Mont Sainte-Victoire* haunting it, the gestalt of the discourse of Surrealism via Pollock in the understated images that are really there, soak-stained colour/space became an empty signifier. Or rather it signalled, as Frankenthaler put it 'the end of painting'.

Her other remark about endings 'I no longer feel like dying for the sake of work', swings us away from the situation of colour within the formal system of painting and towards its situation in painting considered as a *practice,* that is as an activity of an embodied subject – a painter. Kristeva proposes that colour is situated in the

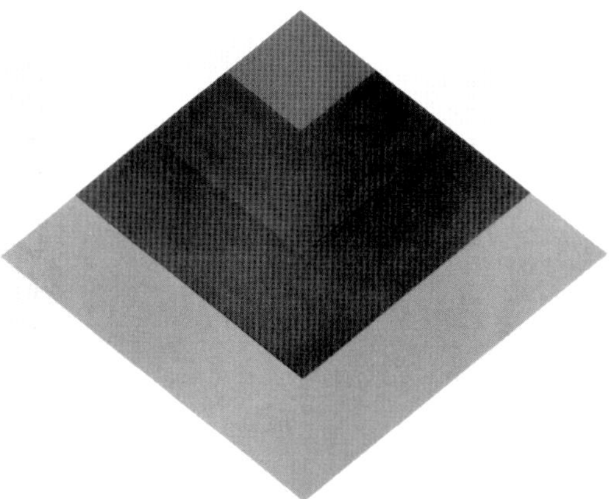

Fig. 9
Kenneth Noland, *Dark Sweet Cherry*, 1966,
acrylic on canvas, 56 x 70 in (142.2 x 177.8 cm)

scopic field as a sign of the hinge between the 'formation-dissolution' of the subject.[76] She pursues her argument through Freud's first topography of mental life, organised as consciousness, the preconscious and the unconscious, and it centres on what she identifies as a 'triple register' within Freud's concept of 'word-presentation' as a constitutive process of the preconscious system.[77] In his chapter on 'The Unconscious' in 'Papers on Metapsychology' Freud speculates that psychical energy linked to archaic perceptions (the force of some 'impact of the world', to borrow Merleau-Ponty's image) is inscribed in the unconscious as '*thing* presentation'. Freud defines '*thing* presentation' as 'the cathexis, if not the direct memory-images of the thing, at least of remoter memory-traces derived from these'.[78] *Thing* presentations, under the imposition of repression are raised to the level of consciousness when their energy is bound to 'word-presentations'. Only then is it possible for the primary process to be succeeded by the secondary process in which the syntactical operations of condensation and displacement, as metaphor and metonymy, organise conscious thought.

Kristeva understands Freud's term 'thing-presentation' as designating 'the pressure of the unconscious drive linked to (if not provoked by) objects'.[79] Thought, resulting from the imposition of repression, holds 'at bay' thing- presentations and their instinctual pressures. Word-presentation, as a mechanism of censorship in the process of symbolisation, is a relationship involving the perceptual *and* the verbal registers. In support of this argument Kristeva draws attention to the fact that Freud writes: 'But word-presentations, for their part too, are derived from sense perceptions in the same way as thing-presentations are.'[80] Word-presentation, then, represents a pressure of both external and internal origin:

> Word-presentations would then be doubly linked to the body. First, as representations of an 'exterior' object denoted by the word, as well as representations of the pressure itself, which, although intraorganic, nevertheless relates speaking subject to the object. Second, as representations of an 'interior object' an internal perception, and eroticization of the body proper during the act of formulating the word as a symbolic object.[81]

According to Kristeva word-presentation is constituted as a 'triple register' made up of 'a pressure marking an outside, another linked to the body proper, and a sign (signifier and primary processes)'.[82] The work of repression transforms this complex visual/verbal condition of the drive into the communicative system of language proper. Word-presentation as a process of symbolisation at the same time modifies the symbolic level 'affecting' it with the pressure and imprint of *thing*-presentations. Kristeva thus links word presentation with artistic practice, a function distinct from utilitarian communication.

Within the processes of the constitution of the subject in the visual field colour is situated in the triple register:

> as an instinctual pressure linked to external visible objects; the same pressure causing the eroticization of the body proper *via* visual perception and gesture; and the insertion of this pressure under the impact of censorship as a sign in a system of representation.[83]

Threatening the prevailing symbolic order of painting as a system of pictorial representation, colour is invested with a transformative function only within that system. If colour threatens the symbolic order in painting as a formal system, in painting as a practice, of both making and viewing, the chromatic experience necessarily threatens the unity of the subject constituted within the symbolic order. On the side of thing-presentation colour is linked to non-sense, non-being, that is to say the death drive, and experienced as *jouissance*. Colour is pleasure on the side of the death drive. Though involving a momentary destruction of meaning, colour is not an absence of meaning but rather its excess, a *something* Kristeva describes as 'differentiating negativity'.[84] Through the 'shattering' (the word is Kristeva's) effect of colour repressed dimensions of archaic experience are momentarily structured to 'revolutionise' the subject/representational dimension of painting. In Kristeva's fundamentally phallic logic repressed archaic material is necessarily equated with the feminine which is outside symbolisation, and the ground against which the symbolic comes to figure as such – inscription in the feminine indeed *is* a Kristevan impossibility. Nevertheless her theorisation of colour as a 'psycho-graphic' element in painting does allow us to move beyond the poles of either the inadequate, or the comprehensive but confusing, descriptions that currently do service as analysis of the function colour in *Mountains and Sea* in the Frankenthaler literature. It also helps us to understand the vicissitudes of sustaining an ongoing practice of painting in Frankenthaler's case.

In the history of post WWII American painting *Mountains and Sea* indeed *is* characterised as a revolutionary moment in painting linked with colour in the Kristevan sense. And consonant with the structural conditions for revolution elaborated by Kristeva, the *jouissance* of *Mountains and Sea* is recognisable only in the work of men: Louis and Noland's 'joy' was critically linked to *Mountains and Sea* by Greenberg in his 1960 essay 'Louis and Noland'.[85] Furthermore it materialised within the normative representational framework of critical practice, the individually authored critical essay. The sense of what making *Mountains and Sea* 'meant' to Frankenthaler herself enters the literature in 1965 as the anecdotal evidence of her own oddly articulated description embedded in the form of an edited dialogue – the interview. Her words, literally closer to the body, bear its mark as syntactical insecurity: 'I know I had the landscapes in my arms as I did it.' Perhaps now, though, we are in a position to locate Frankenthaler's not quite metaphorical statement in the field of the *matrix* as *metramorphic*. We can then go on to attempt a reading of colour in *Mountains and Sea* in the *matrixial* register.

Winter Palace: what can be seen through or via painting

The idea of a 'transport sign' is good.[86] It diverges from the idea of colour as a sign of censorship – an agent of repression, however complexly constituted in its relation to the drive, still a barrier – a block. If the *matrixial* subjectivising stratum is a filter for archaic intra-uterine corporeal-psychic experience prior to Oedipal splitting, it must necessarily, involve only *partial* subjects and *partial* objects in the different meaning-making relation Bracha Lichtenberg Ettinger names *metramorphosis*. Thus in the *matrixial* register there can be no singular unity – no integrity – of subject/meaning for colour to undo. How, then, does it signify there? As an approach to the question, it is useful to return to two quotations I used earlier and read again what Bridget Riley has to say about colour:

> I...did not realise for a very long time to what a profound extent the basis of colour is instability. An element so responsive to relationships and interaction as colour cannot be absolute and stable in the way that forms described by a line can be...one never sees colour isolated, so you never know exactly what any particular colour is. On a canvas, true, it is physical paint, but a colour is not material. Each shade gives off a different light, and these interact according to what is next to what...

Riley's description suggests the idea that colour in painting as a formal system might be homologous at the level of painting as a subjectivising practice (to stay with Kristeva's model) with *matrixial* partial subjectivities and partial psychic objects in the process of *metramorphosis*. Colour is never anything in itself, it is never 'one', it emerges as 'interaction', a relation. What follows is even more suggestive of a practice marked by the matrixial subjectivising stratum:

> Colour is the proper means for what I want to do because it is prone to inflections and inductions existing only through relationship; malleable yet tough and resilient. I do not select single colours but rather pairs, triads or groups of colour which taken together act as generators of what can be seen through or via the painting.

Bryan Robertson writing about space in Riley's work in 1971 observed that her 'true space, the quintessential and most dramatic space of all, is not confined to the picture plane: it is the distance between the spectator and the canvas'.[87] This is an interesting observation but a generalisation. What precisely does Robertson mean by 'space'? Let us take the specific example of a painting I know well. *Winter Palace* (1981) is one of a group of paintings Riley made in the early 1980s (pl. 7). It is in the collection of Leeds City Art Gallery and I visit it a lot. Each time the painting catches my attention just a few steps over the threshold of the room; in which it hangs. A field, best described as a 'density' (to convey a sense of fine-textured thickness) of cool grey-lilac emanates from the opposite corner of the room it dissipates the moment I move in to find out how the painting generates it. The surface of *Winter Palace* is composed of thin vertical bands of perfectly inert, flat matte oil paint on canvas. The relationship between the size of the canvas and the width of the stripes makes determining the individual colour components of the grey-lilac field a frustrating task. Obviously colour permutation, width of band, size of canvas, their relation, is precisely the crux of the matter, but try counting the bands of each colour, establishing which combinations are repeated at what sorts of intervals across the canvas. Standing close enough to count, moving from the left of the painting to the right, each colour is so destabilised by its neighbours it is hard to keep a tally. In *Winter Palace* colour functions not as something to be seen *on* the canvas, but as *knowledge* that the momentary materialisation (to fade as quickly) of 'the painting' – as a density in the field of vision somewhere *between* the picture plane and 'me' – is precisely a condition of a specific set of relations in which 'I' as viewer am inescapably implicated. 'I' do not so much see colour as apprehend *through* it the existence of an objectivising/subjectivising relation not primarily predicated on opticality: matrixial affect inflects the canonical categorisation of Riley's work as Op-Art.

How, then, does the example of *Winter Palace* help as an approach to thinking about the situation of colour in *Mountains and Sea*? Visually the two works could not be more different. At the most fundamental technical level Frankenthaler and Riley are about as far apart as two painters could possibly be. Frankenthaler's contact with the canvas extends to kneeling or squatting on it, Riley does not touch the canvas at all; assistants paint the works for her. Colour in *Mountains and Sea* works not at all in the way it does in *Winter Palace*. It would be a mistake to understand the soak-stain colour in *Mountains and Sea* as *the* inscription of the matrixial psychic apparatus at work in the painting: the way it functions to blur the distinction between figure and ground and disturbs the field of vision. This would be to define it in accordance with phallic psychic organisation, as in fact it was defined by Greenberg, Louis and Noland when they identified it as the thing, the *one* thing they needed to move forward.

In *Mountains and Sea* the soak-stained application of paint functions in the work like every other element and *with* every other element in the painting in a *partial* way. The blue 'sea' on the right-hand side of the canvas is brushed on and participates in the creation of a section of receding space. In the centre, at the base of the canvas, blue is a mark from Cézanne's watercolour brush enlarged; in the right-hand third it denotes surface more than elsewhere in the painting and is relatively free of connotative value. Red, green, grey and lemon function similarly. Blue is the only colour whose method of application varies slightly in different parts of the canvas. It is brushed, dribbled, splattered and poured. Let us now recall Frankenthaler's description in *Toward a New Climate* of the function of the colour blue in the small painting called *With Blue* (1953). The painting was, she said, 'a demonstration of what I was really about on a much larger scale around the post *Mountains and Sea* period', namely 'the whole problem of ambiguity':

> This blue is essentially the same blue in the same shape in the same part of this canvas, but each stroke and each bleed acts very differently and each one is necessary and they are all the same and doing the same job but they are totally different and not the same at all.

A component of Frankenthaler's description surely is the memory of Matisse's famous statement about how colour functions in painting: '1cm^2 of any blue is not as blue as a square metre of the same blue [88]...the colours, which are the same, are none the less changed; as their quantities differ, their quality also changes.'[89] Yet I think what Frankenthaler has to say about *With Blue* is not simply Matisse's statement half-remembered and badly articulated. I think the syntax is pressured by the attempt to convey something of a different order of the function of colour to the quantity/quality binary to which Matisse refers. Perhaps what we hear in Frankenthaler's description is an attempt to speak the idea of a metramorphic severality of blue in *relations-without-relating* to *partial* aspects of the quantity/quality relation described by Matisse.

5

A PAINTING OF THE ROSENBERG ERA

On June 16 1953 President Eisenhower wrote to his son John, serving in Korea:

> To address myself to the Rosenberg case for a minute. I must say that it goes against the grain to avoid interfering in the case where a woman is to receive capital punishment. Over against this, however, must be placed one or two facts that have greater significance. The first of these is that in this instance it is the woman who is the strong and recalcitrant character. The man is the weak one. She is obviously the leader in everything they did in the spy ring. The second thing is that if there would be any commuting of the woman's sentence without the man's then from here on the Soviets would simply recruit their spies from among women.[1]

Out looking at art

We read this text in the Ikon Gallery, Birmingham, in December 1998. The occasion is the first retrospective exhibition of the work of Martha Rosler.[2]

The extract of Eisenhower's letter to his son is stencilled on a hand towel hanging from a wooden rack whose shelf supports a box of raspberry flavoured JELL-O. A full length, life-size, photo-silk-screened image of Ethel Rosenberg drying dishes at a kitchen sink framed by smaller images – press photos, fashion advertisements, technical diagrams, maps – is installed on the wall beside it. The information panel tells us that this installation, called *Unknown Secrets (The Secret of the Rosenbergs)*, (1988) originally formed part of an exhibition entitled *Unknown Secrets: Art and the Rosenberg Era,* which toured the United States in 1988 (figs. 10 & 11).

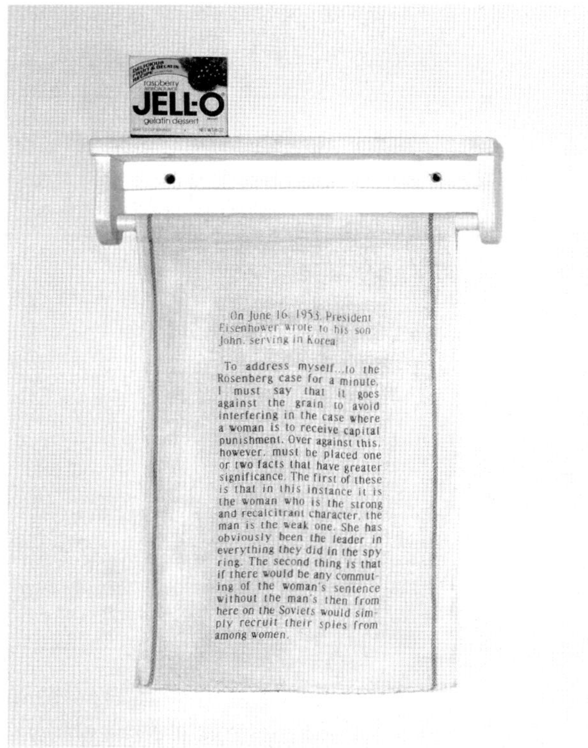

Fig. 10
Martha Rosler, *Unknown Secrets (The Secret of the Rosenbergs)*, 1988, detail of 3-part installation with photo silkscreen, towel rack, JELL-O, box, and text handout

The bare facts of the Rosenberg case are these. Julius and Ethel Rosenberg, a left wing, working-class Jewish couple with two children living on New York City's Lower East Side, were arrested in July 1950 and charged with conspiracy to commit espionage. In March 1951 they were tried and found guilty of conspiring with David Greenglass, Ruth Greenglass, Harry Gold and Anatoly Yakovlev to pass information about America's atomic bomb project to the Soviet Union. On 5 April 1951 Judge Irving Kaufman sentenced Julius and Ethel Rosenberg to death. They were executed by electrocution in Sing Sing Prison on 19 June 1953.[3]

Plotting the trail of events that led to the death of the Rosenbergs through the photocopied text which forms the third element of Martha Rosler's installation, I am reminded that the three years spanning the arrest and execution of the Rosenbergs are those in which Helen Frankenthaler arrived on the scene of advanced American painting. Her professional and personal association with Clement Greenberg began in April 1950, her 'breakthrough' painting *Mountains and*

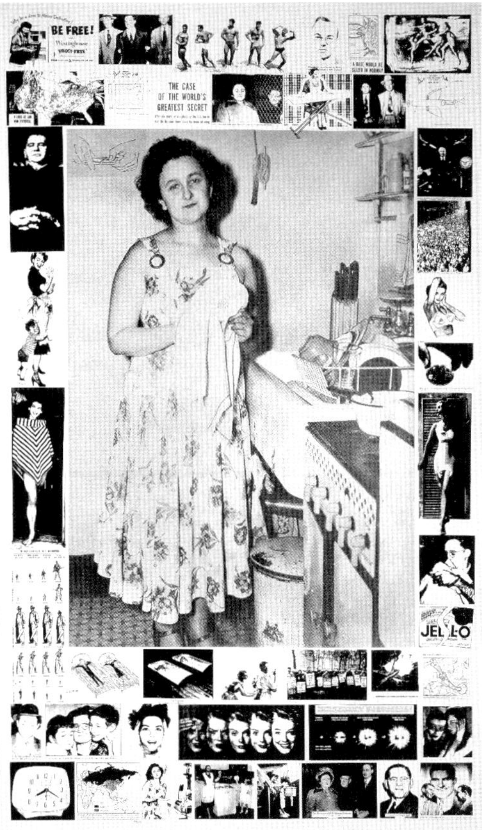

Fig. 11
Martha Rosler, *Unknown Secrets (The Secret of the Rosenbergs)*, 1988, detail of 3-part installation with photo silkscreen, towel rack, JELL-O, box, and text handout

Sea was first exhibited at the Tibor de Nagy Gallery in New York in February 1953. *Mountains and Sea* is, then, centrally, art of the Rosenberg era.

If Serge Guilbaut and T.J. Clark have declared Jackson Pollock's work of the 1950s 'profoundly' of its time, interpreting the formal relationship between 'largeness' and 'smallness' in his practice as enacting a sense of the 'scale of experience' in the age of atomic science, anachronising gestures characterise texts that make a claim for Frankenthaler's place in art history.[4] With Roziska Parker in *Old Mistresses* you tracked the tendency among critics and commentators to mobilise variations on the art historical genre of the pastoral as an interpretative approach to Frankenthaler's practice, noting how viewing the work through the frame of the eighteenth century *fête champêtre* or *fête galante* functions to remove and isolate it from the socio-political contingencies of its own historical moment.[5]

I do not want to follow T.J. Clark's example and in the case of Frankenthaler posit a direct reflective relationship between the morphology of a painting practice and a 'cold war sense of space'.[6] However I do want to explore the possibility that the destruction of Julius and Ethel Rosenberg in the State's obsession with atomic war plans and atomic diplomacy did have implications for the art historical fortunes of *Mountains and Sea.* Implications precisely in relation to the single formal element with which the painting's situation in the canon of 20th American painting is associated, namely soak-stained colour.[7]

Co-poiesis?

How to make the argument – that is the problem: it has to be declared from the outset that what is to come is not strictly speaking 'my' argument. It arises as a relation, a working relation, in conversation (whether actually spoken or as written response) that is not necessarily *about* anything, but rather *with* something we might for the moment call 'painting' or 'art history'. To proceed this way will unavoidably affect the status of the work as 'original research'. More than once in print, Griselda, you have expressed doubts that disciplinary academic art history can survive the impact of questions feminism directs at its fundamentally Oedipal foundations.

'Nichsapha: Yearning/Languishing The Immaterial Tuché of Colour in Painting *After Painting After History*'.[8] You wrote the essay for the catalogue of *Artworking,* an element of *Borderlines,* an exhibition held at the Palais des Beaux-Arts in Brussels in February-May 2000. In an exhibition conceived as a matrixial curatorial event Paul Vandenbroeck set carpets woven by Berber women beside the work of painter Bracha Lichtenberg Ettinger in an installation designed by architect Zaha Hadid. 'Nichsapha: Yearning/Languishing The Immaterial Tuché of Colour in Painting *After Painting After History*', written to accompany Bracha Lichtenberg Ettinger's *Artworking* material, offers a point of departure for an inter-subjective process where *Mountains and Sea* begins to mean as a painting of the Rosenberg era *between* your text and mine. It is an offer I cannot refuse, even though, in truth, I would rather not work with 'Nichsapha' just yet. The text is so new you have hardly had a chance to work through its implications yourself. However, the impossibility of *not* engaging with it at this particular juncture in my text registers, I suspect, something beside the task of working in a mode of inter-subjectivity still phallically determined.[9] I can theoretically underpin this sense of 'something beside' by naming it, with Bracha Lichtenberg Ettinger, a moment of 'trans-subjectivity' in the text, in which meaning for *Mountains and Sea* as a painting of the Rosenberg era is unexpectedly caught up as a singular instance of '*co-poiesis*'.[10] According to Lichtenberg Ettinger's theory of '*co-poiesis*' my sense of something beside the inter-subjectivity of 'our' texts would be the effect of the status of that inter-subjectivity as but one element in a metramorphic movement of 'non-conscious relations without relating' with 'our' traumatising/*jouissance* producing unknown *non-Is*.[11]

If, from my standpoint, the primary manifestation of the impossibility of *not* engaging with your *Artworking* text right now is a not-entirely-pleasurable-not entirely-painful quality of affect we might define as *matrixial*, from the phallic angle, the concept of 'trans-subjectivity' can be approached with a degree of concrete theoretical rigour from the point in the essay where you begin to work with Freud's concept of *nachträglichkeit*.

In *The Language of Psychoanalysis* Laplanche and Pontalis translate the word *nachträglichkeit* in the Freudian context as 'deferred action; action deferred'. (In its double movement the formulation uncannily recalls Friedel Dzubas's description of the place from which Frankenthaler's work appeared on the New York scene in the early 1950s: 'It came out of a kind of 'never never land.')[12] Introducing the concept of *nachträglichkeit* you quote a letter of 1896 from Freud to Wilhelm Fliess in which Freud writes about psychic temporality: 'I am working on the assumption that our psychical mechanism has come into being by a process of stratification: the material present in the form of memory-traces being subjected from time to time to a *re-arrangement* in accordance with fresh circumstances – to a *re-transcription*.[13]

Laplanche and Pontalis provide a useful characterisation of the concept of deferred action:

> It is not lived experience in general that undergoes a deferred revision but, specifically, whatever it has been impossible in the first instance to incorporate fully into a meaningful context. The traumatic event is the epitome of such unassimilated experience.[14]

Work on infantile sexuality led Freud to the notion of primal repression and the proposition that universal fantasy structures, intra-uterine existence, the primal scene, castration, seduction, organise individual human psychic subjectivity. According to Freud primal fantasies acquire 'pathogenic force' only in deferred revision: 'a memory is repressed which has only become a trauma by *deferred action*.'[15]

With Freud we are in the domain of the temporal formation of the psychic subjectivity of the *individual* human subject in primal and other subsequent traumatic events. In the clinical analytic situation as privileged 'fresh circumstance' for the re-transcription of memory traces, however, deferred action is the occasion of an inter-subjective psychic operation connected with the transference. So when I claim that *Mountains and Sea* comes to mean as a painting of the Rosenberg era between your text and mine, this is to say that it is an instance of art historical production as transference-relation involving the 'tug of war of desire on both sides' – on the part both of my text and yours.[16]

In 'Nichsapha: Yearning/Languishing' you suggest that the logic of deferred action has 'immense significance' for feminist moves in cultural analysis'. You write that the concept of *nachträglichkeit* :

> Springs us from the art historical traps of lineages of descent and influence, in which any artist coming after appears at worst derivative, and at best

> locked in an Oedipal struggle with a preceding parent or, if a woman, locked out of precisely that canonising relation…It allows a historical tapestry to emerge as a weaving of threads that may disappear from one area only to emerge, transformed by new interactions, in another part…Grains of possibilities lie unharvested within artworks that are then changed by what a later art work does, making the precedent now reappear as begotten.[17]

Can we extend this feminist theoretical gesture to the practice of writing 'art's histories'?[18]

Your weaving metaphor and the image of grains allude to the materiality of elements in the *Borderline* exhibition, the Berber textiles, the photocopy toner dust in the *Artworking* pieces. They also, though, suggest from within the framework of the concept of *nachträglichkeit* a different pattern, a trace of another psychic temporality caught now and again in the warp and weft of the backwards-forwards/forwards-backwards ineluctable binary movement of deferred action/action deferred. In the matrixial subjectivising strata action is *almost*-deferred; deferral *almost*-happens, a logic which implies the notion of *almost*-traumatic-events, not quite inaccessible. Action *almost*-deferred involves an *almost*-repression and thus what Bracha Lichtenberg Ettinger theorises as 'non-conscious', as distinct from unconscious, formations of fantasy, trauma, desire.[19]

Let us recall Bracha Lichtenberg Ettinger's theorisation of the matrixial borderspace as a zone where psychic subjectivity co-emerges and co-fades as partial and shared, prior to the series of separations and prohibitions constituting individual subjectivity in Freudian/Lacanian phallocentric thought: 'I took the intra-uterine meeting as a model for human situations and processes in which the *non-I* is not an intruder, but a partner in difference.'[20] Subjectivity co-emerges as shared in a specific way then, namely between *non-I's unknown* to one another. However they are the 'most intimate and the most distanced' of partial unknowns, the infant to be and the mother to be, yet to be established as individual subjects 'mother' and 'child' in the phallic *après coup*.[21] Metramorphosis as the figure for a continual asymmetrical subjectivising process of adjustments of 'distance-in-proximity' in 'relations-without-relating' between *partial I(s)* and unknown *non I(s)* constituting a matrixial complex of fantasy, therefore *differences* (to use your term) inter-subjective relations between discrete individuals known to one another.[22]

At this juncture it is useful to return to the particular way Freud articulated the direction of his research in the 1896 letter to Fliess, which you quote in your *Artworking* essay: 'I am working on the assumption that our psychical mechanism has come into being by a process of stratification: the material present in the form of memory-traces being subjected from time to time to a *re-arrangement* in accordance with fresh circumstances – to a *re-transcription.*' The idea of re-arranging memory-traces 'in accordance with fresh circumstances' suggests creative production – poietic activity. From the Freudian/Lacanian phallic perspective memory traces are subjected to *re-transcription* through metaphor and metonymy, discrete linguistic figures that *represent*. In the previous chapter I outlined Freud's account, and Kristeva's elaboration of, the relationship between thing-presentation and word-presentation and how they structure ideational representations of psychic events in the unconscious.[23] For Bracha Lichtenberg Ettinger:

> ...one obstacle to relativizing basic phallic assumptions is the prevailing idea that a distinct representation should correspond to each psychic event, and that the most archaic traces are already representations.[24]

In metramorphosis as not a figure for, but rather the movement of subjectivising inscriptions in the matrixial stratum:

> ...meaning and memory emerge which are not based on a concrete inscription of distinct experiences or on distinct representations. Thus, matrixial experiences are not entirely foreclosed, since they trace connectionist webs.[25]

In Freudian thinking the structure of psychic temporality is a closed system, unique to each individual, as such it is 'autopoietic'.[26] In the matrixial borderspace psychic traces of traumatic events are necessarily and unavoidably 'trans-scribed' between 'several individuals unknown to each other, or between several uncognized partial-subjects' – "parts" of individuals who know each other'. [27] Bracha Lichtenberg Ettinger defines such a 'trans-subjective matrixial alliance' as *'co-poiesis'*: 'A non-cognitive mode of knowledge that reveals itself in...ontogenetic witnessing-together, in *wit(h)nessing*.':

> ...trans-scription is a dispersed subsymbolic and affective memory of event, paradoxically both forgotten and inoubliable, a memory charged with freight that a linear story can't transmit...Traces circulate in a trans-subjective zone by matrixial affects and non-conscious threads, that disperse different aspects of traumatic events between the *I(s)* and *non-I(s)*. Thus as I cannot fully handle events that concern me profoundly, they are fading-in-transformation while my *non-I(s)* become wit(h)nesses to them. It may happen that because of their high traumatic value I cannot physically handle 'my' events at all. In the matrixial psychic sphere, 'my' traces will be trans-scribed in others, thus my others will process these events for me...In the matrixial borderspace a specific aesthetic field comes into light, with metramorphosis as an aesthetic process with ethical implications.[28]

What, then, is the nature of matrixial transference? Something like telepathy? *Tele* is Greek for far (off). The New Shorter Oxford English Dictionary defines *tele* as 'psychic affinity between people separated by time or space. *Pathy*, from the Greek *patheia*, means suffering. So while the dictionary definition of telepathy is 'The communication or perception of thoughts, feelings, etc., by (apparently) extrasensory means', strictly speaking, it can be characterised as a psychic affinity between suffering people separated by time or space: a startlingly matrixial definition.

1933, 1953, 1963/1963, 1953, 1933

Quite early on in 'Nichsapha':Yearning/Languishing', Warhol's *Disaster* series makes an unexpected appearance unprecedented in your previous writing around the work of Bracha Lichtenberg Ettinger, Griselda. I wonder is it possible that, perhaps unknown to you, Warhol's repeated image from a found photograph of an electric chair, possibly the chair at Sing Sing prison (pl. 8), emerges as a trace in your essay in 2000, of our encounter in 1998 with Martha Rosler's *Unknown Secrets (The Secret of the Rosenbergs)*?[29] Whether you know it or not is beside the point. The astonishing conjunctions that tip into view as I begin to work with its appearance in 'your' text in the space of 'mine' are what matters. For instance, you write that the *Disaster* series was made in 1963, that is to say precisely a decade after the execution of the Rosenbergs. This prompts some solid social history of art questions. Was the tenth anniversary of the event commemorated publicly? If so, how, and was it a factor in Warhol's choice of imagery that year? It certainly appeared in Sylvia Plath's novel *The Bell Jar* published in January 1963 whose opening line reads: 'It was a queer, sultry summer, the summer they electrocuted the Rosenbergs.'[30]

In the spring of 1953, when Ethel and Julius Rosenberg were still in the Death House of Sing Sing prison awaiting execution, Morris Louis's first solo show of paintings opened at the Workshop Center Gallery in Washington DC. The fact comes to mind as I read what you write in the *Artworking* essay about the function of colour in Warhol's *Disaster* series, which concerns the *tuché* in your title. In Seminar XI, *The Four Fundamental Concepts of Psychoanalysis,* Lacan borrows the word *tuché* from the work of Aristotle, where it refers to the element of chance in reasoning. Lacan translates it for his purposes as *'the encounter with the real'* and locates it in the psychoanalytical context as follows:

> The function of the *tuché,* of the real as encounter – in so far as it may be missed, in so far as it is essentially the missed encounter – first presented itself in the history of psycho-analysis in the form that was in itself already enough to arouse our attention, that of trauma.[31]

Lacan's elaboration of the gaze as *objet a* in Seminar XI implicates painting with the *tychic* point of the missed encounter in the scopic field.[32] Thus Lacan links painting and trauma. The link structures your *Artworking* essay, and Warhol's *Disaster* series functions as the hinge upon which turns a double elaboration of the temporal structure of trauma, and colour as the *tuché* in painting. Here is what you write about colour in the *Disaster* series:

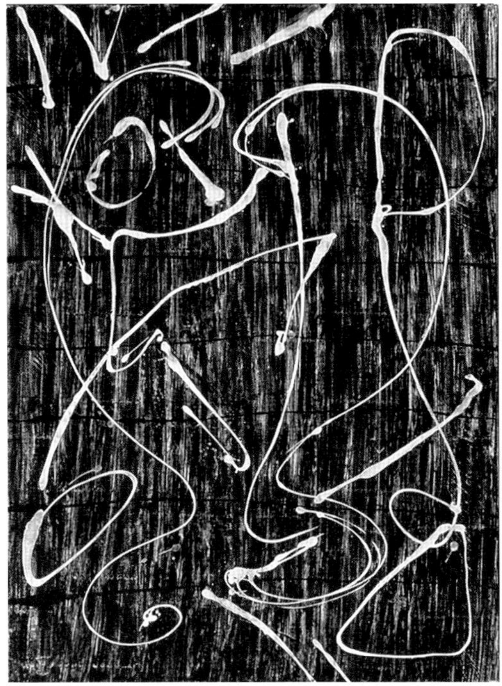

Fig. 12
Morris Louis, *Charred Journal: Firewritten IV*, 1951, acrylic resin (magna) on canvas, Copenhagen, Louisiana Museum of Modern Art

> Whatever affectivity there is in Warhol's image lies…in the veils of colour – red, orange, lavender – that sweep across these serially repeated readymade images. A resounding submission to the formalist discoveries of the high modernist painting Warhol worked to supersede allows each image to move beyond the irony of appropriation and its antithesis, originality, and to achieve a hyper-affectivity that hinges on the valences of colour itself because of the way colour creates its own irreal spatiality that vibrates, at the level of the semiotic, with rhythms that line our subjectivity. A colour field transforms these works into the realm of *painting*, dissolving the proper boundary between subject and object, between viewer and painting into an experience that can be named, using Lacan's late concept, 'extimacy'. Thus Warhol's work operates on that hinge between the draining of all reference in pursuit of aesthetic purity that characterizes high American modernist theory, and the negotiated re-engagement with a world envisioned as not only totally commodified, but catastrophically charged and haunting.[33]

This passage is a condensation of many of your concerns as art historian and

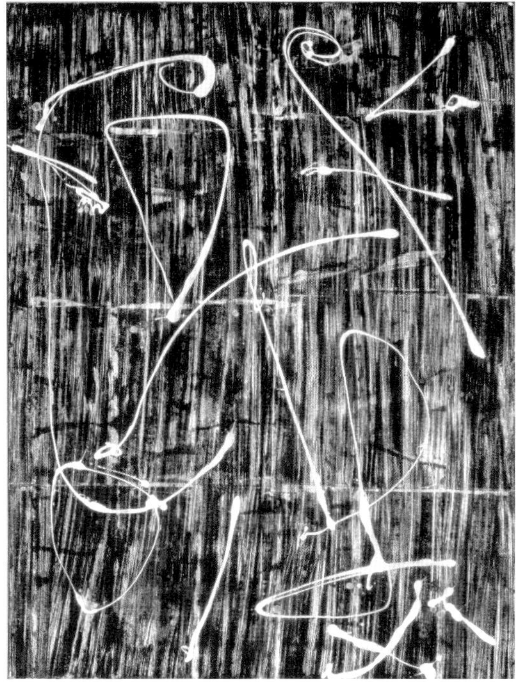

Fig. 13
Morris Louis, *Charred Journal: Firewritten V,* 1951, acrylic resin (magna) on canvas, 34 x 36 in (86.3 x 91.4 cm) New York, The Jewish Museum

cultural theorist. It also opens onto/opens up questions I pose about the art historical life of soak-stained colour in and beyond *Mountains and Sea* at two points specifically. The first is where you touch upon the art historical meaning of colour field painting, and the second when you allude to Kristeva's exploration of the situation of colour in painting *vis à vis* formal system and subjectivity. The interface has a particular temporal logic to which we must attend if the relational nature of this enterprise is to be apprehended in its specificity.

Not long after our visit to *martha rosler: positions in the life world* in Birmingham, you gave me a photocopy of an article from an issue of *The Jewish Quarterly* because it was about the work of Morris Louis. Morris Louis was born Morris Louis Bernstein in 1912 in Baltimore to Russian Jewish immigrant parents. He adopted the name Morris Louis for professional purposes in 1938. The article focuses on a series of seven paintings Louis made in 1951 entitled *Charred Journal: Firewritten* (figs 12 & 13). They were included in his first solo exhibition in Washington in April 1953. Judging solely on the evidence of their surface matter, poured trails of white pigment on predominantly black grounds, critics have dismissed the paintings as 'Pollock-pastiche', the work of an immature artist struggling to make his own move in the field of avant-garde painting in the early 1950s. In his *Jewish Quarterly* article 'Keeping Watch Over Absent Meaning', Mark Godfrey suggest that there is another dimension to the *Charred Journal* series. He argues that the paintings represent Morris Louis's public engagement with 'the memory of the Holocaust'.[34]

Godfrey freely admits that the argument he mounts rests on the 'associative operation' of the series title, *Charred Journal: Firewritten*, in conjunction with a press review of the 1953 Washington exhibition which claimed that the paintings were 'based, according to the artist, on the book burnings of the Nazis', a claim neither confirmed nor denied by Louis himself.[35] Mark Godfrey employs the rhetorical figures of synecdoche and metonymy to link title and dark materiality of the paintings. He writes that while the words 'Charred Journal' 'initially signal the book burnings of 1933', beyond that specific event they recall a wider campaign against the 'contamination of the German language by Jewish usage' in a project to 'exclude the Jew from Western culture'. Reading metonymically:

> As the Jews are 'the people of the book', the charred journal or burnt book might suggest the destruction of Jewish *bodies* in a manner that respected the ultimate resistance of that idea to representation.[36]

However by the end of the article Godfrey doubts the value of his own reading, admitting that although meaning for the words 'Charred Journal' and 'Firewritten' can be drawn from the surface matter of the paintings, 'independent of the titles, many of the arguments simply collapse'. The abstract paint marks on canvas 'refuse to be linked to history by any chains that we can forge'. Invoking Maurice Blanchot's belief that any attempt to produce meaning from the Holocaust inevitably belittles it, Godfrey concludes that the value of the *Charred Journal* series is precisely in its status as work that plays out the collapse of meaning. In that sense Louis's practice as a painter fulfils the role Blanchot advocates for the writer after the Holocaust, to 'keep watch over absent meaning'.[37] In a postscript to the essay, Godfrey introduces two interesting questions raised by the re-examination of the *Charred Journal* series in the light of the later practice for which Louis is recognised in art history. 'How,' he asks, 'could a painter who sought to address the Holocaust immerse himself so easily in a world of colour and light?' 'Why did a man who made efforts to tell the Washington press about the book burnings leave the titling and exhibiting of later paintings to others?'[38]

The two questions loop back to my own about where modernist-formalist art history locates *Mountains and Sea* on the basis of the particular treatment of colour in the painting. The material caught up in that loop interrupts the direct relation Mark Godfrey posits between the *Charred Journal* series and the 'memory of the Holocaust' and involves your extension, Griselda, of Freud's concept of *nachträglichkeit* to cultural analysis in 'Nichsapha: Yearning/Languishing'. Godfrey's argument, that the *Charred Journal* series represents an act of public engagement with the memory of the Holocaust from within the field of an

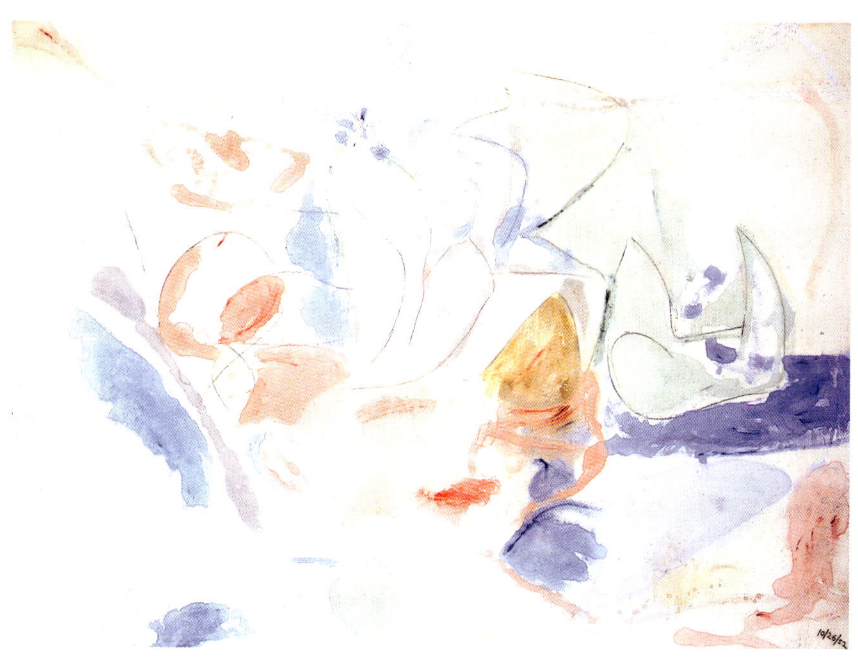

Pl. 1

Helen Frankenthaler, *Mountains and Sea,* 1952, oil and charcoal on canvas, 86 ⅝ in x 117¼ in (220 x 297.8 cm) Collection: Helen Frankenthaler Foundation, Inc. (On loan to the National Gallery of Art, Washington D.C.) © 2007 Helen Frankenthaler

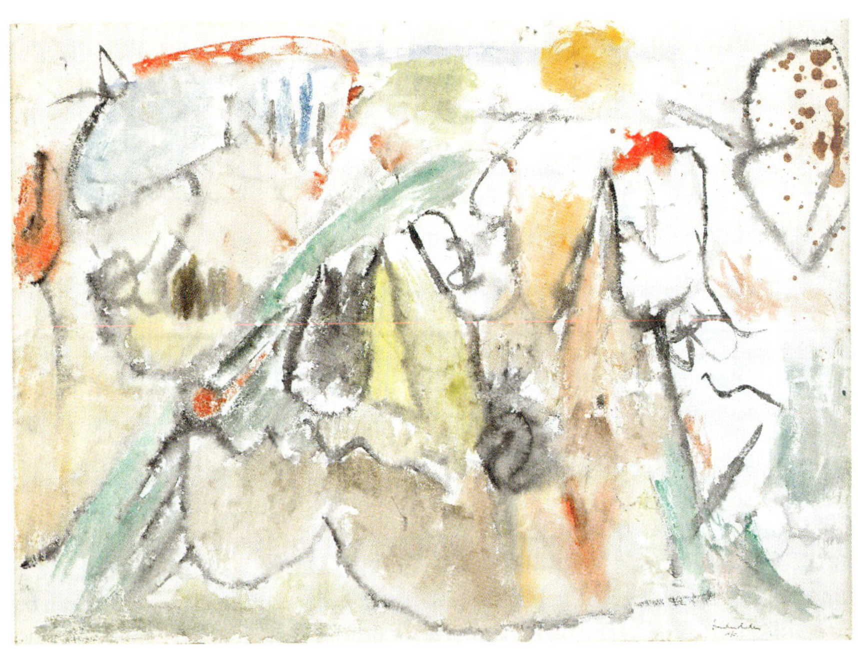

Pl. 2
Helen Frankenthaler, *Great Meadows*, 1951, watercolour and synthetic polymer on paper, 22 x 30 ½ in (56 x 77.4 cm) New York, Museum of Modern Art. © 2007 Helen Frankenthaler

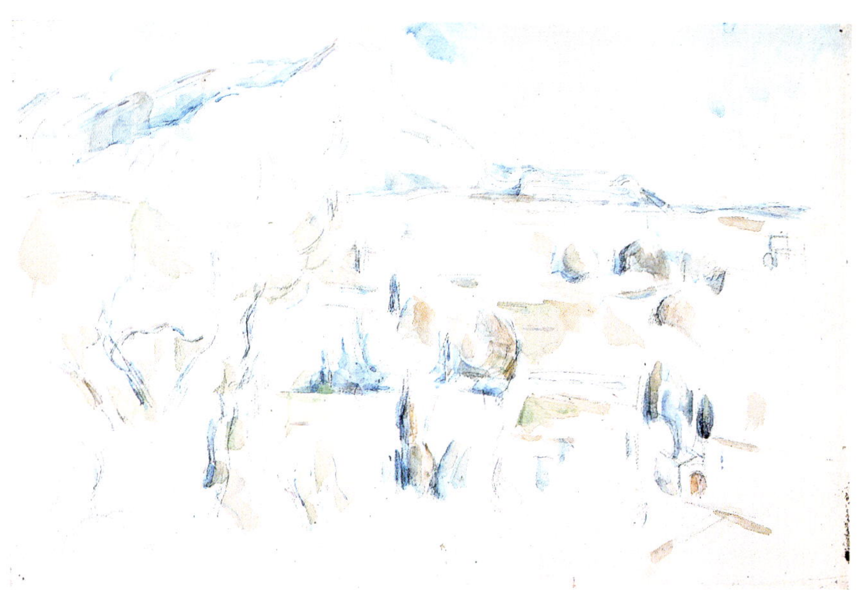

Pl. 3
Paul Cézanne, *Mont Sainte-Victoire (La Montagne Sainte-Victoire Vue des Lauves en Hiver)*, c.1901-1906, watercolour and graphite on pale buff wove paper; 12 ¼ x 18 ¾ in (31 x 47.6 cm) The Henry and Rose Pearlman Foundation

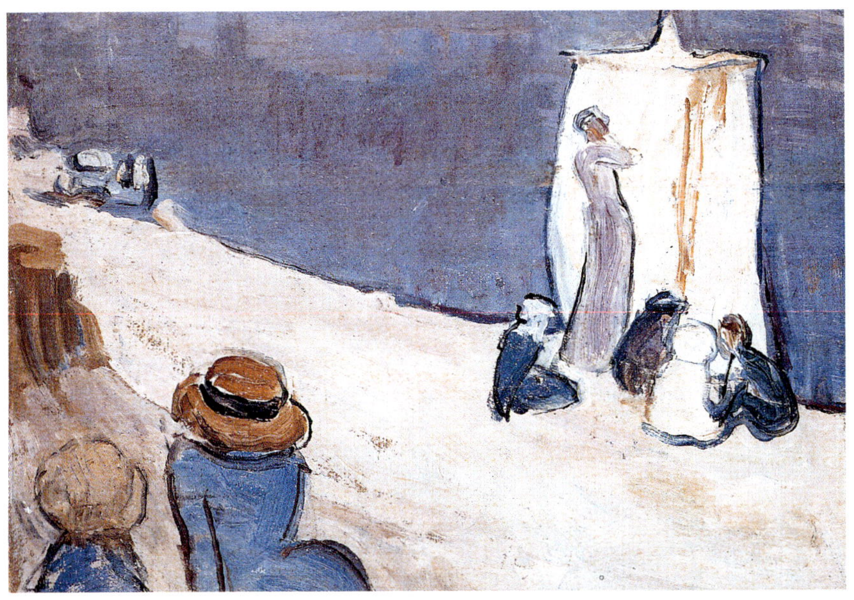

Pl. 4

Vanessa Bell, *The Beach Studland*, c.1911, oil on board, 10 x 13 ½ in (25.5 x 34.5 cm) Private Collection,

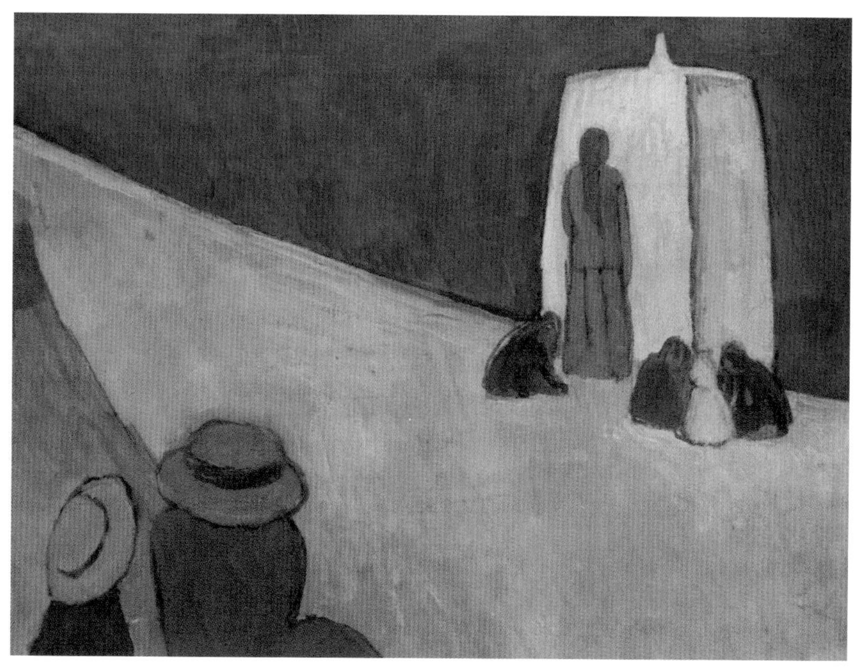

Pl. 5
Vanessa Bell, *Studland Beach,* c.1912, oil on canvas, 30 x 40 in (76.2 x 101.6 cm) Tate Gallery, London.

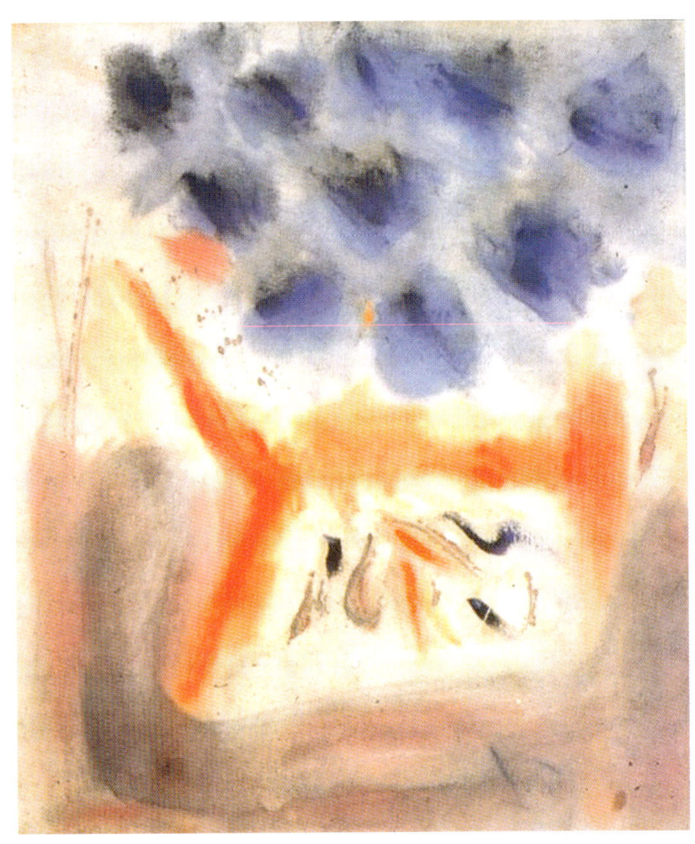

Pl. 6
Helen Frankenthaler, *With Blue,* 1953, oil on canvas,
35 x 31 in (89.9 x 78.7 cm) Private Collection. © 2007 Helen Frankenthaler

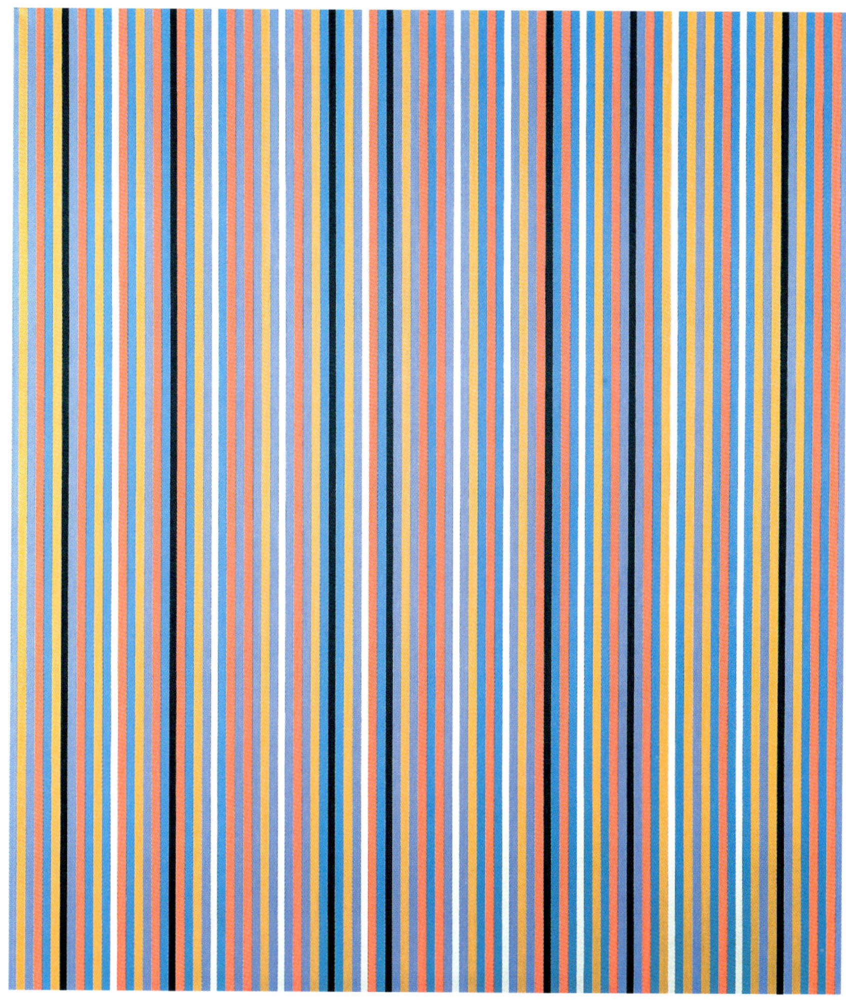

Pl. 7
Bridget Riley, *Winter Palace*, 1981, oil on linen,
83 ½ x 72 ¼ in (212.1 x 183.5 cm) Leeds City Art Gallery. © The artist

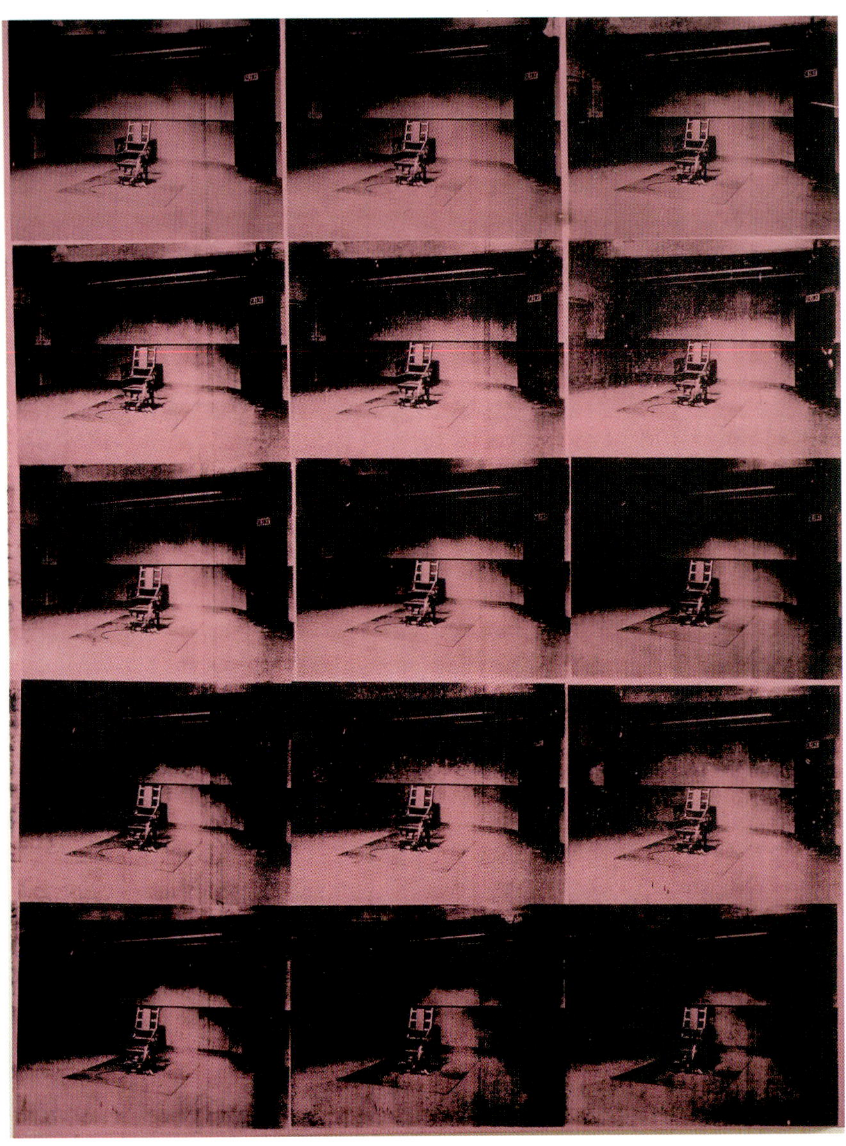

Pl. 8
Andy Warhol, *Lavender Disaster,* 1963, acrylic and silkscreen ink on canvas, 108 x 82 in (274 x 208 cm) The Menil Collection, Huston.

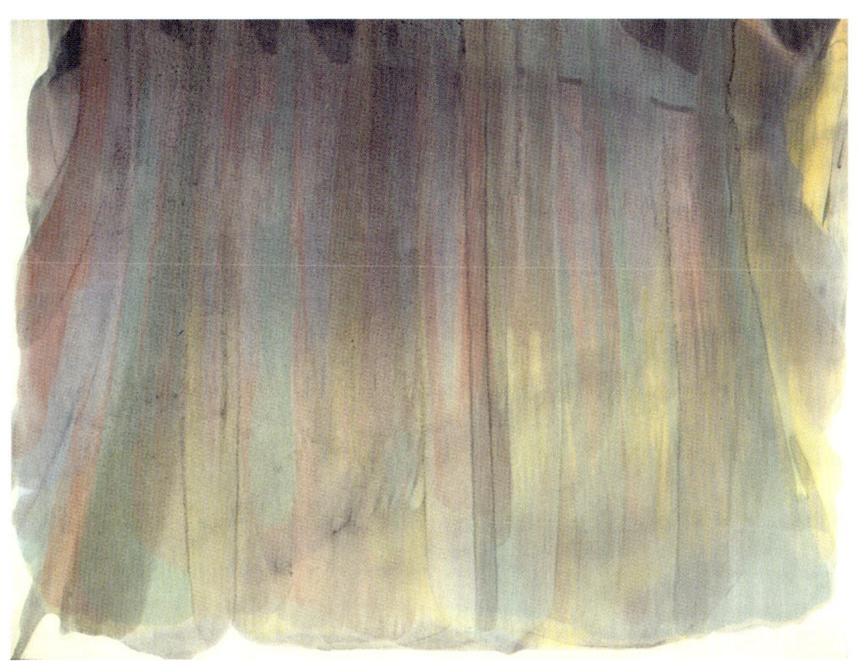

Pl. 9
Morris Louis, *Salient*, 1954, acrylic on canvas, 74 ½ x 99 in (189.2 x 252 cm)
Courtesy The Donald and Barbara Zucker Family Foundation.

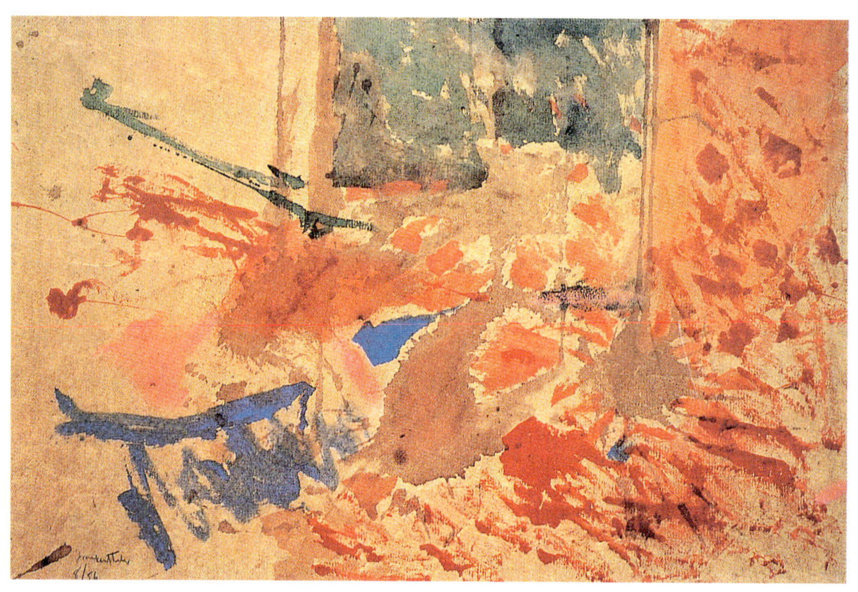

Pl. 10
Helen Frankenthaler, *Hôtel du Quai Voltaire*, 1956, mixed media on paper, 15 3/8 x 23 in (38.1 x 58.4 cm) Private Collection. © 2007 Helen Frankenthaler. Image © courtesy Geoffrey Clements/Corbis

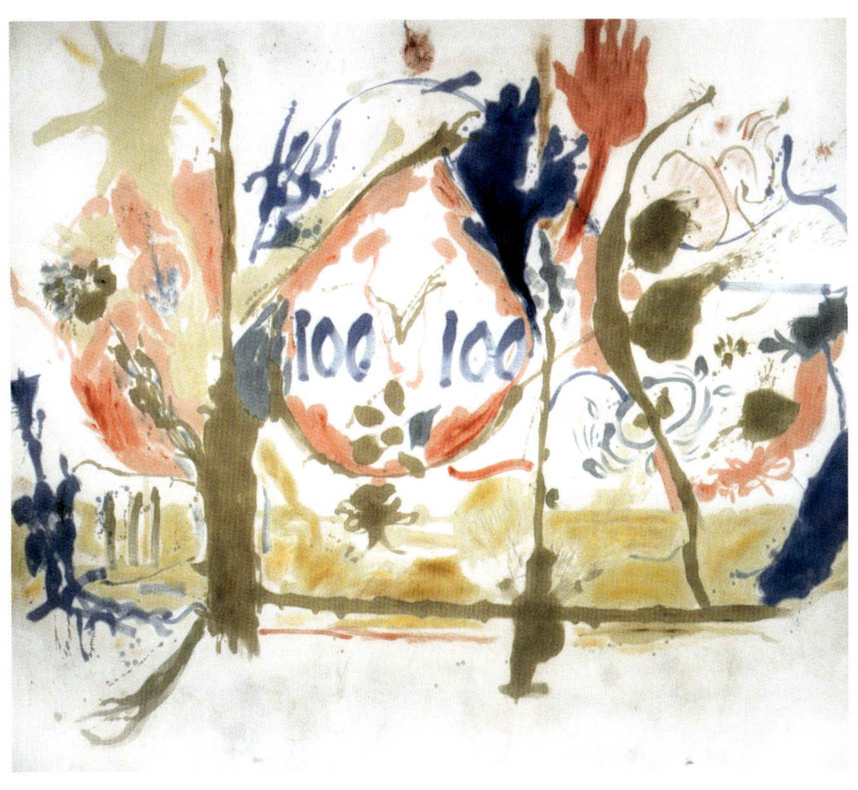

Pl. 11
Helen Frankenthaler, *Eden*, 1956, oil on canvas,
103 x 117 in (261.6 x 297.2 cm) Private collection.
© 2007 Helen Frankenthaler. Image © courtesy Geoffrey Clements/Corbis

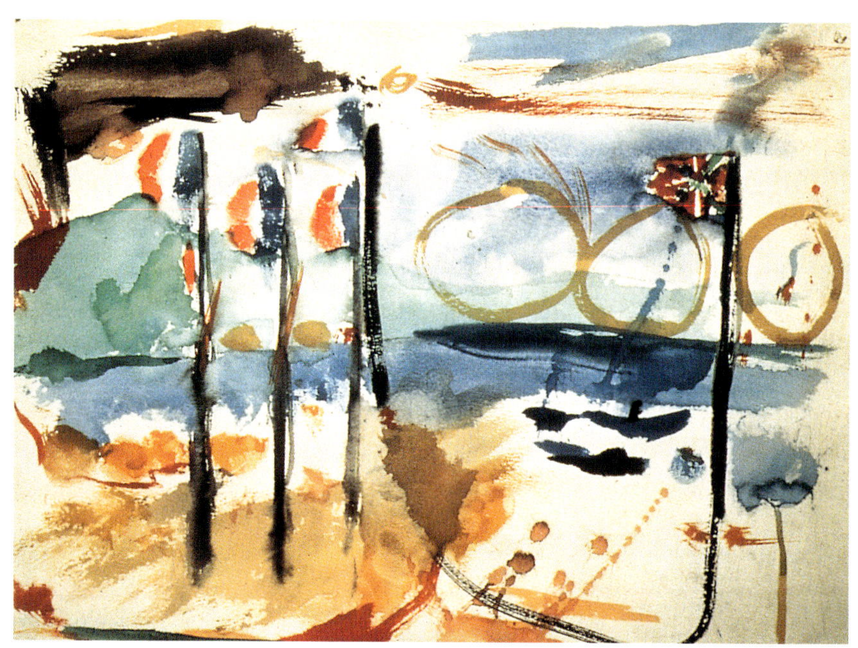

Pl. 12
Helen Frankenthaler, *Landscape (Nice, France)*, 1956, watercolour on paper, 9½ x 12 ½ in (22.8 x 30.4 cm) Private Collection. © 2007 Helen Frankenthaler

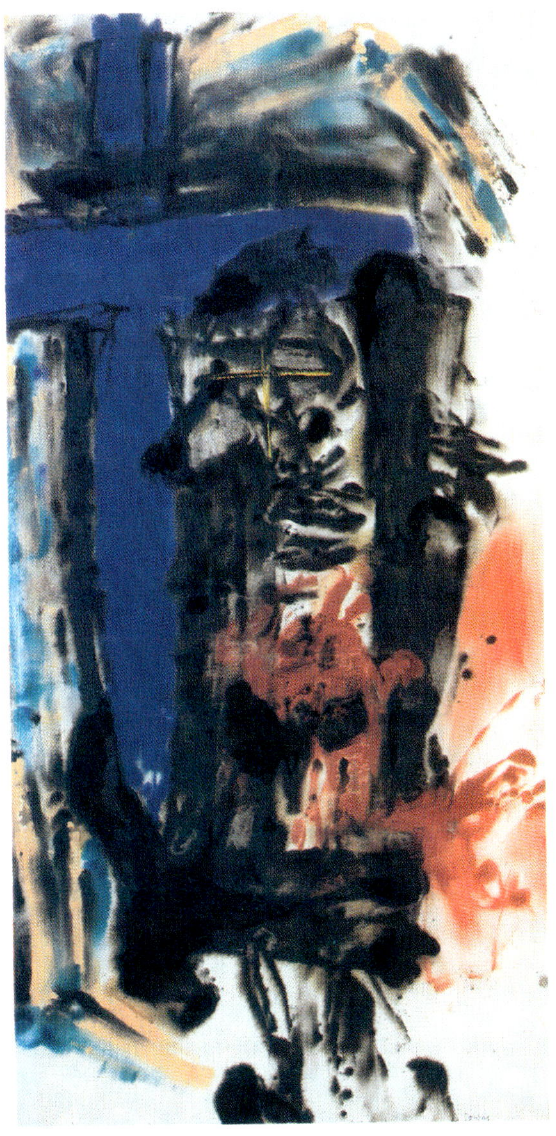

Pl. 13
Friedel Dzubas, *Early Grave,* 1957, oil on canvas,
96 ½ x 47 in (240.9 x 120 cm) Courtesy of the Elkon Gallery, Inc., New York City

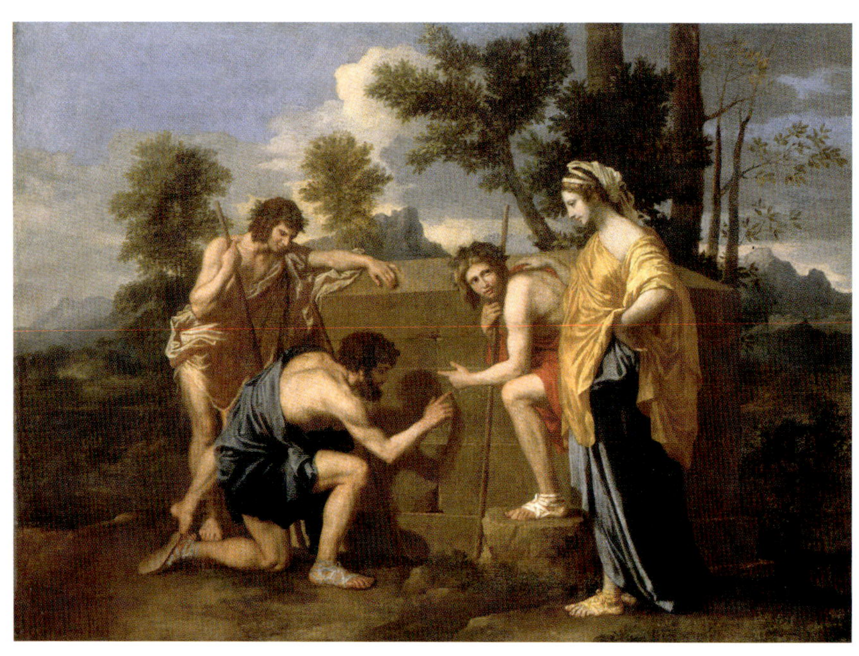

Pl. 14
Nicolas Poussin, *The Arcadian Shepherds*, also known as 'Et in Arcadia Ego', c.1638-40, oil on canvas, 33 ½ x 47 ¾ in (85 x 121 cm) Paris, musée du Louvre. Photograph RMN/© René-Gabriel Ojéda

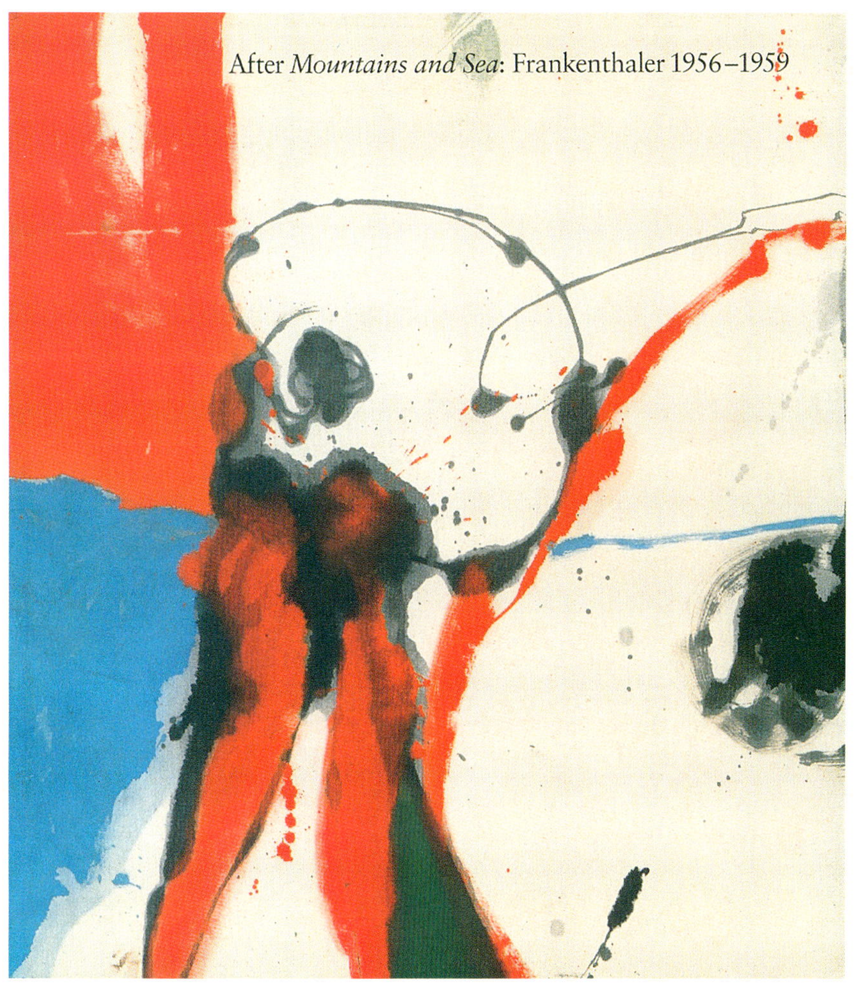

Pl. 15
Helen Frankenthaler, *Mother Goose Melody*, 1959, © 2007 Helen Frankenthaler.
Detail of the cover of the catalogue for the exhibition
After Mountains and Sea: *Frankenthaler 1956-1959*,
Solomon R. Guggenheim Museum, 1998

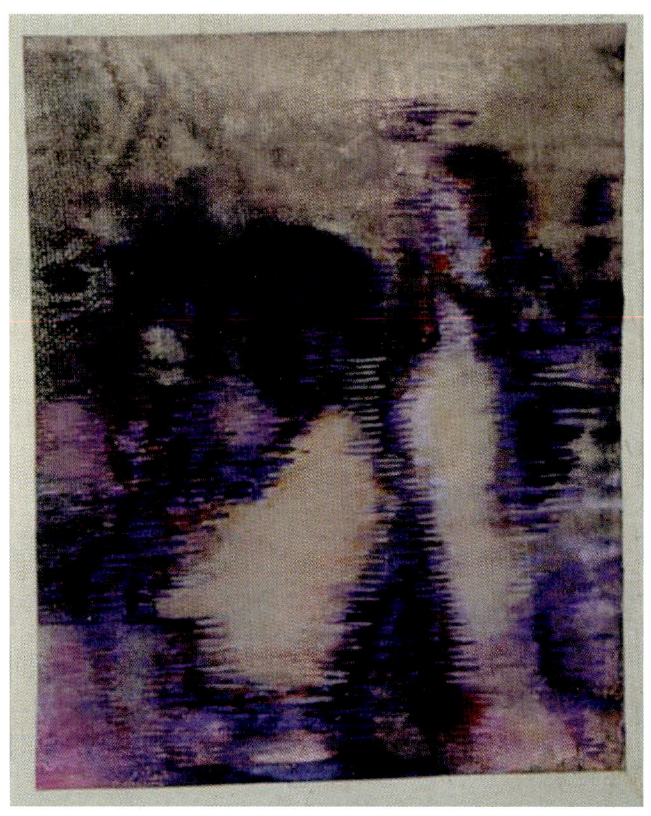

Pl. 16
Bracha Lichtenberg Ettinger, *Eurydice, no. 13*, (1994-1996),
black photocopy toner and pigment on paper mounted on canvas. Courtesy the artist

abstract avant-garde painting driving towards the expurgation of all narrative content, revolves around another question. He poses this question not at the end, but towards the beginning of the essay. 'If,' he asks, 'the critics who propelled Louis to success' dismissed the 1951 series as 'Pollock-pastiche', why did Louis choose, two years later, to show the paintings in his first solo exhibition in Washington in 1953?[39] Reasons begin to suggest themselves if we attend closely to dates.

To recapitulate: Louis's show opened at the Workshop Center Gallery in Washington in April 1953, when Ethel and Julius Rosenberg were still awaiting execution. 'I'm stupid about executions,' confesses Esther Greenwood the narrator in *The Bell Jar*:

> The idea of being electrocuted makes me sick, and that's all there was to read in the papers – goggle-eyed headlines staring up at me on every street corner and at the fusty, peanut-smelling mouth of every subway. It had nothing to do with me, but I couldn't help wondering what it would be like, being burned alive all along your nerves.
>
> I thought it must be the worst thing in the world.[40]

Sylvia Plath's excruciating image of the impending fate of the 'Jewish bodies' of Julius and Ethel Rosenberg prompts speculation. If the *Charred Journal* series was an engagement with the 'memory of the Holocaust' did that engagement undergo the kind of *re-inscription* 'according to fresh circumstances' Freud defined as deferred action? The situation of Julius and Ethel Rosenberg surely resonated in the socio-political field in which Louis was positioned as a Jewish-American with Eastern European roots as he prepared for his first solo exhibition in 1953. Was this event the occasion, almost a decade after the catastrophe of the Holocaust, for the *re-inscription* of its 'memory' as an instance of deferred revision we might in the field of aesthetic practice call poiesis? Sylvia Plath's passage from *The Bell Jar* also gives a sense of the intense media coverage and debate that surrounded the Rosenberg case.

When I return to look at Martha Rosler's *Unknown Secrets (The Secret of the Rosenbergs)* in reproduction, I recognise some of the small images framing the large central one of Ethel Rosenberg.[41] I encountered them again spooling through *The New York Times, The Washington Post, Time* and *Life* magazines from 1950 to 1953 on microfiche reels in the New York Public Library. Just above Ethel Rosenberg's head in the Rosler piece there is a photograph of Julius and Ethel Rosenberg with the headline 'The case of the World's Greatest Secret'. It appears on the microfiche screen as page p. 53 of *Life* on 16 April 1951 (fig. 14). The photo was taken in a prison vehicle as the Rosenbergs were driven away from the court after hearing their sentence. Prominent in the photograph is a wire-mesh screen separating the couple. 2 March 1953, again in *Life* magazine, I stop the machine to catch an image of haunting desolation. More wire-mesh, a fence this time, and a watchtower. In the middle of an expanse of concrete slabs, the wide road of a

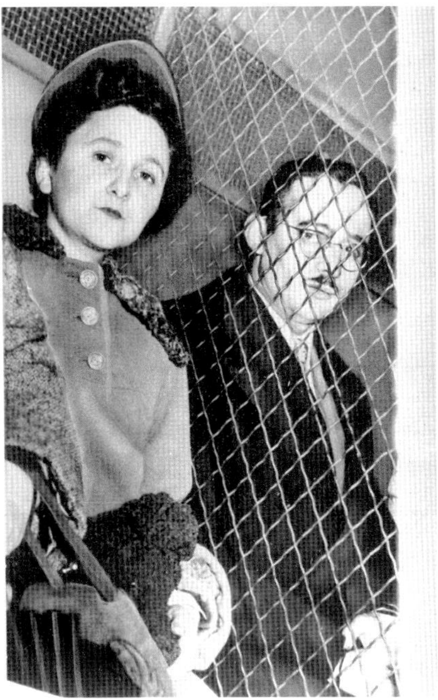

Fig. 14
'Ethel and Julius Rosenberg are separated by a wire screen as they are transported to Sing Sing Prison,' *Life*, 16 April 1951

compound, two little boys in hats and coats walk behind a man in a trilby and overcoat. He is on the edge of the frame. The boys have lagged behind a bit and a space opens up between them. The by-line reads in bold, '**SONS AT A PRISON**'; the text beneath it explains:

> Julius and Ethel Rosenberg's lawyer brought two small visitors to see his clients at Sing Sing on Feb.14. The visitors were their sons, Michael, 9, and Robert 5, who walked solemnly into the prison to give their mother some valentines and have a talk with their father.[42]

Although first shown in Louis's first solo exhibition in 1953, the *Charred Journal: Firewritten* paintings were made, we remember, in 1951. Was exposure to such images accompanying the press reports of the arrest, trial and prison life of the Rosenbergs registered at some level in the *Charred Journal* series as the paintings evolved in 1951? Were they again a factor in Louis's decision to show the paintings in April 1953?

In his introduction to an exhibition of Morris Louis's work at the Hayward Gallery in London in the summer of 1974, John Elderfield writes that the *Charred Journal* paintings testify to the fact that Louis had engaged with Jackson Pollock's work from around 1950. He makes an interesting observation about what happens to the idea of Pollock's work in the *Charred Journal* paintings:

> …whereas Pollock's calligraphy is somehow disembodied and untactile in feeling and inseparable from the surface it creates, Louis's version of it resembles bent wires floated against a background.[43]

Elderfield's image of wire links with an element common to the three *Charred Journal* paintings chosen for inclusion in Mark Godfrey's *Jewish Quarterly* article which shows up clearly in reproduction. Fine horizontal and vertical lines form a grid that sits on top of, in spatial terms it closes off, the dark ground behind. The 'calligraphic' marks are made over the grid. In *Charred Journal: Firewritten IV* and *V* it is difficult not to read the 'bent wire' shapes as figures, a pair… The idea resonates with Sylvia Plath's image of execution by electrocution: the human nervous system as burned-out fuse wire.

Recall that for Helen Frankenthaler Jackson Pollock's black and white paintings of 1951 offered a point of departure. What Frankenthaler found compelling about them was 'the understated image that was really present: animals, thoughts, jungles, expressions'.[44] To my mind the *Charred Journal* series testifies to more than Louis's interest in Pollock's work in general. It signals an engagement with Pollock's 1951 show of black and white works at Betty Parsons Gallery specifically, and the move they sanctioned, namely engagement with the 'understated image' which the painter might key to contemporary public events in associative ways with material. Is there something of the April 1951 *Life* magazine black and white photograph of Julius and Ethel Rosenberg in the back of the police van separated by a wire-mesh screen in *Charred Journal: Firewritten IV and V* for instance? Could it even have triggered the *Firewritten* series as a whole? Was the initial significance of making the series in 1951 recalled for Louis by the *Life* photo-feature of Michael and Robert Rosenberg's visit to Sing Sing published in March 1953, just one month before the opening of his Washington show? Did Louis identify with the two young boys with backgrounds not dissimilar to his own? Why did Louis decide to show paintings easy to dismiss as bad derivatives of 1951 Pollock in his first one man show, surely an occasion crucial to the public perception of his position as an ambitious American painter? Was it a coded act of empathy and solidarity with Ethel and Julius Rosenberg, a form protest against their execution?

The colour of the Rosenberg Era

> Whatever affectivity there is in Warhol's image lies, however, in the veils of colour-red, orange lavender – that sweep across these serially repeated readymade images.[45]

Were you thinking of Morris Louis when you chose the word 'veils', Griselda? *Veils* is, of course, the title of two separate sets of paintings made by Louis, one in 1954, the other between 1957 and 1960, in which colour became an autonomous element (pl. 9). It is not certain that Louis chose the name *Veils* himself; we know that Clement Greenberg suggested titles for some of Louis's work. Which brings me back to the two questions with which Mark Godfrey ends 'Keeping Watch over Absent Meaning': 'How could a painter who sought to address the Holocaust immerse himself so easily in a world of colour and light?' And, 'Why did a man who made efforts to tell the Washington press about the book burnings leave the titling and exhibiting of later paintings to others?' By 'others' I take it that Godfrey is alluding to Greenberg primarily. John Elderfield cautions that 'Greenberg's influence on Louis should not be underestimated; neither should it be misunderstood. Louis's final decisions were his alone.'[46] I want to argue that the involvement of Greenberg in Louis's professional life both provides a connection between Godfrey's two questions, and offers a possible answer to them.

Mark Godfrey's article is propelled by a desire to demonstrate that Louis's decision to exhibit the *Charred Journal: Firewritten* series in 1953 signalled his engagement with the 'memory of the Holocaust' in the *public* arena. This in contrast to his mentor and critical supporter to be, Clement Greenberg, who in 1950 declared his position on the American-Jewish response to the Holocaust in an article entitled 'Self-Hatred and Jewish Chauvinism: Some Reflections on "Positive Jewishness"'. For Greenberg it was a matter of private self-reflection:

> No matter how necessary it may be to indulge our feeling about Auschwitz, we can do so only temporarily and privately; we certainly cannot let them determine Jewish policy either in Israel or outside it...The main struggle, at least for us in America, still has to be fought inside ourselves. It is there, and only there, that we can convince ourselves that Auschwitz, while it may have been a historical judgement, was not a verdict upon our intrinsic worth as a people.[47]

'Self-Hatred and Jewish Chauvinism: Some Reflections on "Positive Jewishness"' was published in *Commentary*, the monthly journal sponsored by the American Jewish Committee. Greenberg was an associate editor of *Commentary* from 1945 to 1957. Louis Kaplan has argued that the theme of self-criticism as the most appropriate approach to living as a Jewish subject in post-WWII America appears in a displaced form in Greenberg's art writing in *Partisan Review* and the *Nation*.[48] He identifies its precise location in the frequent invocation of the name Immanuel Kant in Greenberg's criticism during the 1950s, culminating in the declaration in 'Modernist Painting' in 1960 that Kant was 'the first real modernist' because he was 'the first to criticise the means itself of criticism'.[49] For Greenberg self-criticism lies at the heart of modernist art:

> It quickly emerged that the unique and proper area of competence of each art coincided with all that was unique to the nature of its medium. The task

> of self-criticism became to eliminate from the effects of each art any and every effect that might conceivably be borrowed from or by the medium of any other art.[50]

Returning to 1950 and 'Self-Hatred and Jewish Chauvinism', if we again pay careful attention to dates, another dimension of the article emerges. 'Self-Hatred and Jewish Chauvinism' appeared in *Commentary* in November 1950, three months after the arrest of Julius and Ethel Rosenberg. Characterised by Mark Godfrey as a piece 'occasioned by the need to counter a new belligerence in public American-Jewish life sparked by reactions to the Holocaust', the article has a clear subtext. Greenberg links Jewish Chauvinism, which he defines as 'rabid nationalism', with 'the oppressed, frustrated, or backward peoples of Central and Eastern Europe':

> The East European background of most of the present leaders and spokesmen of Jewish nationalism is another factor that tends to exaggerate it. They cannot, in their political function, wholly escape the effects of the backward environment in which they grew up...This is why so much of what goes as Jewish political and cultural thought in this country ...is so utterly irrelevant to the lives actually led by American Jews – even more irrelevant than the imported Bolshevism of the 30s, another product of the political backwardness of Eastern Europe, was to the lives of Americans in general.[51]

The linking of Jewish nationalism of Eastern European immigrant origin with Bolshevism from the same source alerts us to a more immediate event than the Holocaust demanding Greenberg's polemical intervention, namely the arrest of Ethel and Julius Rosenberg and the debates surrounding the case in the Jewish community. David Suchoff writes:

> The New York intellectuals – the largely Jewish, anti-Stalinist writers and critics that surrounded *Partisan Review* – vigorously denied that anti-Semitism was at work in the Rosenberg case. The charge of Jewish persecution was poisoned for the anti-Stalinist left when the Communist Party trumpeted the Rosenbergs as victims of American anti-Semitism, while it remained silent as Stalin persecuted and executed Yiddish writers and other Jews in the Soviet Union.[52]

Suchoff also notes that the American Jewish Committee, for which *Commentary* was the mouth-piece, 'led the way in calling for the Rosenbergs' execution rather than clemency, fearing that the '"non Jewish public may generalize from these activities and impute to the Jews as a group treasonable motives and activities."'[53] It would not be unreasonable, then, to suggest that Greenberg's argument in 'Self-Hatred and Jewish Chauvinism' – for the need to counter the rise of Jewish nationalism and separatism in America as a response to the Holocaust, is haunted by the spectres of Julius and Ethel Rosenberg. They surely loomed large for Greenberg, a Yiddish-speaking child of immigrant parents from the 'Lithuanian Jewish enclave in northeastern Poland'.[54] For as David Suchoff explains, the Rosenbergs were associated with 'the working class, immigrant Jewish past…most New York intellectuals thought they had left far behind'.[55]

If this was a background Greenberg worked hard to leave behind in his reflections on the situation of Jews in post World War II American life in his work for *Commentary*, it must have made an uncomfortable return in his other field of intellectual endeavour, as arbiter of value in contemporary American art when, just seven months before the publication of 'Self-Hatred and Jewish Chauvinism', he met Helen Frankenthaler. Greenberg's growing professional and personal intimacy with the brilliant and cultivated young painter from a privileged German Jewish background must have exacerbated the sense of the 'inferiority' of his own immigrant Jewish origins.[56] At the same time, however, she also must have provided an irresistible model of the displaced Jewish self-criticism Greenberg advocated. Frankenthaler was someone to whom dominant high culture was 'fed with a silver spoon' from an early age, as Anne M. Wagner has put it. Frankenthaler 'comes across as a haunter of museums herself haunted in turn by the grand tradition as an inescapable inheritance, masterpieces to internalize and explode'.[57] And the first of Frankenthaler's significant engagements with the grand European tradition of painting was the object of Morris Louis and Kenneth Noland's famous visit to her New York studio organized by Clement Greenberg on 4 April 1953 – the spring of the 'sultry summer they executed the Rosenbergs'.

Greenberg's diary entry for that day reads, '"At 6pm Louis and Noland, along with Chas. Egan, George McNeil, Franz Kline, Leon and Ida Berkowitz & Margaret Brown and I visited Helen Frankenthaler's studio, where some of us stayed until 11."'[58] Leon and Ida Berkowitz were co-directors of the Washington Workshop Gallery where Louis's show, including the *Charred Journal* series, was showing that month. What did Louis and Noland see there? What did Greenberg show them? Recalling the occasion in the formal context of his 1960 *Art International* article 'Louis and Noland', Greenberg wrote:

> His first sight of the middle period Pollocks and of a large and extraordinary painting done in 1952 by Helen Frankenthaler, called *Mountains and Sea*, led Louis to change his direction abruptly. Abandoning Cubism with a completeness for which there was no precedent in either influence, he began to feel, think, and conceive almost exclusively in terms of open colour.[59]

Greenberg's ambivalence towards Pollock's 1951 exhibition of black and white works shows in his review for *Partisan Review* in January 1952 entitled '"Feeling is All"'.[60] We might read as significant his citing of the 'middle period Pollocks' as an influence on Louis in terms of his dismissal of the more obvious connection between the painter's later black and white paintings and Louis's *Charred Journal* series. We could infer from it a dismissal of the *Charred Journal* paintings themselves as indicative of precisely the degenerate slide into narrative and Surrealistic 'academicism' towards which Pollock's black and white works beckoned. All the more undesirable a development when tagged with allusive titles freighted not only with the 'memory of the Holocaust', but perhaps also with the current dangerous manifestation of its unfinished business in the form of the Rosenberg case. We now know that the title of Greenberg's review 'Feeling is All' is a quote from a remark made by Helen Frankenthaler who at the beginning of 1952 was making her own moves in painting in the domain of 'open' colour.[61]

Let us imagine Morris Louis viewing *Mountains and Sea* on the evening of 4 April 1953 fresh from hanging his Washington exhibition, including the *Charred Journal* paintings. From the evidence we have in the literature it is safe to surmise that the implications of the soak-stain application of liquid pigment in *Mountains and Sea* were high on the agenda for discussion. Ideas later crystallised in Greenberg's 1960 Kantian characterisation of Louis's practice as one of thinking and conceiving by first *feeling* through colour as *disembodied* and therefore more 'purely optical' (the 'unique and proper area of competence' of painting) were surely nascent in conversation in Frankenthaler's studio that evening and had a particular resonance for Louis. The 'feeling' connected with the destruction of Jewish bodies 'remembered' by the painter making *Charred Journal: Firewritten* in literal darkness of pigment supporting ghostly understated figurative imagery, linked associatively to a title indulgent by Greenberg's standards, might in a way less dangerously partisan, less ethnically backward looking and more culturally avant-garde, be conveyed 'almost exclusively by colour'.

As a photograph

> Whatever affectivity there is in Warhol's image lies…in the veils of colour – red, orange, lavender – that sweep across these serially repeated readymade images… [62]

So perhaps you did have Louis's work in mind when you wrote that passage in 'Nichsapha:Yearning/Languishing'. Or perhaps it emerges in the text only in my reading of it. You write that 'colour creates its own irreal spatiality that vibrates, at the level of the semiotic, with rhythms that line our subjectivity'. I take it that you mean semiotic in the Kristevan sense. If so, the affectivity of colour of which you write is the revolutionary moment Kristeva theorises in *Giotto's Joy* when colour at once threatens and rejuvenates the prevailing symbolic order of both painting as a system, and the unity of the psychic subject constituted in that symbolic order. In Kristeva's theorisation colour has the capacity to carry affective values independent of those, social and ideological, signified by prevailing narrative and representational conventions. However, colour emerges as independent only in relation to the 'everpresent norm'. Here I am redrawing the lines of my own argument in the previous chapter hoping to configure it with the argument of this one.

If, as Mark Godfrey suggests, work on the *Charred Journal* paintings in 1951, and their exhibition two years later in 1953, signalled Louis's engagement with the memory of the Holocaust, it is significant that it should occur in precisely the period spanning the trial and execution of Julius and Ethel Rosenberg. To my mind the fact registers the operation of deferred revision occasioned by that event. It is in this sense that Louis's encounter with *Mountains and Sea* on 4 April 1953 when the Rosenbergs were still in prison awaiting execution, lends the work significance as a painting of the Rosenberg era. We could read the trajectory of Louis's work *after* the 1953 visit to Frankenthaler's studio against the grain of modernist criticism as over compensation for the traumatic 'Real', the mass destruction of the materiality of Jewish bodies, behind the affect that surfaced as he painted works like the *Charred Journal* series. An over compensation that was the effect of the impact of Louis's other encounter that evening, namely with Clement Greenberg. Louis's subsequent drive to push the affective potential of colour he recognised, or was shown, in *Mountains and Sea* to the point of a pure disembodied opticality marks his adoption of Greenberg's Kantian aesthetics as displaced Jewish self-criticism: the most appropriate response for an American citizen to the 'memory of the Holocaust' in the field of ambitious art.

Responding to the unexpected appearance of Warhol's *Disaster* series in your 'Nichsapha' essay allows me to make a further move, Griselda. You suggest that the *Disaster* works themselves might reflect the process of *nachträglichkeit:*

> Thus while Warhol's work belongs to a forward thrust that initiated aspects of Pop Art and the disaffected postmodern attitude itself, art made now may allow us to read within it an unwitting anticipation of current preoccupations with the disaster and the trauma of twentieth-century death. The work registered a freight that was not critically or theoretically spoken. No one spoke much about the Holocaust then.[63]

Conversely, viewed from the perspective of April 1953, the photograph of the empty electric chair in Warhol's 1963 series of images awaits the bodies of Julius and Ethel Rosenberg. In Warhol's found photograph the repressed of Louis's practice after 1953, in Kristevan terms, the social and ideological norms signified by narrative and representation, returns in 1963 with a vengeance. You write: 'Whatever affectivity there is in Warhol's image lies...in the veils of colour – red, orange, lavender – that sweep across these serially repeated readymade images.' The 'whatever' is telling because although *Giotto's Joy* informs your thinking in this passage, colour in Warhol's *Disaster* images does not carry affectivity in the Kristevan sense. Indeed we might diagnose in them the status of colour as a symptom of precisely the death of its revolutionary potential, initiated by Louis when he extracted its revolutionary moment ***in*** the still allusive *Mountains and Sea* and pursued it exclusively ***as*** painting for and in itself. Warhol's gesture with colour in the electric chair images is premeditated and mechanical. Colour does not, 'tear itself from the symbolic norm, bypass it, absorb it, go beyond it, do something else, but always in relation to it.'[64] In the *Disaster* images narrative signified and colour as signifier of painting as such are always already distinct elements. Warhol's gesture of throwing veils of colour over the monochrome readymade image is a knowingly desultory one. You summarise the historical weight it carries:

> Warhol's work operates on that hinge between the draining of all reference in pursuit of aesthetic purity that characterizes high American modernist theory, and the negotiated re-engagement with a world envisioned as not only totally commodified, but catastrophically charged and haunting.[65]

As the electric chair *Disaster* images play here between your text and mine a different quality of affect arises through them. The unfinished business of Louis's *Charred Journal: Firewritten* emerges in Warhol's work both as a photograph, and like a photograph forming in a bath of transparent colour that no longer veils but now functions as active agent of its delayed visibility. The effect is uncanny.[66]

6

EDEN: ET IN ARCADIA EGO

> Julius and Ethel Rosenberg have gone to the electric chair. The first to go into the death chamber was Julius Rosenberg...The first volts of electricity entered his body at about 8:04 p.m...She died a lot harder. When it appeared that she had received enough electricity to kill an ordinary person, and had received the exact amount that had killed her husband, the doctors went over and pulled down the cheap prison dress, a little dark green printed job, and placed the sethe...[he stumbles over the word] I can't say it...stethoscope to her and looked around and looked at each other dumbfounded, and seemed surprised she was not dead.
>
> Believing she was dead, the attendants had taken off the ghastly strapping and electrodes and black belts and so forth. These had to be readjusted again and she was given more electricity which began again the ghastly plume of smoke that rose from her head and went up against the skylight overhead. After two more of those jolts, Ethel Rosenberg had met her maker, and she'll have a lot of explaining to do.[1]

Ethel Rosenberg

The man in a hat delivers his account to camera, blanched against the night sky in a glare of floodlights. The official observer's report to the press is a stark encapsulation of the dimension of the Rosenberg case Martha Rosler stressed when she set the photo silk-screened image of Ethel Rosenberg at her kitchen sink beside Eisenhower's letter to his son printed on the hand-towel in *Unknown Secrets (The Secret of the Rosenbergs)* namely, the working of the ideology of gender in/as representation.[2]

Among those directly involved in the Rosenberg case much was made of Ethel Rosenberg's dominant, unwomanly behaviour. Judge Irving Kaufman sentencing the Rosenbergs to death emphasised Ethel Rosenberg's role in the alleged conspiracy: 'Instead of deterring him [Julius] from his ignoble course, she encouraged and assisted the cause. She was a mature woman, almost three years older than her husband, and almost seven years older than her younger brother. She was a full-fledged partner in the crime.'[3] Ethel Rosenberg's demeanour at

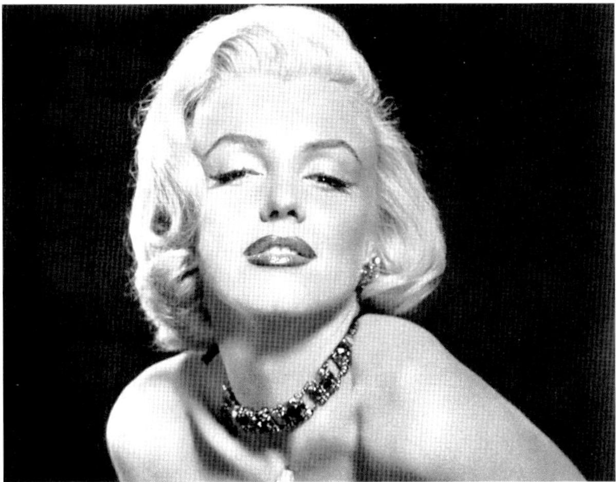

Fig. 15
Marilyn Monroe in a strapless dress and hairstyle favoured in the mid 1950s. Publicity Still

her trial, her failure to lose her composure on the witness stand, her repeated recourse to the Fifth Amendment, created an impression amongst legal experts and jurors alike of a cold 'unnatural' woman lacking 'normal feminine characteristics'.[4] Yet it was precisely an excess of warmth, the unseemly behaviour of a body in its need for physical contact that shocked the prison authorities into placing a table between the couple when Ethel Rosenberg embraced her husband on the occasion of their first meeting in Sing Sing. Carol Hurd Green writes: 'Their open sexuality was intolerable to their guards: asserting her body into the political conversation was more proof, if any was needed, of her guilt.'[5] Hurd Green's adjective fails, though, to convey the racial dimension of the reaction, which a visual juxtaposition might serve to catch. In your essay 'Killing Men and Dying Women' you, Griselda, reproduced a publicity still of glamorous, blonde Marilyn Monroe as exemplary representation of feminine desirability in early 50s America (fig. 15). Set beside it Martha Rosler's image of dark, homely Ethel Rosenberg (see fig. 11) and the possibility emerges of a reaction from the guards more visceral than intolerance: one of revulsion.[6]

Most monstrously, Ethel Rosenberg transgressed the defining role of 'natural' femininity in 50s America, that of the good mother, foundation of wholesome family life. Judge Kaufman condemned Ethel and Julius Rosenberg as spies *and* as bad parents: 'the defendants Julius and Ethel Rosenberg...were conscious that they were sacrificing their own children, should their misdeeds be detected...Love for their cause dominated their lives – it was even greater than their love for their children.'[7] In her essay *A Bond of Sisterhood* Joyce Antler draws attention to the Jewish dimension of good mothering as it was represented in American popular culture during the Rosenberg years. Antler points out that Ethel Rosenberg was not the most famous Jewish woman of the early 1950s; that distinction went to Molly Goldberg, 'the Yiddish-accented immigrant heroine of the long-running hit radio and TV series *The Goldbergs*'. Antler argues:

> No greater contrast could be drawn between the Molly Goldberg motherhood ideal of the 1950s – friendly, garrulous, kindhearted, family oriented, noncontroversial, and nonpolitical – and the public image of Ethel Rosenberg: silent and mysterious, conspiratorial and political, dominating and evil. Blindly loyal to her husband at the cost of abandoning her own children, she seemed, above all – and perhaps most dangerously – a neglectful and uncaring mother. Many Americans who loved Molly Goldberg were deeply shocked by Ethel Rosenberg.[8]

To sum up: it was a woman's body, a Jewish woman's body, the body of Ethel Rosenberg that emerged at the beginning of the 1950s as the spectacularly public signifying site of almost all that was dangerously other to post-war, Cold War, American Dream ideology. It was a foreign body, Jewish, alien – attached to the evil (Soviet) empire – and it performed acts of 'unnatural' femininity: overly sexualised and inadequately maternal, coolly intellectual and politically committed.

Revulsion, fear, hatred and retributive violence accumulate in the crude language of the official observer of the execution of the Rosenbergs to produce his narration of the death of Ethel Rosenberg as a disturbingly pornographic scene.

Marjorie Morningstar

> The Marjorie Morningstar of the art world – Helen Frankenthaler – was one of the few women painters of the fifties who did not act as if her gender were a biological mishap. She always seemed to like being a woman, in total contrast to painters such as Joan Mitchell and Grace Hartigan, who seemed confronted and enraged by their femininity. Women artists like these often made a point of sleep-and-tell, when ostensibly their aim was to be buddies at the bar. No crude words ever crossed the lips of Helen Frankenthaler. She was a tall, willowy girl with large, Picassoesque eyes, flawless skin, and a radiant smile. She dressed with taste and elegance, even at her most casual. Clearly a well brought up girl, Helen did not mind the image she presented. She was not about to transform herself into an aggressive, with-it artist, but there was nothing namby-pamby in her attitude about her work or her position among her contemporaries.[9]

Marjorie Morningstar is the eponymous Jewish heroine of a popular novel by Herman Wouk published in 1955 who, after a sudden insight into her true calling as an actress, changes her name from Morgenstern to Morningstar by 'a mere translation of the German compound'. Gruen's comparison is superficial: fictional character and actual painter share little more than certain physical characteristics, taste and elegance in dress, and the manners of a 'well brought up girl'. The designation functions primarily as signifier of Frankenthaler's Jewishness. In the novel Marjorie Morningstar's background and aspirations are closer to those of Clement Greenberg than Helen Frankenthaler:

> 'El Dorado' was perfectly suited to an apartment building on Central Park West. It had a fine foreign sound to it. There were two categories of foreignness in Marjorie's outlook: high foreign, like French restaurants, British riding clothes, and the name El Dorado; and low foreign, like her parents. By moving to the El Dorado on Central Park West, her parents had done much, Marjorie believed, to make up for their immigrant origin. She was grateful to them for this, and proud of them.[10]

Marjorie's aspirations for a career in acting come to nothing. Her flirtation with the left leaning, Jewish fringes of theatrical bohemia end when, on her return from a cathartic trip to Europe, she marries Milton Schwartz, a young lawyer with 'decidedly old-fashioned' ideas on religion and politics, and becomes mother of four children.[11]

The inside flap of the dust jacket of *Marjorie Morningstar* carries a note 'from the author'; it reads:

> *Marjorie Mornigstar* is a picture of an American girl in love: perhaps I should add, a somewhat old-fashioned American girl. Old fashions are having a revival in the United States, in things that go deeper than ladies' waistlines and gentlemen's lapels. I believe my heroine is very much a girl of the moment.[12]

Although published in 1955, Wouk's novel opens in 1933 as Marjorie Morgenstern writes out her new name, 'Marjorie Morningstar', followed by the date, May 7, 1933. The date is significant for a Jewish author beginning a new book. As the fictional Marjorie Morgenstern in New York effaces her Jewish name in the translation 'Morningstar' written across a blank page of her biology notebook, in Berlin in the real world, the Nazis are burning books. It might be argued that *Marjorie Morningstar* is Herman Wouk's own engagement with the 'memory of the Holocaust' in the domain of popular culture, just as the *Charred Journal* series was Louis's in the realm of high culture.

If the Rosenberg case was the occasion of deferred revision of that historical trauma for Louis, does the event also resonate in Wouk's fictional invention of Marjorie Morningstar? Why the emphasis on her American-ness on the dust jacket note? Why should her old-fashionedness make her a girl of the moment in 1955? Is the repressed of *Marjorie Morningstar* the figure of Ethel Rosenberg? [13]

Marjorie Morningstar hears the news of Hitler's invasion of Czechoslovakia in

1939 when she is on board the *Queen Mary* crossing the Atlantic to Europe in the company of a mysterious fellow passenger called Michael Eden. It transpires that, under the cover of transacting foreign business for a chemical company, Eden is engaged in helping Jewish families with small children escape from Nazi Germany. While Wouk's novel looks back to the impending catastrophe of the Second World War, the reality of contemporary events resonates in the name he chooses for Marjorie's shipboard acquaintance.

The legacy of WWII in the Middle East in the formation of State of Israel in May 1948, and the subsequent Tripartite Declaration of May 1950, was driving international affairs in 1955. The Tripartite Declaration was the expression of the claim of the three Western powers, the United States, Britain and France, to the Middle East as their exclusive sphere of influence both politically and economically. It affirmed their sole responsibility for containing the Arab-Israeli conflict and for directing Middle East defence. The intervention of the three Western powers, each in pursuit of its own interests, eventually led to the outbreak of the Second Arab-Israeli War in October 1956. Three specific events precipitated it. Britain's withdrawal from the Suez Canal under the Evacuation Treaty signed with Egypt in 1954, the Czech arms deal of 1955, in which Egypt secured a massive arms package from the Soviet Union, and Egypt's seizure of the Suez Canal in July 1956 with the intention of nationalising it. The man with responsibility for British involvement in the Middle East, British Foreign Secretary in Winston Churchill's cabinet since 1951, and in April 1955 his successor as Prime Minister, was Anthony Eden.[14]

Another summer, another holiday

At the height of diplomatic attempts in August 1956 to secure a peaceful resolution to the Suez crisis, Helen Frankenthaler was in Europe visiting France, Germany, Austria and the Netherlands. She returned from the trip with a small coloured drawing on paper called *Hôtel du Quai Voltaire*, signed and dated in the bottom left-hand corner '8/56' (pl. 10). According to John Elderfield Frankenthaler made the drawing in Paris. He describes *Hôtel du Quai Voltaire* as 'wonderfully limpid and made on that hotel's brown drawer-lining paper, using nail polish and lipstick to supplement her watercolours'.[15] Before it makes an appearance in John Elderfield's 1989 Frankenthaler monograph, *Hôtel du Quai Voltaire* is discussed by Maurice Poirier in a review of a retrospective of Frankenthaler's works on paper entitled, *Frankenthaler: Works on Paper 1949 to 1984*, at the Guggenheim Museum in New York.[16] Poirier describes the drawing in very different terms from Elderfield:

> *Hôtel du Quai Voltaire*, [is] perhaps the most feverishly painted of all the works in the exhibition...Compelled to express her feelings in visual form, Frankenthaler pulled out the brown paper lining the drawers of the bureau in her hotel room and began to sketch in watercolor from a kit she carried with her. Finding the kit too limited, she turned to the hotel's blue green ink

> and to her own lipstick and nail polish. The result is an explosive, frenzied display of color splashes, suggesting a high state of agitation. The work becomes even more moving when one discerns at the right a woman's face with a troubled expression – presumably a self portrait.[17]

The description suggests that the drawing was a response to an event, the nature of which is known to Poirier, but that he chooses not to divulge to the reader. What was it that 'compelled' Frankenthaler to 'express her feelings in visual form'? What was the cause of her 'high state of agitation'? Why is a self-portrait presumed to be included in the drawing, and why would that make it all the more moving, in fact, why is the drawing moving at all?

The air of mystery in Poirier's approach to *Hôtel du Quai Voltaire* also pervades John Elderfield's treatment of a painting made by Frankenthaler in the autumn of 1956 on her return home to America from Europe. He considers it one of her greatest works and describes it as a 'synoptic "interior" landscape of the artist's imagination'.[18] The title of the painting is *Eden*. He does not, however, disclose what he believes or knows it summarises. There is an air of self-censorship about the reluctance in the critical commentaries to speculate about links between events on and off the canvas, not just in *Hôtel du Quai Voltaire* and *Eden*, but in general in Frankenthaler's work throughout the 1950s, a result perhaps of taking the artist at her word. As recently as 1992 in an interview published in *Partisan Review* when Hilton Kramer asked Frankenthaler a question about the relationship between politics and art as she lived it in the 1950s, she answered:

> Politics *per se*, the news of the world at large, were often a passionate concern. But these considerations were apart from the passionate concerns of art. Striving to make beautiful new paintings that worked was one issue: McCarthyism, the Cold War were something else. When art is really beautiful and moving, it brings with it not only growing pleasure but a sense of truth. This truth, this reality – something so spiritual and unnameable, unprovable – is and always has been a political force in itself. Any other kind of political persuasion is usually empty fashion, or dangerous, or both.[19]

Insulated by wealth and privilege from the necessity of direct political engagement with the realities of American life as Ethel Rosenberg experienced it, Helen Frankenthaler was free to pursue the 'unnameable, unprovable' truths of painting undisturbed. Nevertheless she did live and work beside the hideous facticity of the execution of the Rosenbergs, inhabiting a body that resembled Ethel Rosenberg's in two uncomfortable respects. It was a Jewish body, and in its activity as a painter it occupied another position 'uncharacteristic of normal femininity' in 1950s America.[20] But was the compartmentalisation of 'the news of the world at large' and 'the passionate concerns of art', really as watertight as Frankenthaler's statement would have us believe? In a discussion of the legacy of Jackson Pollock's black and white paintings in the artist's work after *Mountains and Sea*, John Elderfield remarks:

> Still little realized…is the way in which her interpretation of Pollock's figuration to create an art of floating symbols opened the way for the most interesting other forms of 1950s referential art, namely that of Larry Rivers and Robert Rauschenberg who in the mid 50s adopted the diaristic, episodic approach to picture making.'[21]

A crucial figure is missing from Elderfield's genealogy of purely visual artists. The poet Frank O'Hara, well known for his development of a diaristic and episodic poetic form, was a friend of Larry Rivers and an admirer and the most perceptive critic of Frankenthaler's work in the 1950s. He wrote the catalogue essay for her first major solo exhibition at the Jewish Museum, New York, in 1960. I think we can attribute to Frankenthaler herself an approach to picture making in which diaristic and episodic elements also figure, though in radically condensed forms. Was it not precisely this aspect of Frankenthaler's work O'Hara recognised, and to which he responded so strongly?[22]

It is not difficult to guess the circumstances under which Frankenthaler produced *Hôtel du Quai Voltaire* in Paris in August 1956. We know that the painter Lee Krasner was also in Paris in July and early August that year, and that she met with other American art world friends there, including Helen Frankenthaler. It was in Paris on 11 August 1956 that Lee Krasner received the news of Jackson Pollock's death in a car crash by telephone from Clement Greenberg in America.[23] These are reasonable grounds then, for speculation that this is the distressing event to which Maurice Poirier alludes, and that *Hôtel du Quai Voltaire* was connected with Frankenthaler's response to the death of Jackson Pollock. I want to take issue, however, with Poirier on two counts. First with the scene he conjures up in his story of how the drawing was made. Taking the study itself as evidence, I find his scenario of a distraught Frankenthaler pulling brown paper lining out of bureau drawers in a grief-stricken frenzy to 'express her feelings' in the immediacy of the moment, rather histrionic. A painter who carries a watercolour kit usually carries paper. If we accept that there is an element of visual diary to Frankenthaler's paintings in the mid-1950s, then a more convincing explanation of the artist's choice of support suggests itself. Perhaps Frankenthaler used the drawer lining paper in its status as a material fragment, a memento, of the place – the hotel of the title – in which she received the news of Pollock's death. Her choice of support was a conscious decision, and conscious decision-making slows down the working process. *Hôtel du Quai Voltaire* is a remarkably well composed drawing. The touch is light and controlled (note the pair of steady vertical lines in the left-hand third of the canvas), nothing catches or clogs. It belies Poirier's description of the facture as explosive and splashed. John Elderfield's adjective 'limpid' is more accurate.

Secondly, I question Poirier's interpretation of the configuration of marks in the top right side of the drawing. The four marks he sees as eyes, nose and mouth of a women's face are larger than life: cavernous patches of darkness in a heart-shaped area of wash. They are the holes where eyes, nose and mouth once were. It may be a face but not a living one: it is a skull, a death's head. This reading offers the possibility of moving beyond Poirier's anecdotal account of *Hôtel du Quai Voltaire* as a one-off sketch recording a personal experience, towards speculation about its place in a larger structure of historical and cultural meaning in Frankenthaler's work in the mid 1950s in which the small drawing is fundamentally connected with *Eden,* the big painting made in the autumn of 1956.

Eden?

At the Guggenheim Museum in New York in 1998, the scale of the painting surprised me.[24] *Eden* (pl. 11) measures 103 x 117 in (261.6 x 297.2 cm), less than seventeen inches higher and close to the same width as *Mountains and Sea.* In the space of the gallery, however, *Eden* seems like a bigger painting. In *Mountains and Sea* shapes of poured or brushed translucent colour stack up from the drawn blue baseline to the top of the canvas functioning to flatten the picture plane. Spatial recession occurs only in its right, vertical third. Consequently, against the expectations of the landscape dimensions of the canvas, a sense of height characterises the experience of viewing *Mountains and Sea.* While *Eden* is a composition similarly divided vertically roughly into thirds, in which the shallow stage-like foreground of *Mountains and Sea* is repeated but reversed, it is spatially consistent across the whole of the picture plane. This is a result of its dominant technical resource, drawing with fluid colour, by means of which an equally balanced, open relation between figure and ground is maintained with great skill and economy. The relationship between the size of the canvas and the scale and disposition of its pictorial elements is finely judged to achieve a sense of immense spatial expansion, both in width and in depth, beyond the actual dimensions of the frame. Translucent pale yellows, browns and reds combine with off-white, untouched, unprimed ground to create an environment of air and light. The painting breathes. *Eden*'s focus is a pair of numbers, 100 100, inscribed in blue within a teardrop shape situated close to the centre of the picture between two thin, brown vertical lines. To the right, beside a pool of blue, a hand shape painted red shoots up to the top of the canvas, its fingers touching the edge. Is it the back of a right hand, or the front of a left hand? It's not clear. The hand is balanced in the top left of the canvas by a pale yellow spiky form of a similar size. Scribbles and scrawls, blobs and splatters swirl and eddy around these distinctive elements of the composition, animating and energising them. The picture looks windblown. What sense, though, are we to make of its idiosyncratic imagery?

Over reliance on the title of the painting as the key to unlocking its meaning has led to critical interpretations of *Eden* both astonishing for their banality, and bizarre in their narrative logic. Barbara Rose writing in 1971 starts out from a formalist position:

> Although Frankenthaler never uses so rigid a system as absolute symmetry, the paintings of 1957 are more symmetrical than most she has done. *Eden*, for example, is bisected by a rounded red form alluding perhaps to the legendary apple or to a metaphorical target with 100 (bull's-eye) inscribed on each side. Several critics have commented on the wit of the allusions in Eden – the presence of the snakes as well as of the big red hand of God at the top right, which balances the pronged form of the yellow sun at the upper left.[25]

For John Elderfield writing in 1989, *Eden* is:

> As astounding and sudden invention in some respects as *Mountains and Sea* itself, it tells of an ideal and abstracted world of sensuous delight, cut off in the ironical form of its representation from any real landscape. Hoisted into the trees, the winning 100 scores of prelapsarian perfection are marvellously witty inventions that also carry extraordinary visual force.[26]

Only Edward Carmean in 1989, surveying the critical commentaries on *Eden* from the moment of its first exhibition at the Tibor de Nagy Gallery in 1957, challenges the basis of such interpretations of the work:

> These readings raise some curious theological and iconographic questions, foremost being why the artist would identify perfection – the winning 100s – with the forbidden fruit, the apple. But more importantly, there is little about the picture aside from its title to specifically support such identification.[27]

It is Carl Beltz, however, who really goes to town with the title, building upon Barbara Rose's assessment of Frankenthaler as 'essentially an intuitive and natural painter not an intellectual one', whose work is fundamentally lyrical and pastoral in tone.[28] Beltz writes:

> For all its general richness, Helen Frankenthaler's *Eden*, painted in 1957, is not primarily muscular, and for all its firmness of structure, it is not bound to a formal idea...It is grand in its physical presentation, yet it contains a wealth of intimate detail; it eschews the programmatic in favour of spontaneity and adventure.[29]

His choice of adjectives genders the formal characteristics of the painting in a series of crude cultural stereotypes. The work is not virile or intellectual ('bound to a formal idea'), rather its qualities are the feminine ones of intimacy and thoughtless spontaneity. 'Landscape associations are encouraged by many of the motifs in *Eden.*' But at the same time:

> The gestures in nearly all cases are abstract, signs of what the painter and her materials can do in creative collaboration, yet several are also plainly referential – the glowing sun, the pair of '100s' (emblems of some perfect score?) in the centre of the composition and the flaming, forbidding red hand that rises above all other images. These add an engaging freshness to the painting, a childlike naiveté that is especially meaningful in view of its title.[30]

Combining 'intimacy' and 'spontaneity' with 'childlike naiveté' Beltz conflates feminisation and infantilisation to represent the painting as the site of regression to a pre-symbolic and a-temporal condition culturally equated with the feminine. 'Intellectually I knew that *Eden* had taken time to evolve, but I felt as though it had been shaped all at once,' he writes in a sentence striking as a structure of disavowal, but unsurprising in assigning the intellectual capacity to himself.[31]

I agree with Beltz's intellectual assessment of *Eden* as a painting that took time to evolve, but want to forestall his swift, defensive closure of any consideration of specific developmental movements. To start with I think it is productive to think about *Eden*'s evolution in relation to the coloured drawing *Hôtel du Quai Voltaire*. A major art historical study contemporary with both works by Frankenthaler offers a suggestive structural model for exploring this idea.

In 1955 Doubleday & Company of New York published a collection of essays by the art historian Erwin Panofsky under the title *Meaning in the Visual Arts*.[32] The book contains the revision of an essay, first published in 1936 as '*Et in Arcadia ego:* On the Conception of Transience in Poussin and Watteau', under the new title, '*Et in Arcadia ego:* Poussin and the Elegiac Tradition'.[33] *Meaning in the Visual Arts* was reviewed in the May 1956 issue of the journal *Arts*, in which reviews of Frankenthaler's work also appeared in the 1950s. The book's epilogue is an essay entitled, 'Three Decades of American Art History in the United States: Impressions of a Transplanted European'. The essay opens autobiographically. Panofsky writes of his move to America after his dismissal as professor of the history of art in Hamburg when in the spring of 1933 the Nazis removed all Jewish officials from their positions. The main body of the essay is a comparison of the evolution of the discipline of art history in Germany and America. It ends, however, with protest against the curtailment of intellectual and academic freedom in American universities and cultural institutions by McCarthyism. Panofsky warns of 'the terrifying rise of precisely those forces which drove us out of Europe in the 1930s: nationalism and intolerance.'

> ...we cannot blind ourselves to the fact that Americans may now be legally punished, not for what they do or have done but for what they say or have said, think or have thought. And though the means of punishment are not the same as those employed by the Inquisition, they are uncomfortably similar: economic instead of physical strangulation, and the pillory instead of the stake.[34]

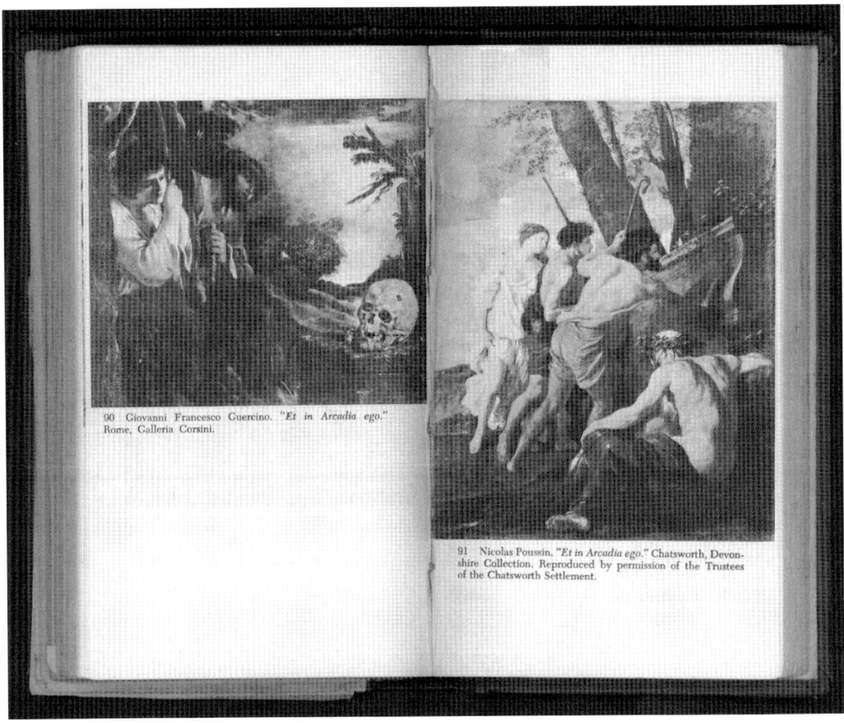
90 Giovanni Francesco Guercino. "*Et in Arcadia ego.*" Rome, Galleria Corsini.

91 Nicolas Poussin. "*Et in Arcadia ego.*" Chatsworth, Devonshire Collection. Reproduced by permission of the Trustees of the Chatsworth Settlement.

Fig. 16
Illustrations in *Meaning in the Visual Arts* by Erwin Panofsky, 1955

'Three Decades of American Art History in the United States' was originally published as 'The Cultural Migration: The European Scholar in America' in 1953, at the time when the execution of Julius and Ethel Rosenberg was a highly public physical manifestation of state punishment.[35]

The publication of *Meaning in the Visual Arts* in 1955, or at least the review of the book in the May 1956 issue of *Arts*, was surely noted by Clement Greenberg, a contributor on the visual arts to *Partisan Review*. The book's epilogue touching upon the situation of the Jewish intellectual in post war America cannot have been without interest to him in his role as editor of *Commentary*. The resonance between events surrounding the emergence of the painting Frankenthaler named *Eden* and the theme of Panofsky's '*Et in Arcadia ego:* Poussin and the Elegiac Tradition', the most significant essay in the newly published collection, is so striking it demands attention.[36]

'*Et in Arcadia ego:* Poussin and the Elegiac Tradition' is concerned with the change in interpretation of the Latin phrase *Et in Arcadia ego* in the Western literary tradition from the grammatically correct translation, 'death is even in Arcadia', to

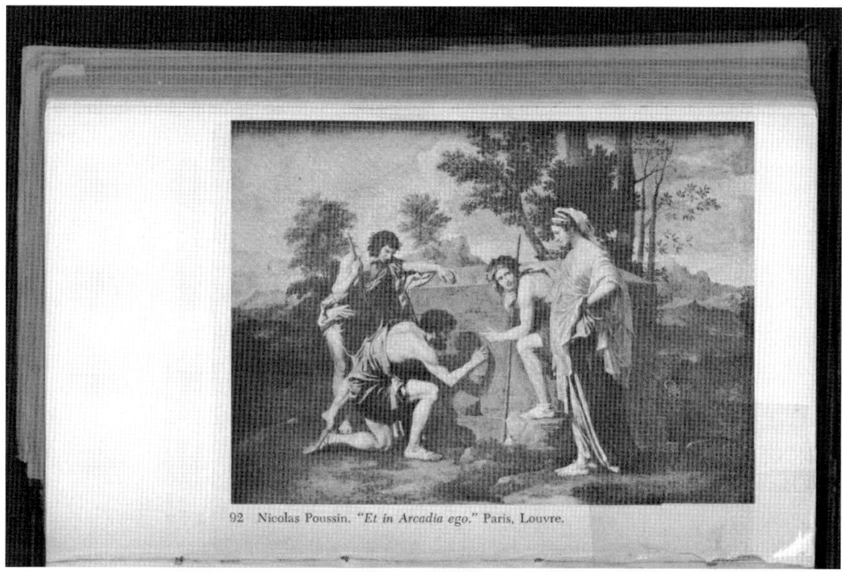

Fig. 17
Nicolas Poussin, *The Arcadian Shepherds* as illustrated in *Meaning in the Visual Arts* by Erwin Panofsky, 1955

its modern meaning, 'I, too, was born, or lived, in Arcady'. Panofsky identifies the moment of change, not in the field of literature, but in a painting: Nicolas Poussin's treatment of the theme of death in Arcady in *The Arcadian Shepherds* (1638-40) now in the Louvre, Paris. Panofsky traces the first appearance of the theme in painting to a picture by Giovanni Francesco Guercino made in Rome between 1621 and 1623. He describes it as follows:

> In this painting two Arcadian shepherds are checked in their wanderings by a sudden sight...a huge human skull that lies on a mouldering piece of masonry and receives the attentions of a fly and a mouse, popular symbols of decay and all-devouring time. Incised on the masonry are the words *Et in Arcadia ego*, and it is unquestionably by the skull that they are supposed to be pronounced...the accepted symbol of death personified...[37]

The young shepherds are surprised by death in the present happiness of their pastoral existence. The picture functions as a *memento mori* and thus remains faithful to the grammatically correct interpretation of the inscription *Et in Arcadia ego* as 'Death is even in Arcadia'. Panofsky argues that Poussin took Guercino's painting as the model for the first of his two versions of *Et in Arcadia ego*, the painting now in the Devonshire Collection at Chatsworth in England (fig. 16). In Poussin's interpretation the skull has become 'small and inconspicuous' and the shepherds, 'seem to be more intensely fascinated by the inscription than they are shocked by the death's-head'. Nevertheless Panofsky argues that the phrase *Et in Arcadia ego* can still be understood to issue from the mouth of the skull as death personified.[38] Therefore it still can be translated as 'Death is even in Arcadia' in the context of the visual events in the picture.

When Poussin returned to the theme five or six year later he treated it differently (fig. 17). The death's-head has disappeared completely, and with it the element of drama and surprise. Instead of an unexpected encounter with a terrifying phenomenon the shepherds are depicted calmly deciphering the inscription on the tomb, watched by a thoughtful female figure:

> Here, then, we have a basic change in interpretation. The Arcadians are not so much warned of an implacable future as they are immersed in mellow meditation on a beautiful past. They seem to think less of themselves than of the human being buried in the tomb – the human being that once enjoyed the pleasures which they now enjoy, and whose monument 'bids them remember their end' only in so far as it evokes the memory of one who had been what they are. In short, Poussin's Louvre picture no longer shows a dramatic encounter with Death but a contemplative absorption in the idea of mortality. We are confronted with a change from thinly veiled moralism to undisguised elegiac sentiment.[39]

A memento (mori)

Imagine, now, Helen Frankenthaler, passionate about painting and deeply interested in the European tradition, installed at the *Hôtel du Quai Voltaire* at the beginning of August 1956. With its history of artist residents, and situated on the right bank of the Seine facing the Louvre on the opposite side of the river, the hotel provided the perfect base for daily visits to the museum to view paintings significant, compelling, beloved, that formed part of Frankenthaler's archive as a painter. We know that the artist spent her evenings in Paris dining with American friends, sometimes followed by dancing at a club.[40] Into this happy holiday environment broke the shocking news of Jackson Pollock's violent and self-destructive death.

Hôtel du Quai Voltaire made under these circumstances on the hotel's brown drawer lining paper could be understood to function not only as a material reminder of an event, a memento, but also, symbolically as a *memento mori,* in the mode of Guercino's picture of the Arcadian Shepherds theme true to the grammatically correct translation of *Et in Arcadia ego* as 'Death is even in Arcadia'. Panofsky's essay, illustrated in the 1955 pocket sized Doubleday edition with black and white reproductions of the Guercino and Poussin pictures, serves as a reminder that, to count as such, significant cultural representations of even this shocking human experience are *artful.* I would like to wager that the exquisite *Hôtel du Quai Voltaire* was not the only drawing the artist made in that particular working session. It survives because it represents the material resolution of both an impulse *and* an idea. Is it self-portrait or is it a skull? We can read the configuration of marks to which Poirier draws our attention as either and as both. As self-portrait they register the immediate impact upon the artist of the shocking news of Jackson Pollock's death, as skull they reference a history, a tradition of the theme of mortality in painting.

An elegy

In the case of *Eden* there is some hard evidence to suggest that the compositional framework of the painting evolved from another small work on paper made in Europe during the summer of 1956.[41] Maurice Poirier discusses it in his 'Working Papers' article immediately before he turns his attention to *Hôtel du Quai Voltaire.* He refers to the study as *St Caste Landscape* (pl. 12). The work's title has been subsequently corrected to *Landscape (Nice, France).* He describes it as, 'a view of a bay. Windblown flags fly high above the horizon line, and three gold circles look as if they might be large suns. The work radiates a sense of boundless exhilaration.'[42] If we compare *Landscape (Nice, France)* with *Eden*, two significant elements of the study's composition are recognisable in the painting. In *Landscape (Nice, France)* four 'flagpoles' are grouped closely together on the left side of the drawing, and one stands alone on the far right. Two of three roughly drawn circles fill the space on the horizon between them; the third circle is caught between the flagpole on the right and the edge of the canvas. In *Eden* of the three 'golden circles' only one remains, slightly compressed, as the teardrop shape caught between two thin vertical brown marks, the residual trace of the *Landscape* 'flagpoles'.

The *Landscape (Nice, France)* watercolour study measures 9½ x 12½ in (22.8 x 30.4 cm), *Eden*, as we know, is a large painting measuring 103 x 117 in (261.6 x 297.2 cm). If *Landscape (Nice, France)* was a starting point for *Eden*, what encouraged the painter to begin on such a grand scale? Nothing more, perhaps, than the need to stretch back in the studio after the confinement of working small while travelling, or did the quality of 'boundless exhilaration' Poirier described as characterising the Nice *Landscape* study demand a bigger arena for its full expression? One where, quite literally, the boundaries were not always in sight in a practice of painting that involved working on lengths pulled out from a roll of canvas and tacked to the studio floor? According to Helen Frankenthaler, however, the painting did not start with images at all but with numbers, '100, 100'.[43] This suggests another possibility: that the scale of *Eden* is connected as much with issues of conceptual and historical weight as it is with physical expansiveness, in other words with an exhilarating drive to *think* big.

Recall Panofsky's analysis of the function of Poussin's second treatment of the Arcadian shepherds theme in the painting now in the Louvre:

> Here, then, we have a basic change in interpretation. The Arcadians are not so much warned of an implacable future as they are immersed in mellow

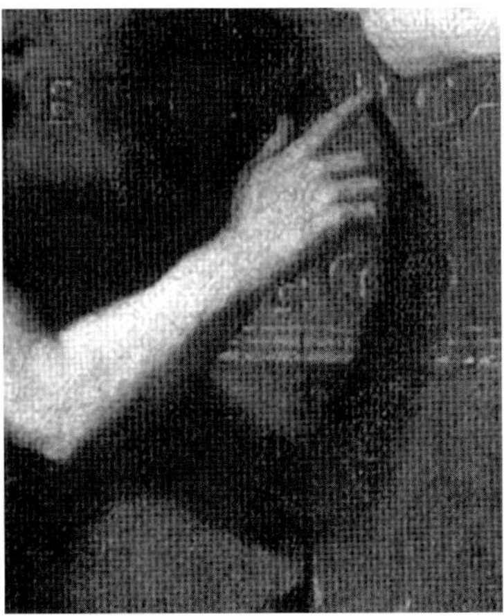

Fig. 18
Nicolas Poussin, *The Arcadian Shepherds*, c.1638-40, oil on canvas, 33 ½ x 47 ¾ in (85 x 121 cm) Paris, musée du Louvre (detail)

> meditation on a beautiful past. They seem to think less of themselves than of the human being buried in the tomb – the human being that once enjoyed the pleasures which they now enjoy, and whose monument 'bids them remember their end' only in so far as it evokes the memory of one who had been what they are. In short, Poussin's Louvre picture no longer shows a dramatic encounter with Death but a contemplative absorption in the idea of mortality. We are confronted with a change from thinly veiled moralism to undisguised elegiac sentiment.[44]

In a recent catalogue essay for the exhibition *Friedel Dzubas: Critical Painting*, Timothy McElreavy discusses a painting called *Early Grave* (pl. 13) made in 1957, a year after *Eden*. He has this to say about it:

> Critics had connected this particular painting with Pollock's tragic and untimely death a year earlier, as a comment on the loss of a friend and colleague. However, this grave is being dug not for Pollock personally but for his art. With Pollock gone and his mythical stature firmly ensconced in the canons of art history, Dzubas could now be free to work through and be rid of the chimerical myth of gestural, automatic painting.[45]

In other words, McElreavy interprets *Early Grave* as the triumphant moment of Dzubas's Oedipal struggle with his artistic father.[46] As you, Griselda, argue in 'Killing Men and Dying Women', this is also a struggle for women who paint, shaped by the demands and conditions of their professional environment.[47]

It is in *Eden* in 1956 and not *Mountains and Sea* in 1952 that Pollock's particular legacy to Frankenthaler in his black and white works of 1951 is fully accepted and freely elaborated. The 'drawn' articulation of colour in *Eden* is an ambitious revision of Pollock's technique in works like *Echo: Number 25*, 1951, and *Number 14*, 1951. Furthermore the painting is a bold, unequivocal statement of the element of Pollock's work to which Frankenthaler told Geldzahler she responded in 1951, namely, 'the understated image that was really present'. However I puzzle with Edward Carmean about a theological and iconographic logic that would make sense of the combination of snakes, apples, prelapsarian perfect scores and the red hand of God commentators claim as the imagery of *Eden* when they spin out their interpretations from the hook of the title. I propose that the fundamental logic of the painting's imagery is pictorial rather than iconographic.

Let us take a closer look at Poussin's Louvre *Arcadian Shepherds*, (pl. 14) specifically at a detail near the centre of the picture. The bent arm and pointing finger of the kneeling shepherd of the group casts a looping shadow on the wall of the tomb (fig. 18). It forms a drop-like open shape, not unlike the so-called apple in *Eden*. Caught within it is a fragment of the inscription on the tomb, the word 'EGO'. The top horizontal bar of the letter E is obscured by the shepherd's hand. The upright stroke of the capital G almost meets the top of the curve of the letter, and its horizontal bar is short. What we read as the word EGO can also be seen as the number 100. If we work with this detail as an idea about the pictorial logic of *Eden*, then the 'big red hand' fits in and its origin is human rather than divine, a transposition of the bare, terra-cotta coloured arm and hand of the kneeling shepherd pointing to the inscription on the tomb. Another pairing leads us elsewhere: Arcadia Greek, Eden Hebrew. Not God but his messenger, a red robed angel with outstretched arm and pointing finger expels Adam and Eve – two beings once perfect – from the garden of Eden in Masaccio's painting on the wall of the Brancacci Chapel in the church of Santa Maria del Carmine in Florence. The Poussin and the Masaccio pictures are both top scorers in a history of painting about mortality, and recollections of them both may have played a part in the evolution of the imagery of *Eden*. Title notwithstanding, however, the *mise-en-scène* of Frankenthaler's painting is not the chilly wastes awaiting Adam and Eve beyond the gates of Eden in Masaccio's *Expulsion*, but rather the golden landscape of Poussin's Arcadia. *Eden* is the tiny holiday *Landscape (Nice, France)* sketch writ large with knowledge of a history of European painting, by a painter ambitious to re-animate its resources in the contemporary American context.

In his essay 'Cézanne and the Unity of Modern Art', Clement Greenberg reminds the reader that Cézanne had the Louvre Arcadian Shepherds picture tacked to the studio wall as he worked on his last great landscape paintings, struggling to 're-do Poussin after nature' and 'make Impressionism something solid and durable like the Old Masters'.[48] As I have argued in the opening chapter of this book in the early 1950s Cézanne's last landscape studies in watercolour were, in turn, a resource for Helen Frankenthaler starting out on an ambitious project to get to grips with Jackson Pollock's groundbreaking innovations in painting, and find her own point of departure from them. The elegiac sentiments of Poussin's great, culturally transitional Arcadian Shepherds picture could not have been more apposite to her situation as a painter in the autumn of 1956. 'Et in Arcadia ego', I too was born, or lived in Arcady: the voice from the tomb is Jackson Pollock's, and it addresses the painter working in the studio in New York who, alive, remains to contemplate mortality in 'the utopian happiness of painting'.[49] Sole female member of the band of Arcadian Shepherds, self-contained and attentive to his words to her they mean most; spoken by the top scoring painter of the last generation, addressed to the potential top scoring painter of the present generation: 100, 100.

Commentators recognise *Eden* as a major painting in Helen Frankenthaler's practice in the 1950s but are unable to specify its significance. The events condensed in the painting remain mysterious in John Elderfield's description of it as a 'synoptic "interior" landscape of the artist's imagination'. They are altogether inaccessible when Carl Beltz relegates them to a pre-symbolic, and thus a-temporal realm that he associates with the position of the feminine in culture.[50] Panofsky, Poussin, Pollock and Frankenthaler in Arcadia is a conceit woven around the coincidence on the cultural scene in New York in the middle of the 1950s of two public events that touch upon one another in a remarkable way: the publication of Panofsky's '*Et in Arcadia ego:* Poussin and the Elegiac Tradition' in *Meaning in the Visual Arts,* and the death of 'the greatest living painter in the United States'.[51] Not entirely fanciful, this poietic Arcadian encounter offers a glimpse of an aspect of *Eden* to which the art historical and critical literature had been blind in its occlusive repetition of the disciplinary structures and discourses of phallocentric culture: *Eden* is a profound instance in American avant-garde painting at the beginning of the second half of the 1950s of the inscription of a specifically 'feminine filial' engagement with the 'anxiety of influence'.[52]

Coda

The short report of the car crash on the Montaulk Highway in which Jackson Pollock was killed appeared on the front page of the *New York Times* for Sunday, 12 August 1956. Columns devoted to diplomatic attempts to secure peace in the Middle East surrounded it. Official notice of the painter's death was posted in the *New York Times* on 15 August, in a week when the paper was full of news of the planned conference on the Suez crisis to be held in London between 16 and 26 August. Interest focused on British Prime Minister Anthony Eden's position on the situation: 'Labourites break with Eden on use of force in Egypt', 'Eden to continue stress on Crisis'. In the context of events in the summer of 1956, association with the urgent temporality of 'news of the world at large' inflects the prelapsarian title of Frankenthaler's key painting of that year.

POST FACTUM

Not quite death – a different life?

…the thing is, I suppose I'm disappointed. After all this to have it end with fathers and death is not what I expected. And what about Frankenthaler painting into the 1980s in the belief that painting ended with Noland's final chevrons in the middle of the 1960s?

Painting was not at the cutting edge of visual art practice even as *Mountains and Sea* momentarily glimmered into view in Greenberg's prose between the lines of 'Louis and Noland' in 1960.[1] Allan Kaprow was already taking 'The Legacy of Jackson Pollock' elsewhere: out of painting and towards *Assemblages, Environments and Happenings*.[2] Prospective fathers themselves were decamping, or else, like Rauschenberg, Johns, Warhol, camping up the authority of the position itself. I think, however, that we can trace Frankenthaler's particular relation to artistic practices of living and dying, that is to say to the prevailing critical discourse of beginnings and endings, back further: even before *Eden*.

After Mountains and Sea: *Frankenthaler 1956-1959* was the title of an exhibition curated by Julia Brown for the Guggenheim Museum in New York in 1988. The cover of the catalogue for the exhibition is a colour reproduction of a detail from *Mother Goose Melody* (fig. 19) painted in 1959.[3] According to John Elderfield, who takes the painting as the starting point for his study of Frankenthaler's work, its *mise-en-scène* is the nursery. All the elements of the picture 'combine to tell of a benign and idyllic, if fragile, domain of innocence and pleasure'.[4] The detail from *Mother Goose Melody* chosen as the cover for the catalogue for *After* Mountains and Sea: *Frankenthaler 1956-1959*, uncannily figures the fragility of the world of childhood and recalls another scene (pl. 15).

In Virginia Woolf's novel *To the Lighthouse* the skull of a dead pig nailed to the nursery wall by her brother James so terrifies Cam that she cannot sleep in the room at night until Mrs Ramsay covers the object with her old green shawl. The gradual unravelling of the folds of the shawl to reveal the skull beneath once more is the image that represents the passage of time and the process of decay in the empty house in *Time Passes*, the central section of the novel following the sudden death of Mrs Ramsay. The change in the meaning of *Et in Arcadia Ego* that Panofsky

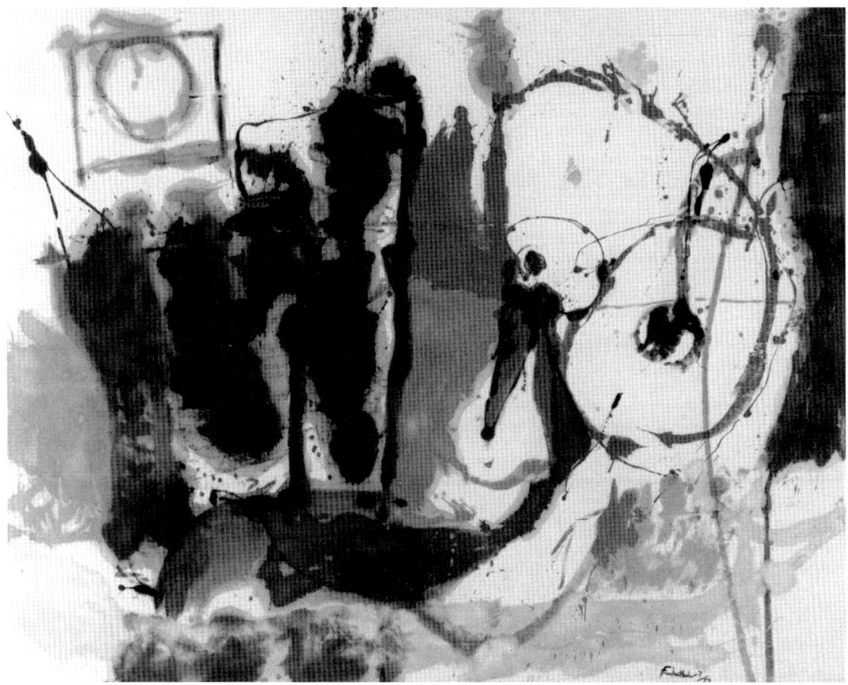

Fig. 19
Helen Frankenthaler, *Mother Goose Melody*, 1959, oil on canvas, 82 x 104 in (208.3 x 264.1 cm)
Virginia Museum of Fine Arts, Richmond. © 2007 Helen Frankenthaler

attributed to Poussin's second version of the Arcadian Shepherds theme can be read in the structure of *To the Lighthouse*, the novel in which Woolf began to come to terms with the death of her mother. The devastatingly abrupt narration of Mrs Ramsay's death in the novel is a representation of *Et in Arcadia ego* as 'death is even in Arcadia'. Lily Briscoe's return to the summer place ten years later to meditate upon Mrs Ramsay's death through the activity of painting marks a shift in the meaning of the novel to the elegiac form of *Et in Arcadia Ego* as 'I too was born, or lived, in Arcadia'.[5]

The small skull-like form embedded in *Mother Goose Melody* reproduced large as a detail on the cover of the catalogue for *After* Mountains and Sea: *Frankenthaler 1956-1959* eerily figures the perplexing absence at the centre of an exhibition in which the inclusion of *Mountains and Sea* itself, painted in 1952, is in the capacity of an ending. *After* Mountains and Sea: *Frankenthaler 1956-1959*. So what happened to Frankenthaler 1953-1955? John Elderfield has this to say about the artist's work in those years:

> The discovery of the stain method was a revelation. But consistency of technique could be an unbearable constraint. For these and other reasons

> Frankenthaler's mid-1950s pictures, though not her best works, do not separate themselves from her *oeuvre* as, say, Morris Louis's comparable works of this period do from his; neither did she have to repudiate them, as he did, in order to advance.[6]

Indeed if the 1953 encounter with *Mountains and Sea* marked the beginning of Morris Louis's drive towards 'pure opticality', for the maker of the painting herself it had no such effect. After *Mountains and Sea,* a brilliantly economical formal resolution of the problem of integrating tradition and innovation, Frankenthaler returned to the wider possibilities offered by the resources of painting. The stained ground of *Façade* (1954) for example, is almost entirely covered with passages of heavy impasto.

John Elderfield's characterisation of Frankenthaler's practice immediately after *Mountains and Sea* re-articulates the view expressed by the painter herself in print in 1965 in the Geldzhaler interview:

> Often what I seem to fight is the idea that I'm on to something and going to drive it into the ground. I tend to side-develop, not to hang on, but in seeming to side-develop that's the way I really show my mark and continuity.[7]

I have argued, through Kristeva's theorisation of the 'revolutionary' function of colour in painting as a) a representational system and b) a subjectivising practice, that by extracting what they recognised as the revolutionary dimension of colour in *Mountains and Sea,* Morris Louis and Kenneth Noland led painting to its eventual end. It ended because, in Kristevan terms, the potential of colour to revolutionise painting as a system of representation lies precisely in its *relation* to the prevailing norms of that system. In the work Frankenthaler identifies as the site of painting's end, Noland's final chevrons, colour comes to *be* the norm of the system. Following the logic of Kristeva's theorisation of the concurrent function of colour in painting as a practice linked to psychic subjectivising processes, this inevitably involves the death of the *subject of painting*: namely the painter. We might read Warhol's *Disasters* as the kitsch death of the subject of painting as avant-garde father, suffocated between the two inert surfaces of the ready-made found photograph, mechanically reproduced on canvas with commercial silk-screen techniques, and the non-porous plastic film of acrylic colour screed across it. At the site of Helen Frankenthaler's practice, however, painting and the painting subject *never quite* died.

In an essay on Bracha Lichtenberg Ettinger's work in painting, Christine Buci-Glucksmann puzzles about the function of the colour violet. Unlike Warhol's lavender it does not seal off what is underneath, which in the case of Lichtenberg Ettinger's work is not underneath at all but beside: violet *beside* a disaster, touching upon it in careful approaches with a fine brush, working at once to draw it in and paint it out (pl. 16). The disaster *was* a photograph, a found image of a group of women and children, part of the archive of the Holocaust. But it is at once beyond, and has not yet achieved, the integrity of Warhol's photo-silk-screen reproductions. Brian Massumi provides a precise description of Lichtenberg Ettinger's technical process:

> You can stop the photocopy machine mid-run. Just open the door. Time it right and you can catch the toner before it has set. It still has the graininess of its pre-packaged powder form, but the warmth of the machine has already given it a certain stickiness, in anticipation of the heat-binding of the copying's next phase. As you remove the paper from the machine, the image smudges slightly. It lightly blurs. Detail is lost. The image has degenerated. But it hasn't disappeared. You might say instead that it has been caught appearing, bearing degeneracy as a birthmark.[8]

Bracha Lichtenberg Ettinger entitled her notes on painting *Matrix Halal(a) – Lapsus*. Christine Buci-Glucksmann notes the recurrence of 'Halala' in the artist's writing and proposes a relationship between the (a) of Halal(a) and the violet of Lichtenberg Ettinger's *Austistwork*. She writes:

> Perhaps this strange violet is but the trace and transposition of an invisible signifier which recurs in the writings of Bracha Lichtenberg Ettinger: 'Halala'. [6] While as a masculine substantive 'halal' is common and used to signify both dead and space (one could say, the space of the dead), the feminine 'halala', absent in modern Hebrew, on the other hand, is gifted with a particularly strong significance: it points back to the acts of desacralization and profanation in ancient Hebrew. The painting in its violet, in its 'halala', would be this act of profaning ('hiloul') a space of the dead ('halal'), indeed it would be the conquest of an impurity as ambiguous as the colour violet. The magic pad of *Austistwork* could then be interpreted in the following manner: it brings into contact a *photo-halal* – shadow-space, death-space – and a *painting-halala*, a power of life as troubling as the aggressive metaphysical violet it makes from a kind of transparent lighting, the *inner space of painting* with its modulations and resonances.[9]

Such critical responses to the material processes and resources of Bracha Lichtenberg Ettinger's work in the 1990s catch its matrixial potential to restage painting in history, to engage again with a tradition of history painting, with a political moment and with death, but in a practice hospitable to metramorphic, trans-subjectivising movements towards life and the future – the libidinal energy of feminine 'corpo-*Real*ity'.[10] In contact with Bracha Lichtenberg-Ettinger's practice today, what counted as painting for Helen Frankenthaler 'after' *Mountains and Sea* and through the 1950s, makes sense. That is to say, with a matrixial awareness we can recognise it as a process of 'halal(a)', of profaning the space of the dead.[11]

At the point in our conversation in 1998 when Frankenthaler wearily admitted that she thought the end of painting was with Noland's final chevrons, I replied that when I had looked at *Mountains and Sea* and *Eden* and other works in the exhibition at the Guggenheim Museum, there seemed many possibilities yet to be explored in painting. Frankenthaler's answer was an interesting one; she said: 'Yes, what I'm really about is drawing.' At once she was animated indicating on the tablecloth with the pencil from her diary how she wanted to interlock line and colour in new work. What was revealed at that moment in 1998 was the persistence of a concern recorded in the Frankenthaler literature as long ago as 1967. Describing her earliest engagements with picture making, Frankenthaler explained to Gene Baro: 'My conscious interest was more in drawing and the *drawing of colour* than in colour alone.'[12]

Eden is the exemplary instance of the 'drawing of colour' in Frankenthaler's work in the 1950s. Colour in *Eden* does not cluster around drawn 'guide-posts', Cézanne-like, as in *Mountains and Sea,* and there are far fewer areas where it spreads into broad patches. Neither is it drawing *as* painting like Pollock's thrown skeins of pigment. Instead colour in *Eden* engages with Pollock's painting as *drawing* in the black and white works of 1951. It is an expansion of the halo of seeping oil around the black lines of pigment soaked into unprimed canvas. It works into and opens out their edges, where, as John Elderfield noted when he claimed the process for *Mountains and Sea*, they were 'softened by the capillary action of the contiguous area of untreated canvas'.[13] Take as an example the yellow line in *Eden* that opens out at its top end into the spiky form in the top left of the picture that commentators have referred to as the 'sun'.

Clement Greenberg regarded Pollock's 1951 show of black and white works at Betty Parsons as less than cutting edge, a sign of waning ambition. While his review of the exhibition for *Partisan Review* includes his assessment of Pollock as 'the best painter of a whole generation', there are passages in the article that inflect the statement with the sentiment of an epitaph.[14] For example, he sees hints of 'innumerable un-played cards in the artist's hand', yet judges the composition of the new work to be 'modulated in a more traditional way, no longer stating itself in one forthright piece'.[15] I have argued that *Eden* is a painting linked in fundamental psychological ways to the actual death of Jackson Pollock. In *Eden* as a formal engagement with Pollock's 1951 work, to which, as we have seen, Frankenthaler was attracted for the possibilities it held for her own artistic development, she touched upon the monochrome space of Pollock's *creative* death, a dead-space of painting, quickening it, *drawing* it into another kind of life with *colour. Eden* is not elegiac, it is too forward-looking, but neither is it a categorical formal advance. Compare *Eden,* with *Salient,* (see pl. 9) one of the earliest of Louis's *Veil* paintings, made two years before Frankenthaler's painting (and two years after *Mountains and Sea*). In *Salient* the element of 'drawing' in Frankenthaler's sense, 'the drawing of colour', is little more than a residual effect of tonal modulation where the pour of one colour overlaps and glazes the edge of another. I have argued that *Eden* is *not enough* an unconscious sign of a triumphant break with an artistic father to be recognised in the critical literature as the inscription of a process of subjectivisation intimately connected with the death of Jackson Pollock. Not enough, rather than not at all, because nobody disputes the ambition and the sheer *joie de vivre* of the painting, but *Eden* manifestly is not equivalent to the painted cross erected on the artist's grave that symbolises Friedel Dzubas's Oedipal struggle with Pollock in the psychic logic of the phallus.[16] We cannot deny that the emergence of human subjectivity entails loss, killing acts and the work of mourning; the matrix does not *replace* the phallus as a subjectivising structure, each moderates the other, and the same object or event can be 'phallic at one moment and matrixial in the next'.[17] Losses are not denied in the sub-symbolic network of the matrix:

> within a matrixial network, what is lost to the one can be inscribed as traces in the other, and metramorphosis can allow the passage of these traces from *non-I* to *I* in the enlarged stratum of subjectivization. As both parts of the same stratum, traces belonging to *I* as well as to *non-I* can be redistributed anew after their initial distribution, the borderlines between what one has and what one has lost, becoming therefore, thresholds.[18]

In *Eden* relations-without-relating with what is lost, and also with what is to be gained from Pollock, are inscribed as the continuity of a practice in which the innovations and regressions of both partners are neither appropriated nor rejected. *Eden* is the inscription of a 'feminine-matrixial filiation' – a potential for both sexes – oriented towards future metramorphoses, which is also to say towards a matrixial future for painting.[19] Ambiguity, that quality so valued by Frankenthaler she publicly celebrated it in the title of a painting, might also be understood matrixially as an acute, 'non-conscious' awareness of the exemplary material potential of painting as a metramorphic space of borderlines becoming thresholds, hospitable to inscriptions of a psychic stratum of co-emergence in difference.[20]

In the mid 1950s when, as John Elderfield observed, Morris Louis's 'advance' beyond the formal innovations of Jackson Pollock involved a radical separation from previous work, it included the repudiation of titles freighted with associations of historical events, like *Charred Journal: Firewritten,* that touched upon the painter's subjectivity as a Jew. As they disappeared from Louis's pictures, titles with openly Jewish associations began to appear in Frankenthaler's oeuvre starting with *Holocaust* in 1955, breaching the boundary the artist herself wished it to be known she maintained between the 'passionate concerns' of the world at large and the equally 'passionate concerns of art', then focused on the project of painting's formal self-sufficiency.[21] From a matrixial angle the connection, impossible to name in the culture and political environment of New York in 1955, between the painting and its name, *Holocaust*, emerges in the 1990s in the work of Bracha Lichtenberg Ettinger as it re-engages with the structural possibilities of modernist painting, colour, mark, touch, together with the drawing-like limits of reprographic technology now to desecrate the dead/killing over-exposure of images of a photographic archive of subjects of the Holocaust.[22]

Art historically, Helen Frankenthaler's practice never has had much of a life after *Mountains and Sea*. While her work has been critically acclaimed, solo exhibitions have taken place primarily within the USA.[23] There is only one painting by Frankenthaler in a public collection in the United Kingdom. The Ulster Museum in Belfast, Northern Ireland owns *Sands* (1964), and there has been only one major exhibition of her work in England in London at the Whitechapel Gallery in 1969.[24] When I approached Julia Brown and her assistant Susan Cross about the possibility of bringing their exhibition After *Mountains and Sea:* Frankenthaler 1956-1959 to London, they wrote to say that the Guggenheim Museum had contacted several institutions there and, 'none were able to be part of the show's tour'.[25] When I asked Helen Frankenthaler why she thought there was so little interest in her work among curators in England she replied: 'Well there's not really that much interest in it here…even Hilton [Kramer] thinks painting has to look worked – worked over. A lightness, an openness, a few marks…(she waved away the idea with a movement of her hand) – it's the result of just as much work. It takes years.'

In Frankenthaler's statement I hear an echo of Virginia Woolf's fears about the perception of her experiments with writing displaced in the characterisation of Lily Briscoe's anxiety about her painting in *To the Lighthouse*. Would her narrative and rhetorical experiments with the novel to make sense of an awareness of the 'reality' of character in fiction as 'moments of being' – a matrixial awareness – read as etherealised, 'pale' and 'semi transparent', when actually, she worked so hard to achieve 'a thing you could ruffle with your breath; and a thing you could not dislodge with a team of horses'?[26]

'Well, we must wait for the future to show…'[27]

If this writing were a painting, it ought to resemble a 1950s canvas by Frankenthaler. It is the trace of a process that profanes the dead-space of art history-*halal* offering *Mountains and Sea* and *Eden* another discursive life. Art history as painting: or maybe just history, a history *in the feminine*, an instance of the emergence of events that can be known *through or via painting* in spatio-temporal encounters unthinkable, intolerable, elsewhere.

NOTES

Preface

1 The reference is to Frankenthaler's account of responding to 'the understated image that was really present' in the work of Jackson Pollock, quoted by Henry Geldzahler, 'An Interview with Helen Frankenthaler', *Artforum*, vol. 4, no. 2, (October 1965), p.37.

2 When asked by Hilton Kramer about the relationship between art and politics as she lived it in the 1950s, Frankenthaler replied, 'Politics per se, the news of the world at large, were often a passionate concern. But these considerations were apart from the passionate concerns of art.' Hilton Kramer, 'An Interview with Helen Frankenthaler', *Partisan Review*, vol. 61, no. 2, (1994), p.241.

3 Frank O'Hara, *Art News,* 53, no. 8, (Dec. 1954), p.53.

Mountains and Sea: Cézannes Country

1 Helen Frankenthaler, quoted in Barbara Rose, *Frankenthaler*, (New York: Abrams, 1972), p. 29.

2 Erle Loran Johnson, 'Cézanne's Country', *The Arts,* vol. 16, (April 1930), pp. 521-551.

3 Erle Loran, *Cézanne's Composition: Analysis of his Form with Diagrams and Photographs of his Motifs*, (Berkeley and Los Angeles: University of California Press, 1947), p.1. The book was published under the name of Erle Loran. Johnson was dropped.

4 Ibid., p. 5.

5 John Rewald, 'The Last Motifs at Aix', in *Cézanne: The Late Work*, (London: Thames and Hudson, 1978), p.105.

6 Ibid., p. 85.

7 On the day it was purchased the American committee of Cézanne admirers turned the studio over to the authorities in Aix to preserve it for all time as a museum. See Rewald, p. 106.

8 Karen Wilkin, 'Frankenthaler at the Guggenheim', in *New Criterion,* vol.16, no. 7, (March 1998), p. 44.

9 Barbara Rose, op.cit., and John Elderfield, *Frankenthaler,* (New York: Abrams, 1989).

10 Henry Geldzahler, 'An Interview with Helen Frankenthaler', *Artforum*, vol. 4, no. 2, (October 1965), p. 37.

11 Ibid.

12 John Elderfield, *Frankenthaler*, (New York: Abrams,1989), p. 37.

13 Gene Baro, 'The Achievement of Helen Frankenthaler', *Art International*, vol. 2, no. 7, (Sept. 1967), pp. 32-38. The example I am thinking of here is in Chapter 4 of Irving Sandler's *The New York School: The Painters and Sculptors of the Fifties*, (New York: Harper and Row, 1978) p. 63.

14 John Elderfield, op.cit., pp. 78-79.

15 This term is Fred Orton's. In his introduction to *Figuring Jasper Johns* Orton makes a distinction between the 'subject-matter' and 'surface-matter' of Johns' paintings. *Figuring Jasper Johns*, (London: Reaktion Books, 1994), p. 8.

16 Helen Frankenthaler quoted in Henry Geldzahler, op.cit., p. 36.

17 Barbaralee Diamonstein, 'Larry Rivers', in *Inside New York's Art World*, (New York: Rizzoli, 1979), p. 320. Thanks to Fred Orton for bringing this interview to my attention.

18 Greenberg's assessment of Pollock in 'Feeling Is All', *Partisan Review*, vol. 19, no. 1, (Jan-Feb 1952), reprinted in Clement Greenberg: *The Collected Essays and Criticism*, vol. 3, ed. by John O' Brian, (Chicago and London: The University of Chicago Press, 1993), pp. 99-106.

19 James Fitzsimmons, 'A Cézanne Exhibition, A Definition of Greatness', *Art Digest*, no. 26, (Feb, 1952), p. 7.

20 Erle Loran, 'Cézanne in 1952', *Chicago Institute Quarterly*, no. 46, (Feb. 1952), pp. 1-14.

21 Theodore Rousseau Jr. 'Cézanne as an old master', *Art News*, no. 51, (April, 1952), p. 28.

22 R.M. Coates, 'Exhibition at the Metropolitan Museum', *New Yorker*, vol. 28, no. 86, (April 12 1952), and, 'Cézanne in a loan exhibition in Chicago and New York', *Connoisseur*, (Am. ed.), vol. 30, no. 80, (Sept. 1952).

23 Clement Greenberg, 'Cézanne Gateway to Contemporary Painting', *American Mercury*, June 1952, reprinted in John O'Brian, op.cit., pp. 113-118, p. 118.

24 Mary Emma Harris, *The Arts at Black Mountain College*, (Cambridge Mass. and London: MIT Press, 1987), p. 93.

25 John Elderfield, op.cit., p. 31.

26 Barbara Rose, op.cit., p. 260.

27 Clement Greenberg, 'The Role of Nature in Modern Painting', *Partisan Review*, vol. XVI 16, no. 1, (Jan 1949), p. 78.

28 Ibid., p. 79.

29 Ibid., p. 80.

30 Clement Greenberg, 'Cézanne and the Unity of Modern Art', *Partisan Review*, vol. XVIII 18, no. 3, (May/June 1951), p. 324.

31 Ibid., p. 323.

32 Ibid., pp. 323-324.

33 Ibid., p. 326.

34 Ibid., p. 329.

35 Clement Greenberg, 'Cézanne Gateway to Contemporary Painting', p. 117.

36 Ibid., p. 118.

37 *Cézanne Paintings, Watercolors & Drawings: A Loan Exhibition*, (Chicago: The Art Institute of Chicago, New York: The Metropolitan Museum of Art, 1952) exhibition catalogue. There were none of Cézanne's prints in the exhibition.

38 I am aware that in the opinion of Theodore Reff, Cézanne's late style emerged clearly only after 1895. See Theodore Reff, 'Painting and Theory in the Final Decade' in, *Cézanne The Late Work*, (London: Thames and Hudson, 1978).

39 Karen Wilkin, 'Frankenthaler at the Guggenheim', op.cit., pp. 46-47.

40 Information provided by John Elderfield and Karen Wilkin in conversation with the author, New York, April 1998.

41 James Fitzsimmons, 'A Cézanne Exhibition, A Definition of Greatness', *Art Digest*, no. 26, (Feb, 1952), p. 8.

42 Quoted in John Elderfield, op.cit., p. 66.

43 Ibid., p. 66.

44 Ibid., pp. 68-69. The passage is accompanied by two small black and white reproductions of a watercolour by Marin and a late *Mont Sainte-Victoire* study in oil by Cézanne. Neither image visually supports particularly well Elderfield's argument about watercolour, uncovered areas of white canvas in oil painting, or his subsequent interesting analysis of Frankenthaler's utilisation of Cézanne's unpainted areas of support in *Mountains and Sea.*

45 *La Montagne Sainte-Victoire vue des Lauves en hiver* (1901-1906), no. 584 in John Rewald, *Paul Cézanne The Watercolours: A Catalogue raisonné*, (London: Thames and Hudson, 1983).

46 Gene Baro, 'The achievement of Helen Frankenthaler', *Art International*, vol. 2, no. 7, (Sept. 1967), p. 36.

47 John Elderfield, op.cit., p. 67.

48 Griselda Pollock, 'Killing Men and Dying Women: A Woman's Touch in the Cold Zone of American Painting in the 1950s', in F. Orton and G. Pollock, *Avant-Gardes and Partisans Reviewed*, (Manchester: Manchester University Press, 1996), p. 223.

49 Clement Greenberg, 'Louis and Noland', *Art International*, vol. IV, no. 5, (May 25, 1960), pp. 26-29.

50 Louis and Noland interviewed in James McC. Truitt, 'Art-Arid D.C. Harbours Touted 'New' Painters', *The Washington Post* , Thursday December 21, 1961, p. 20.

51 Clement Greenberg, 'Louis and Noland', *Art International*, vol. IV, no. 5, (May 25, 1960), p. 28.

52 Anne Wagner, 'Pollock's Nature, Frankenthaler's Culture', in *Jackson Pollock: New Approaches*, ed. by Kirk Varnedoe & Pepe Karmel, New York: Museum of Modern Art, 1999, p. 187.

53 John Elderfield, op.cit., p. 66.

54 Helen Frankenthaler in conversation with the author, New York, April 10, 1998.

55 *The Columbia University Bulletin of Information*, 1948-49: Fine Arts 175, Modern Painting from 1848-1900. 'Lectures on painting, with some reference to sculpture and

architecture in Europe and America in the second half of the nineteenth century'.

56 Helen Frankenthaler was not present on April 4, 1953 when Greenberg took Louis and Noland to her studio to see the painting. Information provided by Karen Wilkin in a conversation with the author, New York, April 13, 1998.

57 According to Helen Frankenthaler Clement Greenberg maintained that their private relationship prevented his writing about her work: he regarded it as a conflict of interests. She went on to express the view, however, that fundamentally Greenberg did not believe that women counted as painters. Conversation with the author, New York, April 10, 1998.

58 Helen Frankenthaler in Henry Geldzahler, 'An Interview with Helen Frankenthaler', *Artforum*, vol. 4, no. 2, (October 1965), p. 37.

1927: Other Countries, Other Cézannes

1 Virginia Woolf, *To the Lighthouse*, [1927], 18th edition, (London: Grafton Books, 1977), p. 165.

2 Virginia Woolf, 'A Sketch of the Past' [1939] reprinted in *Moments of Being*, ed. by Jeanne Schulkind, (London: Grafton Books, 1989), pp. 83-84.

3 Ibid., pp. 94-95.

4 Ibid., p. 72. 'As it happens that I am sick of writing Roger's life, perhaps I will spend two or three mornings making a sketch.'

5 Woolf's reference to the 'litter' of *Athenaeum* articles in the extract from 'A Sketch of the Past' leads back to the beginning of Roger Fry's career in art criticism in 1901 when he was appointed chief art critic of the *Athenaeum*.

6 Virginia Woolf, *Roger Fry A Biography*, [1940], 3rd edition (London: The Hogarth Press, 1969), p. 153.

7 Virginia Woolf, 'Character in Fiction', first published as an essay in the *Criterion*, July 1924, substantially derived from a paper read to the Cambridge Heretics on 18 May 1924, reprinted in *The Essays of Virginia Woolf*, vol.3, ed. by Andrew McNeillie, (London: The Hogarth Press, 1988) p. 141.

8 Arnold Bennett, 'Is the Novel Decaying?', *Cassell's Weekly*, (March 28, 1923).

9 Virginia Woolf, 'Character in Fiction', p. 432.

10 Roger Fry, reprinted as 'The French Post-Impressionists' in *Vision and Design*, (London: Chatto and Windus, 1920), Phoenix Library edition, (1928) p. 237.

11 Ibid., p. 238-239.

12 Hermione Lee, *Virginia Woolf*, (London: Chatto and Windus, 1996), p. 239.

13 From the evidence of a letter from Virginia Woolf to Violet Dickenson dated 27th November 1910, the encounter with the paintings themselves in the exhibition was not a particularly significant one for Woolf: 'I hear a great deal about pictures. I don't think them so good as books. But why all the Duchesses are insulted by the post-impressionists, a modest sample set of painters, innocent even of indecency, I can't conceive. However, one mustn't say they are like other pictures, only better, because that makes everyone angry.' *The Letters of Virginia Woolf*, ed. by Nigel Nicolson and Joanne Trautmann, vol. 1, p. 440. Fry's response to Post-Impressionist painting, communicated and tested in

private conversations with the painters in Woolf's circle, Duncan Grant, and sister Vanessa Bell appeared in the public sphere in the three pieces, 'The French Post-Impressionists' (1912), 'Art and Life' (1917), and 'Retrospect' (1920), collected with other of Fry's essays as the book *Vision and Design*, published in 1920, four years before Woolf delivered her lecture.

14 Virginia Woolf, 'A Sketch of the Past', p. 94. In June 1939, just a month after Woolf recorded Gertler's remark in the manuscript of 'A Sketch of the Past', the painter took his own life.

15 *The Diary of Virginia Woolf*, vol. 1, ed. by Anne Olivier Bell, (London: The Hogarth Press, 1977), pp. 140-141.

16 The observation was made by Quentin Bell in *Virginia Woolf: A Biography*, vol. 2, (London: The Hogarth Press, 1973), p. 104.

17 Rebecca Stott, '"Inevitable relations": aesthetic revelations from Cézanne to Woolf', in *The Politics of Pleasure: Aesthetic and Cultural Theory*, ed. by Stephen Reagan, (Buckingham and Philadelphia: Oxford University Press, 1992), p. 97. Stott mistakenly refers to the Cambridge lecture as 'Mr Bennett and Mrs Brown', the much shorter essay out of which 'Character in Fiction' grew. That essay was published in the 'Literary Review' of the *New York Evening Post*, 17th November 1923, the year before Woolf delivered her lecture. The reference to December 1910 does not appear in 'Mr Bennet and Mrs Brown'.

18 Roger Fry, 'Art and Life', in *Vision and Design*, (London: Chatto and Windus, 1920), Phoenix Library edition, (1928), p. 11.

19 Virginia Woolf, *To the Lighthouse*, p. 48.

20 Ibid., p. 22.

21 Virginia Woolf, *To the Lighthouse*, p. 52.

22 Ibid., p. 191.

23 Ibid., p. 23.

24 Ibid.

25 Virginia Woolf, 'A Sketch of the Past', p. 90.

26 For details of the books typeset by Leonard and Virginia Woolf see J. Howard Woolmer, *A Checklist of the Hogarth Press 1917-1938*, (London: The Hogarth Press, 1976).

27 As quoted in Elizabeth Able, *Virginia Woolf and the Fictions of Psychoanalysis*, (Chicago and London: University of Chicago Press, 1989), p. 17.

28 Ibid., p. 10, from Freud 'Lecture 23, 'Introductory Lectures on Psycho-Analysis', [1916-17], in *The Standard Edition of the Complete Psychological Works of Sigmund Freud*, vol. 16, ed. by James Strachey, (London: the Hogarth Press and the Institute of Psycho-Analysis, 1963, 5th edition 1973), pp. 375-376.

29 Roger Fry, *The Artist and Psycho-Analysis*, (London: The Hogarth Press, 1924), p. 4.

30 The term is Griselda Pollock's. See Griselda Pollock, *Differencing the Canon: Feminist Desire and the Writing of Art's Histories*, (London: Routledge, 1999), pp. 13-19.

31 Roger Fry, *The Artist and Psychoanalysis*, pp. 14-15. A young man who paints pictures presents himself to Pfister for treatment, the psychoanalyst first describes and then comments upon a painting called *The Bridge of Death*. Fry quotes Pfister and then provides his own commentary:

'A youth is about to leap away from a female corpse on to a bridge lost in a sea of fog, in the midst of which Death is standing. Behind him the sun rises in blood-red splendour. On the right margin two pairs of hands are trying to recall or hold back the hurrying youth!'

As a result of prolonged investigation of such works Dr Pfister arrives at the conclusion that:

'Artistic or poetic inspiration is to be regarded as the manifestation of repressed desires and, as such, formed in accordance with the laws by which Freud grouped the processes participating in the origin of neurotic symptoms, dreams, hallucinations and related phenomena, save that the whole is created, the deeper psychological significance of which, however, is not perfectly clear to the artist.'

'Everything was present,' he adds, 'poetic creation, substitution, dramatization. The most extensive use was made of symbolism.'

32 Ibid., p. 16.

33 Ibid.

34 Ibid., p. 19.

35 Ibid., pp. 19-20.

36 Lisa Tickner, 'Vanessa Bell: *Studland Beach,* Domesticity, and "Significant Form"' in *Representations,* vol. 8, no. 65, (Winter 1999), p. 63.

37 Ibid.

38 Ibid., p. 75.

39 Ibid., p. 76.

40 Ibid., p. 79.

41 Virginia Woolf, *To the Lighthouse*, p. 149.

42 Ibid., p. 159

43 Lisa Tickner, op.cit., p. 67.

44 Matisse is an obvious point of reference, but as Lisa Tickner suggests with her observations that the works are never entirely drained of 'psychological intensity', and that the 'affect' conveyed by the 1912 work is one of 'monumentality and pervasive melancholy', it is to the Symbolist works of Gauguin and Maurice Denis that *The Beach, Studland* and *Studland Beach* are more deeply indebted.Tickner's language suggests a move into the domain of what Griselda Pollock has called the 'psycho-mythic/psycho symbolic', opening up the possibility for a reading of Bell's paintings as a differently inflected representation of Gauguin's question, *Where do we come from? What are we? Where are we going?* For a discussion of these terms see Griselda Pollock, *Differencing the Canon: Feminist Desire and the Writing of Art's Histories*, pp. 8. & 13.

45 Virginia Woolf, *To the Lighthouse,* p. 147.

46 Theodore Reff, 'Painting and Theory in the Final Decade' in *Cézanne The Late Work,* ed. by William Rubin, (London: Thames and Hudson, 1978), p. 13.

47 *A Change of Perspective: the letters of Virginia Woolf,* vol. 3., ed. by Nigel Nicolson (London: The Hogarth Press 19776) p. 132.

48 Sigmund Freud, 'Beyond the Pleasure Principle' [1920], reprinted in *The Standard Edition of the Complete Psychological Works of Sigmund Freud,* ed. by James Strachey, vol. 18, (London: Hogarth Press, 1955), 7th edition 1973, p. 15.

49 Ibid.

50 Ibid., pp. 15-16.

51 Ibid., p. 16.

52 Ibid.

53 Fry, *The Artist and Psycho-Analysis,* p. 17.

54 Ibid., p. 18.

55 For an account of the development of the terms Thing-Presentation and Word-Presentation in Freud's work see, J. Laplanch and J.-B. Pontalis, *The Language of Psychoanalysis,* London: Karnac Books and The Institute of Psycho-Analysis, 1988, pp. 447-449.

56 Virginia Woolf, *To the Lighthouse,* pp. 22-23.

57 Ibid.

58 Ibid., p. 50-51.

59 Ibid., p. 51.

60 Ibid., p. 53.

61 Ibid., p. 148.

62 Geneviève Monnier, 'The Late Watercolors' in *Cézanne, The Late Work,* p. 116.

63 Virginia Woolf, *To the Lighthouse*, p. 148.

64 Ibid., p. 150.

65 Ibid., pp. 150-151.

66 Ibid., p. 159.

67 Ibid.

68 Ibid.

69 Ibid., p. 160.

70 Ibid., p. 165.

71 Letter dated May 11th, 1927, Appendix to *A Change of Perspective: letters of Virginia Woolf,* vol. 3, pp. 572-3.

A Spatial Feeling Connected with Landscapes

1 The title is taken from a statement by Frankenthaler in an interview with Donald J. Cyr cited in the article 'The Achievement of Helen Frankenthaler' by Gene Baro in *Art International,* vol. 2, no.7, (Sept. 1967) pp. 32-38: 'I think that while it is true that in a good deal of my work people find a natural or landscape feeling, there's less and less of that in it. But I also find that in most pictures I like by anyone today, I have a spatial feeling that I might connect with landscapes.'

2 John I.H. Baur, *Nature in Abstraction. The Relation of Abstract Painting and Sculpture to Nature in Twentieth-century American Art,* (New York: Whitney Museum of American Art Macmillan, 1958), exhibition catalogue, p. 6.

3 Ibid., p. 66.

4 Ibid.

5 Ibid.

6 Ibid.

7 Henry Geldzahler, op.cit., p. 36.

8 Maurice Merleau-Ponty, 'Eye and Mind', (1960 &1964), reprinted in *The Merleau-Ponty Aesthetics Reader: Philosophy and Painting*, ed. by Galen A. Johnson, (Evanston: Northwestern University Press,1993), p. 122.

9 Cathryn Vasseleu, op.cit., p. 28.

10 Maurice Merleau-Ponty, 'Eye and Mind', p. 121.

11 Maurice Merleau-Ponty, 'Eye and Mind', pp. 123-124.

12 Maurice Merleau-Ponty, 'Cézanne's Doubt' in *Sense and Non-Sense,* trans. H.L. & P.A. Dreyfus, (Evanston: Northwestern University Press, 1964), p. 17.

13 Maurice Merleau-Ponty, 'Cézanne's Doubt', p. 13.

14 Maurice Merleau-Ponty, 'Eye and Mind', p. 124.

15 Ibid.

16 Cathryn Vasseleu, op.cit., pp. 26-27.

17 Maurice Merleau-Ponty, 'Eye and Mind', p. 131.

18 Ibid., p. 138.

19 Ibid.

20 Ibid., p. 129.

21 Ibid., p. 127.

22 Ibid., p. 128.

23 Ibid.

24 Ibid., p. 141.

25 Ibid.

26 Bridget Riley in *The Experience of Painting: Eight Modern Artists*, (London: South Bank Centre, 1989), exhibition catalogue, p. 55.

27 Bridget Riley, 'The Pleasures of Sight', in *Working with Colour*, (London: Arts Council of Great Britain, 1984), exhibition catalogue, unpaginated.

28 Maurice Merleau-Ponty, 'Eye and Mind', p. 140. Nowhere is this more apparent than in the late watercolours of *Mont Sainte-Victoire* where there is little else but the revelation of lighting that supports visibility. Giacometti's remark suggests what the painted evidence of the clogged airless early works and many of the later oil studies prior to and even after the late watercolours shows. Contrary to the received wisdom that Cézanne was attempting to assimilate himself to nature his struggle was in the opposite direction, that is to extricate himself *from* it. His practice was a series of attempts to organise mark and ground in order to structure, and thus momentarily to alleviate, the exhilaration/frustration – 'sensation' – of an embodied, contingent, ambiguous lived relation to the perceptual world experienced as over-closeness.

29 Maurice Merleau-Ponty, 'Eye and Mind', p. 141.

30 Ibid., p. 127.

31 During my research in New York neither John Elderfield nor Karen Wilkin, the expert on Frankenthaler's works on paper, could confirm their whereabouts for me.

32 John Elderfield, then Curator at Large of the Museum of Modern Art, New York, told me that in the 1960s a conservator had washed *Mountains and Sea* by putting it through a large washing machine. The blur I am describing here is much more evident in *Jacob's Ladder* (1957) to the extent of hindering its visibility. *Jacob's Ladder* quite radically refuses to come into focus and it is likely that *Mountains and Sea* had more of that quality before it was cleaned.

33 Julia Brown, 'In Pursuit of Beauty: Notes on the Early Paintings of Helen Frankenthaler', in 'After *Mountains and Sea*: Frankenthaler 1956-1959', (New York: The Solomon R. Guggenheim Museum, 1998), exhibition catalogues, p. 50.

34 Maurice Merleau-Ponty, 'Eye and Mind', p. 139.

35 See 'Frankenthaler: The Small Paintings' by Andrew Forge in *Art International,* vol. 22, no.4, (April-May 1978), pp. 28-32.

36 Perry Miller Adato, *Frankenthaler: Toward a New Climate,* produced and directed by Perry Miller Adato, 1978, broadcast in the series *The Originals: Women in Art,* produced by WNET-Channel Thirteen.

37 John I. H. Baur, *Nature in Abstraction,* p. 6.

38 'The thing that interests me is that today painters do not have to go to a subject matter outside themselves. Most modern painters work from a different source. They work from within,' Jackson Pollock in an interview with William Wright taped in 1950 and broadcast on radio station WERI in Westerly, R.I. in 1951, reprinted in F.V. O'Connor and E.V. Thaw, *Jackson Pollock: A Catalogue Raisonné of Paintings, Drawings and Other Works,* (New Haven and London: Yale University Press, 1978), p. 248.

39 Laura Doyle, '"These Emotions of the Body": Intercorporeal Narrative in *To the Lighthouse*', *Twentieth Century Literature,* vol. 40, (1995), pp. 42-71.

40 Ibid., p. 43.

41 Ibid.

42 Virginia Woolf, *To the Lighthouse,* p. 61.

43 Laura Doyle, op.cit., p. 52.

44 Virginia Woolf, *To the Lighthouse,* p. 34.

45 Ibid., p. 113.

46 Laura Doyle, op.cit., p. 46.

47 Virginia Woolf, *To the Lighthouse,* p. 147.

48 Ibid., p. 168.

49 Ibid., pp. 176-177.

50 Ibid., p. 177.

51 Ibid., p. 186.

52 Laura Doyle, op.cit., p. 68.

Something New in Terms of Nature

1 Jacques Lacan, *The Ethics of Psychoanalysis 1959-1960*, ed. by Jacques-Alain Miller, trans. by Dennis Porter (London: Tavistock/Routledge, 1992), p. 89.

2 Maurice Merleau-Ponty, *The Visible and the Invisible*, trans., Alfonso Lingis, (Evanston: Northwestern University Press, 1997).

3 Luce Irigaray, 'The Invisible of the Flesh: A Reading of Merleau-Ponty, *The Visible and the Invisible*, "The Intertwining – The Chiasm"', in *An Ethics of Sexual Difference*, trans. Carolyn Burke & Gillian C. Gill, (London: Athlone Press, 1993), p. 152.

4 This particular conjunction 'maternal-feminine' is Irigaray's as it appears on p. 152 of the essay.

5 To my mind this is because both Doyle and Irigaray take *The Visible and the Invisible* not 'Eye and Mind' as their text for analysis.

6 Bracha Lichtenberg Ettinger, *The Matrixial Gaze*, (Leeds: Feminist Arts and Histories Network, 1995).

7 See Bracha Lichtenberg Ettinger, 'Trans-Subjective Transferential Borderspace', in *Canadian Review of Comparative Literature*, ed. by Brian Massumi, vol. XXIV, no.3, (September 1997), pp. 625-647.

8 Griselda Pollock, 'Preface', in *The Matrixial Gaze*, p. ii.

9 Bracha Lichtenberg Ettinger, ' Metramorphic Borderlinks and Matrixial Borderspace', in *Rethinking Borders*, ed. by John Welchman, (London and New York: Macmillan, 1996), p. 128.

10 See Bracha Lichtenberg Ettinger, 'Woman-Other-Thing: A matrixial* touch' in *Matrix Borderlines*, (Oxford: Museum of Modern Art, 1993), exhibition catalogue, p. 12.

11 Lichtenberg Ettinger refers to matrixial processes as '*sub*-symbolic' in *The Matrixial Gaze*, p. 23.

12 See Chapter 1.

13 Freud in 'Beyond the Pleasure Principle', see Chapter 2

14 Jacques Lacan, *The Ethics of Psychoanalysis*, p. 93.

15 Ibid., p. 93.

16 Sigmund Freud, 'Three Essays on the Theory of Sexuality', [1905], in *The Standard Edition of the Complete Psychological Works of Sigmund Freud*, vol. 17, ed. by James Strachey, (London: The Hogarth Press and the Institute of Psychoanalysis, 1953), 7th edition 1973, pp. 135-243.

17 Sigmund Freud, 'Papers on Metapsychology: Instincts and their Vicissitudes', [1915], in *The Standard Edition of the Psychological Works of Sigmund Freud*, vol. 14, ed. by James Strachey, (London: The Hogarth Press and the Institute of Psychoanalysis,1957), 6th edition 1973, p. 123.

18 Sigmund Freud, 'Three Essays on the Theory of Sexuality', p. 168.

19 Ibid., pp. 203-204.

20 As cited by Laplanche and Pontalis in *The Language of Psychoanalysis*, p. 334.

21 Jacques Lacan, *The Four Fundamental Concepts of Psychoanalysis*, ed. by Jacques-Alain Miller, trans. by Alan Sheridan, (London: Penguin Books, 1994), p. 71.

22 Ibid., p. 73.

23 Ibid., p. 75.

24 Ibid., p. 94.

25 Ibid., p. 89.

26 I borrow the term 'eye beam' from John Donne. It appears in the poem 'Ecstasy', in *John Donne, The Complete English Poems*, (London: Penguin Books, 1982), p. 53. Donne's eroticisation of sight here puts me in mind of Lacan.

27 Jacques Lacan, *The Four Fundamental Concepts of Psychoanalysis,* Penguin Books Ltd. London, 1994, p. 96. In a comparison of the French and English texts of Seminar XI in a close reading of this passage undertaken with Bracha Lichtenberg Ettinger, we discovered that there was an inaccuracy in the English translation. In English the passage reads 'and makes of the landscape something other than a landscape, something other than what I have called the picture.' In French it reads: ' and makes of the landscape something other than landscape, something other than what I have called perspective.' At the end of the paragraph preceding this one Sheridan's translation reads: 'The picture, certainly, is in my eye. But I am not in the picture.' In French this passage reads: 'The picture, certainly, is in my eye. But I am in the picture.' Bracha Lichtenberg Ettinger's correction is crucial to the sense of Lacan's argument about the light/subject relation and his subsequent discussion of ocelli. I thank her for the time she spent working on this text to clear up the nonsense of this section which had always been so puzzling to me.

28 Ibid., pp. 73-74.

29 Ibid., p. 103.

30 Ibid., p. 112.

31 Ibid., p. 59.

32 Bracha Lichtenberg Ettinger provides a useful account of the structural difference between the two types of phallic gazes implied in Lacan's description of these two functions of painting. She defines them as the pre-Oedipal 'passive' gaze, and the Post Oedipal 'active' gaze. *The Matrixial Gaze*, pp. 10-11.

33 Sigmund Freud, 'The "Uncanny"', [1919], in *The Standard Edition of the Complete Psychological Works of Sigmund Freud,* vol.17, ed. by James Strachey, (London: The Hogarth Press and the Institute of Psychoanalysis, 1955), 47th edition 196734, p. 219.

34 Ibid., p. 231.

35 Ibid., p. 224.

36 Ibid., p. 241.

37 Ibid., p. 245.

38 Ibid.

39 Bracha Lichtenberg Ettinger, 'The Matrixial Gaze', p. 8.

40 Ibid., p. 10.

41 Ibid., p. 24.

42 'Jackson Pollock Paints a Picture', *Art News,* (May 1951).

43 Andrew Forge, 'Frankenthaler: The Small Paintings', *Art International* vol. 22, no.4, (April-May 1978), pp. 28-32.

44 Ibid., p. 33.

45 Griselda Pollock, 'Killing Men and Dying Women: A Woman's Touch in the Cold Zone of American Painting in the 1950s', in Fred Orton and Griselda Pollock, *Avant-Gardes and Partisans Reviewed,* (Manchester: Manchester University Press, 1996), p. 257. The description 'metaphorics of masculinity' is T.J. Clark's from 'Jackson Pollock's Abstraction', in *Reconstructing Modernism*, ed. by Serge Guilbaut, (Cambridge Mass.: MIT Press, 1992), p. 29.

46 Griselda Pollock, 'Killing Men and Dying Women', p. 260, and footnotes 80, 82, pp. 292-293.

47 Harold Bloom, *The Anxiety of Influence,* (Oxford : Oxford University Press, 1973).

48 For actual dialogical texts see Alison Rowley and Griselda Pollock, 'Painting in a "Hybrid Moment"', in *Critical Perspectives on Contemporary Painting,* ed. by Jonathan Harris, Liverpool, Liverpool University Press and Tate Liverpool, 2003, pp. 37-73, and Griselda Pollock and Alison Rowley, *Now and Then: Feminism: Art: History, A Critical Response to Documenta 11,* Leeds, University of Leeds CentreCATH Document 2, 2006.

49 Griselda Pollock, 'Killing Men and Dying Women', p. 252.

50 *Jackson Pollock,* produced by Hans Namuth and Paul Falkenberg, music by Morton Feldman, narration by Jackson Pollock, 1951.

51 'Focused fury of creation' is the caption accompanying the stills from Namuth and Falkenberg's film printed in *Life* magazine, 9 November 1959, and reproduced in Griselda Pollock, 'Killing Men and Dying Women', p. 240.

52 The Tate Gallery hosted the Museum of Modern Art's Pollock retrospective in April 1999. The conference held on Saturday 19 April 1999, was called 'Debating Pollock'.

53 T.J. Clark, 'Pollock's Smallness', reprinted in *Jackson Pollock New Approaches*, ed. by Kirk Varnedoe and Pepe Karmel, (New York: The Museum of Modern Art, 1999), p. 22.

54 Ibid., p. 29.

55 Helen Frankenthaler in a conversation with the author, New York, 10 April 1998.

56 My own transcription from *Frankenthaler: Toward a New Climate.*

57 In his memoir of life in the New York art world John Bernard Myers describes Helen Frankenthaler as 'upper class to the nines…Helen's parents were of the old New York Jewish *haute bourgeoisie.*' John Bernard Myers, *Tracking the Marvelous,* (New York: Random House, 1983), p. 154.

58 Transcript of *Toward a New Climate.*

59 Deborah E. Lipstadt, *Beyond Belief: The American Press and The Coming of the Holocaust 1933-1945,* (New York: Free Press,1986).

60 Griselda Pollock, 'Killing Men and Dying Women', pp. 223-224.

61 Transcript of *Toward a New Climate.*

62 'Women Artists in Ascendance': *Life* 42, no.19, May 13, 1957.

63 Griselda Pollock, 'To Inscribe in the Feminine: A Kristevan Impossibility? Or Femininity, Melancholy and Sublimation', *parallax*, vol. 4, no. 3, (July-Sept. 1998), p. 98.

64 Gene Baro, 'The Achievement of Helen Frankenthaler', *Art International* vol. 2, no.7, (Sept 20, 1967), pp. 32-88.

65 See Griselda Pollock, *Avant-garde Gambits: Gender and the Colour of Art History*, (London: Thames and Hudson, 1992), and *Differencing the Canon: Feminist Desire and the Writing of Art's Histories*, (London: Routledge, 1999), p. 4.

66 Virginia Woolf, *To the Lighthouse*, p. 168.

67 Henry Geldzahler, op.cit., p. 38.

68 Transcript of *Frankenthaler: Toward a New Climate.*

69 Julia Kristeva, 'Giotto's Joy', in *Desire in Language*, ed. by Leon Roudiez, (Oxford: Blackwell, 1980), p. 216.

70 Ibid., p. 211.

71 Ibid., p. 215.

72 Ibid., p. 216.

73 Ibid., p. 233.

74 Ibid., pp. 233-234.

75 Henry Geldzahler, op.cit., p. 220.

76 Julia Kristeva, 'Giotto's Joy', p. 220.

77 Ibid., p. 218.

78 Sigmund Freud, 'Papers on Metapsychology: The Unconscious', [1915], in *The Complete Standard Edition of the Complete Psychological Works of Sigmund Freud*, vol. 14, ed. by James Strachey, (London: The Hogarth Press and the Institute of Psycho--analysis, London, 19537), 6th edition 1973, p. 201.

79 Ibid., p. 217.

80 Freud, 'The Unconscious', p. 202.

81 Julia Kristeva, 'Giotto's Joy', p. 217.

82 Ibid., p. 218.

83 Ibid., p. 219.

84 Ibid., 221.

85 Clement Greenberg, 'Louis and Noland', *Art International*, vol. IV, no 5, (May 25, 1960), pp. 26-9.

86 The term was suggested by Griselda Pollock in a seminar with Bracha Lichtenberg Ettinger, in her role as visiting Professor of Psychoanalysis and Aesthetics at the School Department oof Fine Art, History of Art and Cultural Studies, University of Leeds on July 5, 2000, when I presented the problematic of colour in *Mountains and Sea* for discussion.

87 Bryan Robertson, introduction to *Bridget Riley Paintings and Drawings 1951-71*, (London: Arts Council of Great Britain, 1971), exhinbition catalogue, p. 7.

88 Quoted in Louis Aragon, *Henri Matisse: A Novel*, trans. by Jean Stewart, vol. 2, (New York: Harcourt Brace Jovanovich, 1972), p. 308.

89 Matisse in a letter to Alexander Romm, Flam p. 68, quoted by Yve-Alain Bois in *Painting as Model*, (Cambridge Mass., London England: MIT Press, 1993), p. 22.

A Painting of the Rosenberg Era

1 President Eisenhower in a letter to his son John in Korea written on June 16th 1953, quoted in Ronald Radosh and Joyce Milton, *The Rosenberg File: A Search for the Truth,* (New York: Holt, 1983), p. 379.

2 The exhibition *Martha Rosler: Positions in the Life World* was installed at the Ikon Gallery, Birmingham from 5 December 1998 to 30th January 1999.

3 Information gleaned from *Secret Agents: The Rosenberg Case McCarthyism & Fifties America,* ed. by Marjorie Garber & Rebecca L. Walkowitz, (London and New York: Routledge, 1995).

4 T.J. Clark, 'Pollock's Smallness', reprinted in *Jackson Pollock New Approaches*, ed. by Kirk Varnedoe and Pepe Karmel, (New York: The Museum of Modern Art, 1999).

5 Rozsika Parker and Griselda Pollock, *Old Mistresses: Women, Art and Ideology,* Pandora Press, London (1981) pp. 148-9.

'Her art becomes timeless as nature, inexplicably reverting to the eighteenth century even in the midst of the important upsurge in national American art in the 1950s. Frankenthaler is contained and categorised...No one can say simply here is an artist, a woman, who is working in a particular movement and shares its premises but produces something different because she is breaking new ground and saying new things within it. Instead they find themselves only suggesting that here is an art that is inevitably, timelessly and quintessentially feminine.'

6 T.J. Clark, op.cit., p. 29.

7 I use the word 'associated' advisedly to draw attention again to the paradox that it is soak-stained colour not **in** *Mountains and Sea* itself but elsewhere, in the paintings of others, that has determined the art historical meaning, and the art historical place **of** *Mountains and Sea.*

8 Griselda Pollock, 'Nichsapha: Yearning/Languishing The Immaterial Tuché of Colour in Painting *After Painting After History*, in *Bracha Lichtenberg Ettinger, Artworking 1985-1999*, (Ghent-Amsterdam: Ludion, Palais des Beaux-Arts, Brussels, 2000), exhibition catalogue.

9 The phrase 'something beside' is chosen for its resonance with Bracha Lichtenberg Ettinger's theory of the *Matrix* and *Metramorphosis,* in which matrixial psychic subjectivising processes alternate or co-exist with the phallic. See Bracha Lichtenberg Ettinger *The Matrixial Gaze,* (Leeds: Feminist Arts and Histories Network, 1995), espec. pp. 28-29.

10 The concepts of 'trans-subjectivity' and '*co-poiesis*' are elaborated in Bracha Lichtenberg Ettinger, 'Traumatic Wit(h)ness-Thing and Matrixial Co/in-habit(u)ating'. See also my own introduction to that essay, both in *parallax*, Issue 10, January-March 1999, pp. 89-98 and 83-88 respectively. Not only is this chapter theoretically supported by material in 'Traumatic Wit(h)ness-Thing', its actual structure is indebted to the structure of *co-poiesis* outlined there.

11 See Bracha Lichtenberg Ettinger, *The Matrixial Gaze,* Leeds, Feminist Arts and Histories Network, 1995, and my explication of the matrix as a subjectivising stratum in Chapter 4 of this thesis.

12 See Chapter 4.

13 As quoted by Laplanche and Pontalis in *The Language of Psychoanalysis*, p. 112.

14 Ibid.

15 Laplance and Pontalis in *The Language of Psychoanalysis*, p. 113, quoting Freud in 'The Origins of Psychoanalysis', *Standard Edition of the Complete Psychological Works of Sigmund Freud*, vol. 1, ed. by James Strachey, (London: The Hogarth Press, 1954).

16 The phrase is Gayatri Chakravorty Spivak's from 'The Rani of Simur', where she considers Dominick La Capra's use of the transferential model in disciplinary critique. 'The Rani of Simur', *History and Theory*, vol. 24, no. 3, (1985), p. 250.

17 Griselda Pollock, 'Nichsapha: Yearning/Languishing The Immaterial Tuché of Colour in Painting *After Painting After History*', p. 50.

18 This is a reference to *Differencing the Canon: Feminist Desire and the Writing of Art's Histories*, Griselda Pollock, (London, New York: Routledge) 1999.

19 The idea of the matrix and metromorphosis as a 'non-conscious', rather than 'unconscious' dimension of subjectivisation and meaning donation is set out in Bracha Lichtenberg Ettinger, 'Metramorphic Borderlinks and Matrixial Borderspace', in *Rethinking Borders* ed. by John C. Welchman, (London and New York: Macmillan, 1996), p. 126. See also my Chapter 4, pp. 105-6.

20 Bracha Lichtenberg Ettinger, 'Woman-Other-Thing: A matrixial* touch' in *Matrix Borderlines*, (Oxford: Museum of Modern Art, 1993), p. 12.

21 Ibid.

22 Bracha Lichtenberg Ettinger, 'Woman-Other-Thing: A matrixial* touch', pp. 12-13.

23 See Chapter 4, p. 81.

24 Bracha Lichtenberg Ettinger, 'Metramorphic Borderlinks and Matrixial Borderspace', p. 134.

25 Ibid.

26 Bracha Lichtenberg Ettinger, 'Metramorphic Borderlinks and Matrixial Borderspace', p. 134. Lichtenberg Ettinger borrows the term 'autopoietic' from F. Varela's work on biological systems in *Autonomie et Connaissance* (Paris: Seuil, 1989). She quotes from pp. 63 and 45 of the book: 'The ontogenesis of a living system is the history of its identity conservation by the perpetuation of its own autopoiesis in the material space...an autopoietic system is a dynamic system...without entries or exits...The idea of autopoiesis leans on the idea of homeostasis', 'Metramorphic Borderlinks and Matrixial Borderspace', note 16, p. 157.

27 Bracha Lichtenberg Ettinger, 'Traumatic Wit(h)ness-Thing and Matrixial Co/in-habit(u)ating', in *parallax*, vol. 5, no. 1, (January-March 1999), p. 90.

28 Ibid., pp. 91-92.

29 See *Andy Warhol: Death and Disasters* (The Menrill Collection, Huston: Fine Art Press, 1988), pp. 82-83.

30 Sylvia Plath, *The Bell Jar*, first published by William Heinemann, London, 1963, 10th edn. (London and Boston: Faber and Faber, 1988), p. 1.

31 Jacques Lacan, *The Four Fundamental Concepts of Psychoanalysis*, ed. by Jacques-Alain Miller, trans. by Alan Sheridan, (London: Penguin Books, 1994), pp. 54-55.

32 Lacan elaborates the notion of the 'tychic' as the 'missed encounter' with the 'real', the 'too late' of deferred revision of the traumatic event, in his reading of Freud's example of the dream of the sleeping father and burning child in *The Interpretation of Dreams*, *The*

Four Fundamental Concepts of Psychoanalysis, pp. 68-70. See Chapter 4 for my reading of Lacan's theory of the gaze as *objet a* in the scopic field.

33 Griselda Pollock, 'Nichsapha: Yearning/Languishing The Immaterial Tuché of Colour in Painting *After Painting After History*, p. 49.

34 Mark Godfrey, 'Keeping Watch over Absent Meaning: Morris Louis's *Charred Journal* series and the Holocaust', *The Jewish Quarterly*, vol. 46, no. 3, (175) (Autumn 1999), pp. 17-22.

35 Ibid., p. 18.

36 Ibid., p. 20.

37 Ibid., p. 22.

38 Ibid.

39 Ibid., p. 18.

40 Sylvia Plath, *The Bell Jar*, p. 1.

41 *Martha Rosler: Positions in the Life World*, ed. by Catherine de Zegher (Birmingham and Vienna: Ikon Gallery and the Generali Foundation, 1998), pp. 162-163.

42 *Life*, 2nd March, 1953, p. 26.

43 John Elderfield, 'Introduction' in *Morris Louis*, (London: Arts Council of Great Britain, 1974), exhibition catalogue, p. 9.

44 Henry Geldzahler, 'An Interview with Helen Frankenthaler', p. 37.

45 Griselda Pollock, 'Nichsapha: Yearning/Languishing The Immaterial Tuché of Colour in Painting *After Painting After History*, p. 49.

46 John Elderfield, 'Introduction' in *Morris Louis*, note 5, p. 74.

47 Clement Greenberg, 'Self-Hatred and Jewish Chauvinism: Some Reflections on "Positive Jewishness"', *Commentary*, November 1950, reprinted in *Clement Greenberg, The Collected Essays and Criticism*, vol. 3, ed. by John O'Brian, (Chicago and London: The University of Chicago Press, 1993), pp. 45-58, pp. 51 & 53.

48 Louis Kaplan, 'Reframing the Self-Criticism: Clement Greenberg's "Modernist Painting" in the Light of Jewish Identity', in *Jewish Identity in Modern Art History*, ed. by Catherine M. Soussloff, (Berkeley, Los Angeles, London: University of California Press, 1999), pp. 180-199.

49 Clement Greenberg, 'Modernist painting', [1960] *Forum Lectures*, Washington, D.C: Voice of America, reprinted in *Clement Greenberg, The Collected Essays and Criticism*, vol. 3, ed. by John O'Brian, (Chicago and London: The University of Chicago Press, 1993), pp. 85-93, p. 85.

50 Ibid., p. 86.

51 Clement Greenberg, 'Self-Hatred and Jewish Chauvinism: Some Reflections on "Positive Jewishness"', pp. 54-55.

52 David Suchoff, 'The Rosenberg Case and The New York Intellectuals' in *Secret Agents: The Rosenberg Case, McCarthyism and Fifties America*, ed. by Marjorie Garber and Rebecca Walkowitz, (New York and London: Routledge, 1995), p. 155.

53 Internal memo, American Jewish Committee, quoted in David Suchoff, 'The Rosenberg Case and The New York Intellectuals', p. 59.

54 Clement Greenberg quoted in John O'Brian, *Clement Greenberg, The Collected Essays and Criticism*, Vol.1, (1986) p. xix.

55 David Suchoff, 'The Rosenberg Case and The New York Intellectuals', pp. 156-157.

56 Florence Rubenfeld, *Clement Greenberg: A Life,* (New York, Scribner, 1997), see Chapter 2, 'An Inauspicious Beginning'.

57 Anne M. Wagner, 'Pollock's Nature, Frankenthaler's Culture', in, *Jackson Pollock New Approaches*, ed. by Kirk Varnedoe and Pepe Karmel, (New York: The Museum of Modern Art, 1999), p. 181.

58 Florence Rubenfeld, *Clement Greenberg: A Life,* p. 181.

59 Clement Greenberg, 'Louis and Noland', *Art International,* vol. IV, no. 5, (May 25, 1960), pp. 28.

60 In the review Greenberg calls Pollock 'the best painter of a whole generation', however he also writes: 'Some recognizable images appear – figures, heads, and animal forms – and the composition is modulated in a more traditional way, no longer stating itself in one forthright piece'. Clement Greenberg, 'Feeling is All', p. 105.

61 Florence Rubenfeld, *Clement Greenberg: A Life,* p. 160.

62 Griselda Pollock, 'Nichsapha: Yearning/Languishing The Immaterial Tuché of Colour in Painting *After Painting After History*', p. 49.

63 Griselda Pollock, 'Nichsapha: Yearning/Languishing The Immaterial Tuché of Colour in Painting *After Painting After History*, p. 50.

64 Julia Kristeva, 'Giotto's Joy', in *Desire in Language*, ed. by Leon Roudiez, (Oxford: Blackwell, 1980), p. 215.

65 Griselda Pollock, 'Nichsapha: Yearning/Languishing The Immaterial Tuché of Colour in Painting *After Painting After History*', p. 49.

66 That is to say *matrixial,* see Chapter 4.

Eden: Et in Arcadia Ego

1 Transcription from a sequence in *Atomic Café,* produced and directed by Kevin Rafferty, Jyne Loader, and Pierce Rafferty (Los Angeles: Thorn EMI Video, 1982) quoted by Carol Hurd Green in 'The Suffering Body: Ethel Rosenberg in the Hands of the Writers', in *Secret Agents: The Rosenberg Case, McCarthyism and Fifties America,* ed. by Marjorie Garber & Rebecca L. Walkowitz, (New York & London: Routledge, 1995), p. 186.

2 For a discussion of the concept of the ideology of gender, see Teresa de Lauretis, 'The Technology of Gender', in *Technologies of Gender,* (Bloomington and Indianapolis: Indiana University Press, 1987), pp. 1-30. De Lauterits writes: 'The construction of gender is both the product and the process of its representation,' p 5.

3 Carol Hurd Green, 'The Suffering Body: Ethel Rosenberg in the Hands of the Writers', p. 186.

4 Joyce Antler, 'A Bond of Sisterhood', in *Secret Agents: The Rosenberg Case, McCarthyism and Fifties America,* ed. by Marjorie Garber & Rebecca L. Walkowitz, (New York & London: Routledge, 1995), p. 206.

5 Carol Hurd Green, 'The Suffering Body: Ethel Rosenberg in the Hands of the Writers', p. 187.

6 Griselda Pollock, 'Killing Men and Dying Women: A Woman's Touch in the Cold Zone of American Painting in the 1950s', in Fred Orton and Griselda Pollock, *Avant-Gardes and Partisans Reviewed,* (Manchester: Manchester University Press, 1996), p. 228, fig. 42. See also Pollock p. 236 where she quotes Richard Dyer: 'Blondness, especially platinum (peroxide) blondness is the ultimate sign of whiteness.' Richard Dyer, *Heavenly Bodies: Film Stars and Society* (New York: St Martin's Press, 1986), pp. 42-43.

7 *U.S. v. Rosenbergs, Sobell, Yakovlev, and Greenglass, CR 124-125.* Quote from the trial transcript, in Robert Meeropol, 'Rosenberg Realities' in *Secret Agents: The Rosenberg Case, McCarthyism and Fifties America*, p. 241.

8 Ibid., p. 207.

9 John Gruen, *The Party's Over Now: Reminiscences of the Fifties – New York's Artists, Writers, Musicians and Their Friends,* (New York: Viking Press, 1972), p. 184.

10 Herman Wouk, *Marjorie Morningstar,* 1955, 2nd edition, (London: Reprint Society, 1957), p. 12.

11 Ibid., p. 527.

12 Dust jacket of the 1957 Reprint Society edition.

13 Interestingly, Joyce Antler writes that like Margorie Morniningstar, Ethel Rosenberg planned to make a career as an actress and singer before her marriage. Joyce Antler, 'A Bond of Sisterhood', p. 203.

14 I am aware that events surrounding the Suez Crisis are complex and that their meaning is much debated by historians. I have relied for this brief sketch on Michael B. Oren's *The Origins of the Second Arab-Israeli War* (London: Frank Cass, 1992).

15 John Elderfield, *Frankenthaler* (New York: Abrams, 1989), p. 102.

16 *Frankenthaler: Works on Paper 1949-1984,* Solomon R. Guggenheim Museum, February 22-April 21, 1985.

17 Maurice Poirier, 'Working Papers', *Art News*, vol. 84, no. 6, (Summer 1985), p. 83.

18 John Elderfield, *Frankenthaler*, p. 125.

19 Hilton Kramer, 'An Interview with Helen Frankenthaler', *Partisan Review,* vol. 61, no. 2, (December 19924), p. 241.

20 See Sander Gilman, *The Jew's Body,* (New York, London: Routledge, 1991), for a historical study of representations of the female Jewish body.

21 John Elderfield, op.cit., *Frankenthaler*, p. 83.

22 See Frank O'Hara's review in 'Reviews and Previews', *Art News*, vol. 53, no. 8, (Dec. 1954), p 53, and 'Helen Frankenthaler' in *An Exhibition of Oil Paintings by Frankenthaler,* (New York: Jewish Museum, 1960), exhibition catalogue, pp. 5-7. O'Hara also wrote a poem called *Blue Territory* inspired by Frankenthaler's painting of that name (1955), published in *Locus Solus,* 5, (1962), p. 37-39. Frankenthaler herself has described some of her works on paper as 'private' pictures – 'menus, memos, salutations, birthday greetings'. Quoted in, *Frankenthaler: Works on Paper 1949-1984,* by Karen Wilkin, (New York: George Braziller, 1984), p. 26.

23 Stephen Naifeh and Gregory White Smith, *Jackson Pollock: An American Saga* (London: Barrie and Jenkins, 1989), p. 793.

24 *Eden* was part of the exhibition *After* Mountains and Sea: *Frankenthaler 1956-1959,*

curated by Julia Brown at the Solomon R. Guggenheim Museum, New York, in 1998.

25 Barbara Rose, *Frankenthaler* (New York: Abrams, 1971), pp. 86-87. *Eden* was mis-dated 1957 in all the literature until John Elderfield verified that it was made in 1956 and corrected it in his 1989 monograph. Information from my conversation with John Elderfield in New York in April 1998.

26 John Elderfield, *Frankenthaler* op.cit., p. 125.

27 Edward Carmean, JR., *Helen Frankenthaler: A Paintings Retrospective,* (New York: Abrams in association with the Modern Art Museum of Fort Worth, 1989), p. 16.

28 Barbara Rose, *Frankenthaler* op.cit., p. 36. On the subject of the 'feminisation' of Frankenthaler's work in the critical literature see Rozsika Parker and Griselda Pollock, 'Back to the twentieth century: femininity and feminism' in *Old Mistresses: Women, Art and Ideology* (London, Sydney, Wellington: Pandora, 1989) pp. 145-150.

29 Carl Beltz, 'Helen Frankenthaler's *Eden: A* "joyously involved creativity"', *Art News* 80, no. 5, (May 1981), p.157.

30 Ibid.

31 Ibid.

32 Erwin Panofsky, *Meaning in the Visual Arts: Papers in and on Art History* (New York: Doubleday Anchor Books, 1955). The book was published in a small, illustrated pocket sized edition.

33 'Et in Arcadia ego: On the Conception of Transience in Poussin and Watteau', in R. Klibansky and H.J. Paton, eds, *Philosophy and History, Essays Presented to Ernst Cassirer* (Oxford: Clarendon Press, 1963), pp. 223-54.

34 Erwin Panofsky, *Meaning in the Visual Arts,* p. 345.

35 Originally published in 1953 as 'The History of Art' in *The Cultural Migration: The European Scholar in America,* in W.R.C.Crawford, ed., (Philadelphia: University of Pennsylvannia Press, 1953), pp. 82-111.

36 According to a source close to Helen Frankenthaler, the artist did not read Panofsky's book, however the publication in 1955 of a collection of essays entitled *Meaning in the Visual Arts,* written by a major art historian who was Jewish and concerned about intellectual freedom, cannot have gone unnoticed by Helen Frankenthaler, a painter for whom we do know the European tradition was a resource, and by Clement Greenberg in his capacity both as art critic, and as editor of *Commentary* concerned with the nature of Jewish responses in American life to the legacy of World War II in Europe.

37 Erwin Panofsky, *Meaning in the Visual Arts,* p. 354.

38 Ibid., p. 312.

39 Ibid., p. 359.

40 Stephen Naifeh and Gregory White Smith, op.cit., p. 793.

41 It is interesting to note that in the chronology in John Elderfield's study of Frankenthaler's work, *Hôtel du Quai Voltaire* and *Eden* are structurally linked as the only two works mentioned by name in the entry for 1956. See *Frankenthaler*, p. 410.

42 Maurice Poirier, 'Working Papers', pp. 81-2. I am grateful to Karen Wilkin for lending me her slide of this drawing.

43 John Elderfield, *Frankenthaler* op.cit., p. 125.

44 Erwin Panofsky, *Meaning in the Visual Arts*, p. 359.

45 Timothy McElreavy, 'Language Barriers: Critical and Painterly Semantics and the work of Friedel Dzubas in *Friedel Dzubas: Critical Painting*, (Massachusetts: Tufts University Gallery, 1998), p. 29.

46 Dzubas was, as we saw in Chapter 1, Frankenthaler's friend and colleague who witnessed the making of *Mountains and Sea* in 1952.

47 See Griselda Pollock, *Killing Men and Dying Women*, where this is the problematic of the essay, and also Part III, Section 6 in the chapter 'The Female Hero and the Making of a Feminist Canon' in *Differencing the Canon: Feminist Desire and the Writing of Art's Histories* (London and New York: Routledge, 1999) pp. 97-107, for a brilliant analysis of the issues in readings of representations of *Susanna and the Elders* and *Judith Slaying Holofernes* by Artemisia Gentileschi.

48 'Cézanne and the Unity of Modern Art', *Partisan Review*, vol. 18, no. 3, (May/June 1951), p. 234.

49 In his essay 'Panofsky and Poussin in Arcadia', Louis Marin reads the voice from the tomb in a painting by Fragonard, with which Panofsky ends *Poussin and the Elegiac Tradition*, as that of the painter. The painter assigns himself to the tomb by the act of painting the letters EGO on its wall. 'Panofsky and Poussin in Arcadia' in Louis Marin, *Sublime Poussin*, trans., Catherine Porter (California: Stanford University Press, 1995), p. 119.

50 John Elderfield, *Frankenthaler*, p. 125.

51 In August 1949 *Life* Magazine ran an article entitled 'Jackson Pollock, is he the greatest living painter in the United States?' *Life*, 27, 8 August 1949.

52 Griselda Pollock, *Differencing the Canon: Feminist Desire and the Writing of Art's Histories*, pp. 122-123. In relation to the position of Artemisia Gentileschi Pollock writes:

'Making a claim for oneself…would involve not only the murder of certain internalized prescriptions on femininity but also symbolic killing of the fathers, who were both figures of necessary identification and professional rivalry. It required a specifically feminine, filial engagement with the 'anxiety of influence', which Harold Bloom insisted is what gives a work its edge and claim to accede to the canon in the face of which the artist is always a latecomer.'

Post Factum

1 Clement Greenberg, 'Louis and Noland', *Art International*, vol IV. no. 5, (May 25, 1960), pp. 26-29.

2 The references here are to Allan Kaprow's essay 'The Legacy of Jackson Pollock', *Art News*, vol. LVII, (October 1958), pp. 24-26, and his book '*Assemblages, Environments and Happenings* (New York: Abrams, 1966).

3 The title of the painting recalls and perhaps alludes to the musical composition *Mother Goose Suite*, written by Maurice Ravel in 1910.

4 John Elderfield, *Frankenthaler*. p. 11.

5 Analysing changes in Frankenthaler's work in the mid 1950s, John Elderfield notes events in her life in that period, including 'the sudden and tragic death of her mother' in April 1954. *Frankenthaler*, p. 89.

6 John Elderfield, *Frankenthaler* op.cit., p. 99.

7 Henry Geldzahler, An Interview with Helen Frankenthaler op.cit., p. 38.

8 Brian Masumi, 'Painting: The Voice of the Grain', in *Bracha Lichtenberg Ettinger Artworking 1985-1999*, (Ghent – Amsterdam: Ludion, 2000), exhibition catalogue, p. 9.

9 Christine Buci-Glucksmann, 'Inner Space of Painting', in *Bracha Lichtenberg Ettinger Halala-Austistwork*, (Jerusalem: The Israel Museum, Aix en Provence: Cité du Livre, 1995), pp. 65-68.

10 'To my mind, discussing art in the psychoanalytical context is inseparable from debating sexual difference, since we enter the function of art by way of the libido and through extensions of the psyche closest to the edges of corpo-*Real*ity', Bracha Lichtenberg Ettinger, The With-In-Visible Screen in *Bracha L. Ettinger: The Matrixial Borderspace*, Minneapolis, (London, University of Minnesota Press 2006), p. 93.

11 I borrow the phrase 'what counted as painting' from Stephen Melville's essay 'Counting/As/Painting' in the catalogue of the exhibition *As Painting: Division and Displacement*, held between May and August 2001 at Wexner Centre for the Arts, The Ohio State University, and curated by Philip Armstrong, Laura Lisbon, and Stephen Melville, (Columbus: Wexner Center for the Arts and Cambridge Mass., London, England: MIT Press, 2001), pp. 1-26.

12 Gene Baro, op.cit.,'The Achievement of Helen Frankenthaler', p. 33.

13 See Chapter 1.

14 Clement Greenberg, 'Feeling Is All', *Partisan Review*, vol. 19, no.1 (Jan-Feb, 1952), reprinted in *Clement Greenberg Collected Essays and Criticism*, vol. 3, ed. by John O'Brian, (Chicago and London: The University of Chicago Press, 1993), p. 106.

15 Ibid.

16 See *Early Grave*, 1957.

17 Bracha Lichtenberg Ettinger, 'The becoming threshold of matrixial borderlines', in *Traveler's Tales: Narratives of Home and Displacement*, ed. by George Robertson, Melinda Mash, Lisa Tickner and John Bird, (London: Routledge, 1994), p. 41.

18 Ibid., Bracha Lichtenberg Ettinger, p. 60.

19 'This retrospective access to the general human latest prenatal/feminine encounter is facilitated but not conditioned by the fact of having a womb. However, this potential facility for access puts women in a privileged position with respect to this stratum of subjectivization; this is one of the reasons why I see the *matrix* as feminine. This doesn't mean though that having or not having a womb determines different ways of recognition, since the *matrix*, as a symbolic filter that is different from the *phallus*, is at the disposition of both sexes,' Bracha Lichtenberg Ettinger, Ibid., p. 47.

20 'Non-conscious' refers to matrixial almost-repression, rather than the 'unconscious' of phallic repression; see the section 'Something New in Terms of Nature' in Chapter 4. The title to which I refer is Helen Frankenthaler's *Seven Types of Ambiguity*, 1957.

21 Other titles are *Mt Sinai* (1956), and *Jacob's Ladder* (1957).

22 Griselda Pollock has succinctly described this practice as 'a co-emergence of contemporary post-Holocaust subjectivity with the subjects (the non-I's) of that which is also our tragedy.' In 'Femininity: Aporia or Sexual Difference?' by Griselda Pollock, introduction to, *Bracha L. Ettinger: The Matrixial Borderspace*, (Minneapolis, London, University of Minnesota Press, 2006), p. 7.

23 See 'Exhibition History' in *Frankenthaler*, by John Elderfield, pp. 420-433.

24 The exhibition at the Whitechapel Gallery in May/June 1969 travelled to London from the Whitney Museum of American Art where it was shown from February to April 1969.

25 Fax from Susan Cross to the author dated May 26th 1998.

26 *To the Lighthouse*, p.159.

27 Ibid., p. 117.

BIBLIOGRAPHY

Able, Elizabeth, *Virginia Woolf and the Fictions of Psychoanalysis* (Chicago and London: University of Chicago Press, 1989).

Antler, Joyce, 'A Bond of Sisterhood', in *Secret Agents: the Rosenberg case, McCarthyism, and Fifties America*, ed. by Marjorie Garber & Rebecca L. Walkowitz (New York and London: Routledge, 1995), pp. 197-214.

Armstrong, Philip, Lisbon, Laura, Melville, Stephen, *As Painting: Division and Displacement* (Columbus: Wexner Centre for the Arts and Cambridge Mass.: MIT Press, 2001).

Ashton, Dore, 'Helen Frankenthaler', *Studio International*, vol. 170, no. 868 (August 1965), pp. 52-55.

—— *American Art Since 1945* (London: Thames and Hudson, 1992).

Bal, Mieke, *Reading 'Rembrandt': Beyond the Word-Image Opposition* (Cambridge: Cambridge University Press, 1991).

—— 'Reading Art?' in *Generations and Geographies in the Visual Arts: Feminist Readings*, ed. by Griselda Pollock (London and New York: Routledge, 1996), pp. 25-41.

—— *Quoting Caravaggio: Contemporary Art, Preposterous History* (Chicago and London: The University of Chicago Press, 1999).

Badt, Kurt, *The Art of Cézanne*, trans. Sheila Ann Ogilvie (London: Faber & Faber, 1956).

Baro, Gene, 'The Achievement of Helen Frankenthaler', *Art International*, vol. 2, no. 7 (Sept. 1967), pp. 32-38.

Batchelor, David, *Chromophobia* (London: Reaktion Books, 2000).

Baur, John I. H., *Nature in Abstraction* (New York: Macmillan, 1958), exhibition catalogue, pp. 5-14.

Bell, Quentin, *Virginia Woolf: A Biography*, 2 vols, (London: The Hogarth Press, 1972)

Beltz, Carl, 'Helen Frankenthaler's Eden: A "Joyously involved creativity"', Art *News*, vol. 80, no. 5 (May 1981), pp. 156-157.

—— *Helen Frankenthaler and the 1950s* (Waltham: Brandeis University, 1981), Rose Art Museum, exhibition catalogue.

Bloom, Harold, *The Anxiety of Influence* (Oxford: Oxford University Press, 1973).

Bois, Yves Alain, 'Matisse and "Arché-Drawing"', in *Painting as Model* (Cambridge Massachusetts, London, England: MIT Press, 1993), pp. 4-63.

Brach, Paul, 'Helen Frankenthaler', *Art Digest*, vol. 26, no. 5 (December, 1951), p. 18.

Brown, Julia, 'A Conversation *Helen Frankenthaler with Julia Brown*', in *After* Mountains and Sea: *Frankenthaler: 1956-1959* (New York: The Solomon R. Guggenheim Museum, 1998), exhibition catalogue, pp. 27-47.

Buci-Glucksmann, Christine, 'Inner Space of Painting', in *Bracha Lichtenberg Ettinger: Hala-Autistwork* (Jerusalem: Israel Museum, Aix en Provence: Cité du Livre, 1995), exhibition catalogue, pp. 58-68.

Carmean, Jr., E.A., 'On Five Paintings by Helen Frankenthaler', *Art International*, vol. 22, no. 4 (April-May 1978), pp. 28-32.

—— *Helen Frankenthaler: A Paintings Retrospective* (New York: Abrams in association with the Modern Art Museum of Fort Worth, 1989), exhibition catalogue.

Caws, Mary Ann, *Women of Bloomsbury: Virginia, Vanessa & Carrington* (New York and London: Routledge, 1990).

Cézanne. Paintings, Watercolors and Drawings: A Loan Exhibition (Chicago: The Art Institute of Chicago, New York: The Metropolitan Museum of Art, 1952), exhibition catalogue.

Chappuis, Adrien, *The Drawings of Paul Cézanne A Catalogue Raisonné* 2 vols (London: Thames and Hudson, 1973).

Cixous, Hélèn, and Clément, Catherine, *The Newly Born Woman*, trans. by Betsy Wing, Theory and History of Literature, vol. 24 (Minneapolis and London: University of Minnesota Press, 1986).

Clark, T.J., 'Jackson Pollock's Abstraction', in *Reconstructing Modernism*, ed. by Serge Guilbaut (Cambridge Massachusetts: MIT Press, 1992), pp. 172-243.

—— 'Pollock's Smallness', in *Jackson Pollock: New Approaches*, ed. by Kirk Varnedoe & Pepe Karmel (New York: The Museum of Modern Art, 1999), pp. 15-31.

—— *Farewell to an Idea, Episodes from a History of Modernism* (New Haven and London, 1999).

Crawford, W.R., ed., *The Cultural Migration: The European Scholar in America* (Philadelphia: University of Pennsylvania Press, 1953).

de Antonio, Emile, and Tuchman, Mitch, *Painters Painting: A Candid History of the Modern Art Scene 1940-1970* (New York: Abbeville Press, 1984).

de Lauretis, Teresa, *Technologies of Gender: Essays on Theory, Film, and Fiction* (Bloomington and Indianapolis: Indiana University Press, 1987).

de Zegher, M. Catherine, *Inside The Visible: an elliptical traverse of 20th Century, art, in, of and from the feminine* (Cambridge, Mass.: MIT Press, 1996).

—— de Zegher, M. Catherine, ed., *Martha Rosler: Positions in the Life World* (Birmingham and Vienna: Ikon Gallery and the Generali Foundation, 1998).

Deleuze, Gilles, *Cinema 1: The Movement-Image* (London: The Athlone Press, 1992).

Diamonstein, Barbaralee, *Inside New York's Art World* (New York: Rizzoli, 1979).

Domhoff, C. William, *Who Rules America?* (Englewood Cliffs: Prentice Hall, 1967).

—— *The Powers That Be: Processes of Ruling Class Domination in America*, (New York: Vintage Books, 1979).

Donne, John, *John Donne The Complete English Poems* (London: Penguin Books, 1982).

Doyle, Laura, '"These Emotions of the Body": Intercorporeal Narrative in *To the Lighthouse*',

Twentieth Century Literature vol. 40 (1995), pp. 42-71.

Dunn, Jane, *A Very Close Conspiracy Vanessa Bell and Virginia Woolf* (London: Jonathan Cape, 1990).

Elderfield, John, 'Introduction', in *Morris Louis* (London: Arts Council of Great Britain, 1974), exhibition catalogue, pp. 7-11.

—— *Frankenthaler* (New York: Abrams, 1989).

Empson, William, *Seven Types of Ambiguity* (New York: New Directions, 1947).

Felman, Shoshana, *What Does a Woman Want? Reading and Sexual Difference* (Baltimore and London: The Johns Hopkins University Press, 1993).

Felstein, Sam, 'Helen Frankenthaler', *Art Digest*, vol. 27, no. 10 (Feb. 1953), p. 20.

Fer, Briony, *On Abstract Art* (New Haven and London: Yale University Press, 1997).

Fisher, Andrea, *Let Us Now Praise Famous Women* (London: Pandora, 1987).

Fitzsimmons, James, 'A Cézanne Exhibition, A Definition of Greatness', *Art Digest*, no. 26 (Feb, 1952), pp. 6-8.

Forge, Andrew, 'Frankenthaler: The Small Paintings', *Art International*, vol. 22, no. 4 (April-May 1978), pp. 28-32.

Frankenthaler, Helen, artist's statement in the catalogue for the exhibition *Nature in Abstraction*, The Whitney Museum of American Art (New York: Macmillan, 1958), pp. 65-66.

—— *Helen Frankenthaler* (Bennington College, May, 1962), exhibition catalogue.

Frascina, Francis, ed., *Pollock and After: The Critical Debate* (London: Harper and Row, 1985).

Freud, Sigmund, 'Three Essays on the Theory of Sexuality' [1905], in *The Standard Edition of the Complete Psychological Works of Sigmund Freud*, vol. 17, ed. by James Strachey (London: The Hogarth Press and the Institute of Psycho-Analysis, 1953), 7th edition 1973, pp. 135-243.

—— 'Papers on Metapsychology: Instincts and Their Vicissitudes' [1915], in *The Standard Edition of the Complete Psychological Works of Sigmund Freud*, vol. 14, ed. by James Strachey (London: The Hogarth Press and the Institute of Psycho-Analysis, 1957), 6th edition, 1973, pp. 117-140.

—— 'Papers on Metapsychology: The Unconscious', [1915], in *The Standard Edition of the Complete Psychological Works of Sigmund Freud*, vol. 14, ed. by James Strachey (London: The Hogarth Press and the Institute of Psycho-Analysis, 1957), 6th edition, 1973, pp. 161-179.

—— 'Introductory Lectures on Psycho-Analysis' [1916-17], in *The Standard Edition of the Complete Psychological Works of Sigmund Freud*, vol. 16, ed. by James Strachey (London: The Hogarth Press and the Institute of Psycho-Analysis, 1963), 5th edition 1973, pp. 243-463.

—— 'The "Uncanny"' [1919], in *The Standard Edition of the Complete Psychological Works of Sigmund Freud*, vol. 17, ed. by James Strachey (London: The Hogarth Press and the Institute of Psycho-Analysis, 1955), 7th edition 1973, pp. 219-256.

—— 'Beyond the Pleasure Principle' [1920], in *The Standard Edition of the Complete Psychological Works of Sigmund Freud*, vol. 18, ed. by James Strachey (London: The Hogarth Press and the Institute of Psycho-Analysis, 1955), 7th edition 1973, pp.7-64.

Fry, Roger, *Vision and Design* (London: Chatto and Windus, 1920).

—— *The Artist and Psychoanalysis* (London: The Hogarth Press, 1924).

—— *Cézanne A Study of his Development*, [1927], 2nd edition (London: The Hogarth Press, 1952).

Gage, John, *Colour and Meaning* (London: Thames & Hudson, 1999).

Gallop, Jane, 'Annie Leclerc Writing a Letter, with Vermeer', *October*, no. 34 (Fall 1985), pp. 103-118.

—— 'Keys to Dora', in *In Dora's Case: Freud-Hysteria-Feminism*, ed. by Charles Bernheimer and Clare Kahne (New York: Columbia University Press, 1990), pp. 200-220.

Garber, Marjorie and Walkowitz, Rebecca, eds, *Secret Agents: the Rosenberg case, McCarthyism, and Fifties America* (New York and London: Routledge, 1995).

Geldzahler, Henry, 'An Interview with Helen Frankenthaler', *Art Forum*, vol. 4, no. 2 (October 1965), pp. 36-38.

—— *New York Painting and Sculpture 1940-1970* (London: Pall Mall Press Ltd., 1969).

Gill, Carolyn Bailey, ed., *Time and The Image* (Manchester and New York: Manchester University Press, 2000).

Godfrey, Mark, 'Keeping Watch Over Absent Meaning: Morris Louis's *Charred Journal* series and the Holocaust', *The Jewish Quarterly*, vol. 46, no. 3 (Autumn 1999), pp. 17-22.

Goossen, E.C., 'Helen Frankenthaler', *Art International* vol. 5, No. 8 (October 1961), pp. 76-9.

—— *Helen Frankenthaler* (New York: Whitney Museum of American Art, 1969), exhibition catalogue, pp. 8-18.

Gordon, Lyndall, *Virginia Woolf: A Writer's Life* (Oxford: Oxford University Press, 1984).

Greenberg, Clement, 'The Role of Nature in Modern Painting', *Partisan Review*, vol. 16. no.1 (Jan. 1949), pp. 78-81.

—— 'Self-Hatred and Jewish Chauvinism: Some Reflections on "Positive Jewishness"', in *Commentary*, November 1950, reprinted in *Clement Greenberg Collected Essays and Criticism*, vol. 3, ed. by John O'Brian (Chicago and London: The University of Chicago Press, 1993), pp. 45-58.

—— 'Cézanne and the Unity of Modern Art', *Partisan Review*, vol. 18, no.3 (May/June 1951), pp. 323-330.

—— 'Feeling is all', *Partisan Review*, vol. 19, no.1 (Jan-Feb, 1952), reprinted in *Clement Greenberg Collected Essays and Criticism*, vol. 3, ed. by John O'Brian (Chicago and London: The University of Chicago Press, 1993), pp. 99-106.

—— 'Cézanne Gateway to Contemporary Painting', *American Mercury*, June 1952, reprinted in *Clement Greenberg The Collected Essays and Criticism*, vol. 3, ed. by John O'Brian (Chicago and London: The University of Chicago Press, 1993), pp. 113-118.

—— 'Louis and Noland', *Art International*, vol. 4, no.5 (May, 25, 1960), pp. 26-29.

—— 'Modernist Painting', *Forum Lectures*, Washington D.C.: Voice of America, 1960, reprinted in, *Clement Greenberg The Collected Essays and Criticism*, vol. 4, ed. by John O'Brian (Chicago and London: The University of Chicago Press, 1993), pp. 85-93.

Grosz, Elizabeth, 'Lived Spatiality (The Space of Corporeal Desire)', in *Culture Lab*, ed. by B. Boignton (Princeton: Princeton Architectural Press, 1993).

—— *Volatile Bodies: Toward a Corporeal Feminism* (Sydney: Allen and Unwin, & Bloomington and Indiana: Indiana University Press, 1994).

—— *Space, Time and Perversion: Essays on the Politics of the Body* (New York and London: Routledge, 1995).

Gruen, John, *The Party's Over Now: Reminiscences of the Fifties – New York's Artists, Writers, Musicians and Their Friends* (New York: Viking Press, 1972).

Guilbaut, Serge, *How New York Stole the Idea of Modern Art: Abstract Expressionism, Freedom, and the Cold War,* trans. by Arthur Goldhammer (Chicago and London: The University of Chicago Press, 1983).

H.B., 'Helen Frankenthaler', *Art News,* vol. 50, no. 7 (Nov. 1951), p. 48.

Haraway, Donna, and Goodeve, Thyrza, *How Like a Leaf: Donna Haraway An Interview with Thyrza Nichols Goodeve* (New York and London: Routledge, 1998).

Harris, Mary Emma, *The Arts at Black Mountain College* (Cambridge, Massachusetts and London: MIT Press, 1987).

Harrison, Charles, *Essays on Art & Language* (Oxford: Basil Blackwell, 1991).

Harrison, C. & Wood, P., *Art in Theory 1900-1990* (Oxford UK & Cambridge US, 1993).

Harrison, Pegram, *Frankenthaler A Catalogue Raisonné, Prints 1961-1994* (New York: Abrams, 1996).

Hobbs, Robert, *Lee Krasner* (New York: Independent Curators International, 1999).

Hurd Green, Carol, 'The Suffering Body: Ethel Rosenberg in the Hands of the Writers', in *Secret Agents: the Rosenberg case, McCarthyism, and Fifties America*, ed. by Marjorie Garber & Rebecca L. Walkowitz (New York and London: Routledge, 1995), pp. 183-195.

Irigaray, Luce, 'The Invisible of the Flesh: A Reading of Merleau-Ponty, *The Visible and the Invisible,* "The Intertwining – The Chiasm"', in *An Ethics of Sexual Difference,* trans. by Carolyn Burke and Gillian C. Gill (London: Athlone Press, 1993), pp. 151-184.

Janes, Hilly, 'True Colours', *The Observer Magazine*, 4 June (2000), pp. 26-29.

Johnson, Galen A., 'Ontology and Painting: "Eye and Mind"', in *The Merleau-Ponty Aesthetics Reader*, ed. by Galen A. Johnson (Evanson: Northwestern University Press, 1993), pp. 35-55.

Judd, Donald, 'Helen Frankenthaler', in *Donald Judd Complete Writings 1959-1975* (Nova Scotia: Press of the Nova Scotia College of Art and Design, New York: New York University Press, 1975), pp. 13-14.

Kaplan, Louis, 'Reframing the Self-Criticism: Clement Greenberg's "Modernist Painting" in the Light of Jewish Identity', in Sousslof, Catherine M., ed., *Jewish Identity in Modern Art History* (Berkeley, Los Angeles, London: University of California Press, 1999), pp. 180-199.

Kaprow, Allan, *Assemblages, Environments and Happenings* (New York: Abrams, 1966).

Kramer, Hilton, 'An Interview with Helen Frankenthaler', *Partisan Review,* vol. 61, no. 2 (1992), pp. 240-47.

Kristeva, Julia, 'Giotto's Joy', in *Desire in Language,* ed. by Leon Roudiez (Oxford: Blackwell, 1980), pp. 210-236.

Kudielka, Robert, ed., *The Eye's Mind: Bridget Riley Collected Writings 1965-1999*, (London: Thames & Hudson, 1999).

Lacan, Jacques, *The Four Fundamental Concepts of Psychoanalysis*, ed. by Jacques-Alain Miller, trans. by Alan Sheridan (London: Penguin Books, 1994).

—— *The Ethics of Psychoanalysis 1959-1960*, ed. by Jacques-Alain Miller, trans. Dennis Porter (London: Tavistock/Routledge, 1992).

Laplanche, Jean, *Life and Death in Psychoanalysis*, trans. Jeffrey Melman (Baltimore and London: The Johns Hopkins University Press, 1976). \

Laplanche, J. & Pontalis, J.B., 'Fantasy and the Origins of Sexuality' [1964]reprinted in *Formations of Fantasy*, ed. by Victor Burgin, James Donald and Cora Caplan (London and New York: Methuen, 1986), pp. 5-34.

—— *The Language of Psychoanalysis* (London: Karnac and the Institute of Psycho-analysis, 1988).

Lee, Hermione, *Virginia Woolf* (London: Chatto and Windus, 1996).

Lichtenberg Ettinger, Bracha, 'Matrix and Metramorphosis', *Differences*, vol. 4, no. 3 (1992), pp. 176-208.

—— *Matrix Hala(a)-Lapsus: notes on painting* (Oxford: Museum of Modern Art, 1993).

—— 'Woman-Other-Thing: A matrixial* touch', in *Bracha Lichtenberg Ettinger: Matrix Borderlines* (Oxford: Museum of Modern Art, 1993), exhibition catalogue, pp. 11-18.

—— *The Matrixial Gaze* (Leeds: Feminist Arts and Histories Network, 1995).

—— 'The Red Cow Effect', in *Beautiful Translation – Act 2*, ed. by Juliet Steyn (London: Pluto Press, 1996), pp. 82-119.

—— 'Metramorphic Borderlinks and Matrixial Borderspace', in *Rethinking Borders*, ed. by John Welchman (London and New York: Macmillan, 1996), pp. 125-159.

—— 'Transference, or what is left of it, or: Analysts live in perpetual fear', Félix Guattari in conversation with Bracha Lichtenberg Ettinger, in *Doctor and Patient* (Pori Art Museum, 1997) exhibition catalogue, pp. 120-124.

—— 'Trans-Subjective Transferential Borderspace', *Canadian Review of Comparative Literature*, vol. XXIV, no. 3 (September 1997), pp. 625-47.

—— 'Traumatic Wit(h)ness-Thing and Matrixial Co/in-habit(u)ating', *parallax*, vol. 5, no.1 (Jan-March, 1999), pp. 89-98.

—— 'Matrixial Gaze and Screen: Other than Phallic, Merleau-Ponty and the Late Lacan', *'ps', Journal of the Universities Association for Psychoanalytic Studies*, vol. 2, no. 1 (Summer 1999), pp. 3-39.

—— 'Art as the Transport-Station of Trauma', *Bracha Lichtenberg Ettinger Artworking 1985-1999* (Ghent-Amsterdam: Ludion, 2000), exhibition catalogue, pp. 91-116.

Lipstadt, Deborah E., *Beyond Belief: The American Press and The Coming of the Holocaust 1933-1945* (New York: Free Press, 1986).

Loran Johnson, Erle, 'Cézanne's Country', *The Arts*, vol. 16 (April 1930), pp. 521-51.

—— *Cézanne's Composition: Analysis of his Form with Diagrams and Photographs of his Motifs* (Berkeley and Los Angeles: University of California Press, 1947).

Lowenstein, Steven M., *Frankfurt on the Hudson* (Detroit: Wayne State University Press, 1989).

Macey, David, *Lacan in Contexts* (London: Verso, 1988).

Marin, Louis, 'Panofsky and Poussin in Arcadia', in *Sublime Poussin* (Stanford: Stanford University Press, 1999), pp. 104-119.

Marlow, Tim, 'Interview with Helen Frankenthaler', in *Frankenthaler On Paper: 1990 – 1999* (London: Bernard Jacobson Gallery, 2000), exhibition catalogue, pp. 2-8.

McElreavy, Timothy, 'Language Barriers: Critical and Painterly Semantics and the work of Friedel Dzubas', in *Friedel Dzubas: Critical Painting* (Medford: Tufts University Gallery, 1998), exhibition catalogue, pp. 25-49.

Meeropol, Robert, 'Rosenberg Realities', in *Secret Agents: the Rosenberg case, McCarthyism, and Fifties America*, ed. by Marjorie Garber & Rebecca L. Walkowitz (New York and London: Routledge, 1995), pp. 235-251.

Merleau-Ponty, Maurice, *Phenomenology of Perception,* [1945] trans. Colin Smith (London: Routledge & Kegan Paul, 1962).

—— 'Cézanne's Doubt', [1945] in *Sense and Non-Sense,* trans. H.L. & P.A. Dreyfus (Evanston: Northwestern University Press, 1964), pp. 9-25.

—— 'Eye and Mind', [1961], in *The Merleau-Ponty Aesthetics Reader: Philosophy and Painting,* ed. by Galen A. Johnson (Evanston: Northwestern University Press, 1993), pp. 121-149.

—— *The Visible and the Invisible,* [1960] trans. Alphonso Lingis (Evanston: Northwestern University Press, 1997).

Millner, Marion, *On Not Being Able to Paint,* [1950] (Oxford: Heinemann, 1971).

Monniere, Geneviève, 'The Late Watercolours' in, *Cézanne The Late Work*, ed. by William Rubin (London: Thames & Hudson, 1978), pp. 113-118.

Myers, John Bernard, *Tracking the Marvelous* (New York: Random House, 1983).

Naifeh, Stephen, and White Smith, Gregory, *Jackson Pollock: An American Saga* (London: Barrie & Jenkins, 1989).

Nemser, Cindy, 'An Interview with Helen Frankenthaler', *Arts*, vol. 46 (November 1971), pp. 51-54

—— *Art Talk: Conversations with Twelve Women* (New York: Scribner, 1975).

O'Brian, John, *Clement Greenberg Collected Essays and Criticism,* in 4 vols, (Chicago and London: The University of Chicago Press, 1986-1993).

O'Connor, F.V. & Thaw, E.V., *Jackson Pollock: A Catalogue Raisonné of Paintings, Drawings, and Other Works* (New Haven and London: Yale University Press, 1978).

O'Hara, Frank, 'Reviews and Previews', *Art News,* vol. 53, no. 8 (Dec. 1954), p. 53.

—— Helen Frankenthaler', in *An Exhibition of Oil Paintings by Frankenthaler* (New York: The Jewish Museum, 1960), exhibition catalogue, pp. 5-7.

—— 'Helen Frankenthaler' in *Art Chronicles 1954-1966* (New York: George Braziller, 1975), pp. 121-127.

—— *Selected Poems,* ed. by Donald Allen (London: Penguin Books, 1994).

Oren, Michael B, *The Origins of the Second Arab-Israeli War* (London: Frank Cass, 1992).

Orton, Fred, *Figuring Jasper Johns* (London, Reaktion Books, 1994).

—— '(Painting) Out of Time', *parallax*, no. 3 (September 1996), pp. 99-112.

—— 'Footnote One: The Idea of the Cold War', in *Avant-Gardes and Partisans Reviewed*, ed. by Fred Orton & Griselda Pollock (Manchester: Manchester University Press, 1996), pp. 205-218.

Panofsky, Erwin, '*Et in Arcadia Ego:* Poussin and The Elegiac Tradition' in *Meaning in the Visual*

Arts: Papers in and on Art History (New York: Doubleday Anchor Books, 1955), pp. 295-320.

Parker, Rozsika, and Pollock, Griselda, *Old Mistresses: Women, Art & Ideology* (London: Pandora Books, 1981).

Perloff, Marjorie, *Frank O'Hara, Poet Among Painters* (New York: George Braziller, 1977).

Phelan, Peggy, *Mourning Sex: Performing Public Memories* (London: Routledge, 1997).

Plath, Sylvia, *The Bell Jar* (London: William Heinemann, 1963).

Poirier, Maurice, 'Working Papers' *Art News*, vol. 84, no. 6 (Summer 1985), pp. 79-83.

Pollock, Griselda, *Avant-garde Gambits: Gender and the Colour of Art History* (London: Thames & Hudson, 1992).

—— 'Gleaning in history or coming after/behind the reapers', in *Generations and Geographies in the Visual Arts: Feminist Readings*, ed. by Griselda Pollock (London and New York: Routledge, 1996), pp. 268-288.

—— 'Killing Men and Dying Women: A Woman's Touch in the Cold Zone of American Painting in the 1950s', in *Avant-Gardes and Partisans Reviewed*, ed. by Fred Orton, and Griselda Pollock (Manchester: Manchester University Press, 1996), pp. 221-294.

—— 'To Inscribe the Feminine: A Kristevan Impossibility? or Femininity, Melancholy and Sublimation', *parallax*, vol. 4, no. 3 (July-September, 1998), pp. 81-117.

—— *Differencing the Canon: Feminist Desire and the Writing of Art's Histories* (London and New York: Routledge, 1999).

—— 'Nichsapha: Yearning/Languishing The Immaterial Tuché of Colour In Painting *After Painting After History*', in *Bracha Lichtenberg Ettinger: Artworking 1985-1999* (Ghent-Amsterdam: Ludion, 2000) exhibition catalogue, pp. 45-70.

Pollock, Griselda, and Florence, Penny, *Looking Back to the Future* (Amsterdam: G+B Arts International, 2001).

Porter, Fairfield, 'Helen Frankenthaler', *Art News*, vol. 51, no. 10 (Feb, 1953), p. 55.

Preston, Stuart, 'Diverse Showings', *New York Times* (Sunday, Feb. 8 1953).

—— 'About Art and Artists', *New York Times*, Friday, Nov. 19 (1954).

Rewald, John, *Paul Cézanne Letters*, [1941], 4th edition (Oxford: Bruno Cassirer, 1976).

—— 'The Last Motifs at Aix' in *Cézanne: The Late Work*, ed. by William Rubin, (London, Thames & Hudson, 1978), pp. 83-106.

—— *Paul Cézanne The Water Colours: A Catalogue Raisonné* (London: Thames & Hudson, 1983).

Riley, Bridget, 'The Pleasures of Sight' in *Working With Colour*, (London: Arts Council of Great Britain, 1984), exhibition catalogue, unpaginated.

—— *The Experience of Painting: Eight Modern Artists* (London: South Bank Centre, 1989).

—— *Dialogues on Art*, ed., by Robert Kudielka (London: Zwemmer, 1995).

Rivers, Larry, with Carol Brightman, *Drawings and Digressions* (New York: Clarkson N. Potter Inc., 1979).

Robertson, Bryan, 'Introduction and Biographical Note', in *Bridget Riley Paintings and Drawings 1951-71* (London: Arts Council of Great Britain, 1971), exhibition catalogue, pp. 3-24.

Rose, Barbara, *Frankenthaler* (New York: Abrams, 1972).

Rose, Jacqueline, *The Haunting of Sylvia Plath* (London: Virago, 1991).

Rosenberg, Eric M., Saltzman, Liza, & McElreavy, Timothy, *Friedel Dzubas: Critical Painting* (Medford: Tufts University Gallery, 1998), exhibition catalogue.

Rosenberg, Harold, 'Art and Words', in *The De-definition of Art* (Chicago and London: The University of Chicago Press, 1983), pp. 56-68.

Rousseau Jr., Theodore, 'Cézanne as an Old Master', *Art News*, no. 51 (April, 1952), pp. 28-33.

Rowley, Alison, 'An Introduction to Bracha Lichtenberg Ettinger's 'Traumatic Wit(h)ness-Thing and Matrixial Co/in-habit(u)ating', *parallax*, vol. 5, no.1 (Jan-March, 1999), pp. 83-88.

Rubenfeld, Florence, *Clement Greenberg: A Life* (New York: Scribner, 1997).

Salzman, Lisa, 'Reconsidering the Stain: On Gender, Identity, and New York School Painting', in *Friedel Dzubas: Critical Painting* (Medford: Tufts University Gallery, 1998), exhibition catalogue, pp. 9-24.

Sandler, Irving, *The Triumph of American Painting* (New York, Hagerstown, San Francisco, London: Harper and Row, 1970).

—— 'Frankenthaler, Mitchell, Leslie, Resnick, Francis and Other Gesture Painters', in *The New York School: The Painters and Sculptors of the Fifties* (New York, Hagerstown, San Francisco, London: Harper and Row, London: 1978), pp. 57-89.

Schapiro, Meyer, *Cézanne* (New York: Abrams, 1952).

Schyler, James, 'Helen Frankenthaler [de Nagy: Feb 12-March 2]', *Art News*, vol. 55, no. 10 (Feb. 1957), p. 11.

Shiff, Richard, 'Cézanne's physicality: the politics of touch', in *The Language of Art History*, ed. by Salim Kemal and Ivan Gaskell (Cambridge: Cambridge University Press, 1991), pp. 129-180.

Smith Jr., Alexander, *Frank O'Hara A Comprehensive Bibliography* (New York and London, Garlan,1980).

Soussloff, Catherine M., *Jewish Identity in Modern Art History* (Berkeley, Los Angeles, London: University of California Press, 1999).

Spalding, Frances, *Roger Fry; Art and Life* (London: Granada Publishing, 1980).
Vanessa Bell (London: Weidenfeld & Nicholson, 1983).

Spivak, Gayatri Chakravorty, 'Unmaking and Making in *To The Lighthouse*', in *In Other Worlds* (New York and London: Routledge, 1988), pp. 30-45.

—— 'The Rani of Sirmur', *History and Theory*, vol. XXIV, no. 3 (1985), pp. 249-272.

Steedman, Carolyn, *Landscape for a Good Woman* (London: Virago, 1986).

Stone, I. F., *The Haunted Fifties* (London: The Merlin Press, 1963).

Stott, Rebecca, '"Inevitable relations": aesthetic revelations from Cézanne to Woolf', in *The Politics of Pleasure: Aesthetic and Cultural Theory*, ed. by Stephen Reagan (Buckingham and Philadelphia: Oxford University Press, 1992), pp. 87-107.

Suchoff, David, 'The Rosenberg Case and the New York Intellectuals', in *Secret Agents: the Rosenberg case, McCarthyism, and Fifties America*, ed. by Marjorie Garber and Rebecca Walkowitz (New York and London: Routledge, 1995), pp. 155-169.

Swanson, Dean, 'Morris Louis: The Veil Cycle' in *Morris Louis: The Veil Cycle* (Minneapolis: Walker Art Center, 1977), exhibition catalogue, pp. 6-13.

Tickner, Lisa, 'Vanessa Bell: *Studland Beach*, Domesticity, and "Significant Form"', *Representations*, vol. 8, no. 65 (Winter 1999), pp. 63-92.

—— *Modern Life and Modern Subjects: British Art in the Early Twentieth Century* (New Haven & London: Yale University Press, 2000).

Tyler, Parker, 'Helen Frankenthaler [De Nagy; Feb. 18, March 8.]', *Art News*, vol. 54, no. 10 (Feb. 1956), p. 49.

Vasseleu, Cathryn, *Textures of Light: Vision and Touch in Irigaray, Levinas and Merleau-Ponty* (London and New York: Routledge, 1998).

Venturi, Lionello, *Cézanne: son art – son oeuvre*, 2 vols (Paris: Paul Rosenberg, 1936).

Wagner, Anne M., *Three Artists (Three Women)*, (Berkeley, Los Angeles, London: University of California Press, 1996).

—— 'Pollock's Nature and Frankenthaler's Culture', in *Jackson Pollock: New Approaches*, ed. by Kirk Varnedoe & Pepe Karmel (New York: The Museum of Modern Art, 1999), pp. 181-199.

Waldman, Diane, *Kenneth Noland: A Retrospective* (New York: The Solomon R. Guggenheim Foundation, in collaboration with Harry N. Abrams, 1977), exhibition catalogue, pp. 9-36.

Warhol, Andy, *Andy Warhol: Death and Disasters*, The Menil Collection (Huston: Fine Art Press, 1988).

Wilkin, Karen, *Helen Frankenthaler: Works on Paper* (New York: George Braziller, 1984).

—— 'Frankenthaler and her critics', *New Criterion*, vol. 8, no. 2 (October, 1989), pp. 16-23.

—— 'Frankenthaler at the Guggenheim', *New Criterion*, vol. 16. no. 7 (March, 1998), pp. 44-9.

Woolf, Virginia, 'Mr Bennett and Mrs Brown' [1923], reprinted in *The Essays of Virginia Woolf*, vol. 3, ed. by Andrew McNeillie (The Hogarth Press, London, 1988), pp. 384-389.

—— 'Character in Fiction' [1924], reprinted in *The Essays of Virginia Woolf* vol. 3, ed. by Andrew McNeillie (London: The Hogarth Press, 1988), pp. 420-438.

—— *To the Lighthouse*, The Hogarth Press, London [1927] (London: Grafton Books, 1977).

—— 'A Sketch of the Past' [1939], in *Moments of Being*, ed. by Jeanne Schulkind (London: Grafton Books, 1989), pp. 72-173.

—— *Roger Fry A Biography*, [1940], 3rd edition (London: The Hogarth Press, 1969).

—— *The Diary of Virginia Woolf*, 5 vols, ed. by Anne Olivier Bell (London: Hogarth Press, 1977-1984).

—— *The Letters of Virginia Woolf*, 6 vols, ed. by Nigel Nicolson, ass. ed. Joanna Trautman (London: The Hogarth Press, London 1976-1980).

—— *The Essays of Virginia Woolf*, 4 vols, ed. by Andrew McNeillie (The Hogarth Press, London, 1986- 1988).

—— *A Passionate Apprentice: The Early Journals 1897-1909*, ed. by Mitchell A. Leaska (London: The Hogarth Press, 1990).

'Women Artists in Ascendance', *Life*, vol. 42, no. 19 (May 13, 1957), p. 71-74.

Woolmer, Howard J., *A Checklist of The Hogarth Press 1917 –1938* (London: The Hogarth Press, 1976).

Wouk, Herman, *Marjorie Morningstar,* [1955] (London: Jonathan Cape, 1955; The Reprint Society, 1957).

Wylie, Philip, *Generation of Vipers,* [1942] (Illinois: Dalkey Archive Press, 1996).

The Columbia University Bulletin of Information, 1948-49: Fine Arts 175 'Modern Painting from 1848-1900', 'Lectures on painting with reference to sculpture and architecture in Europe and America in the second half of the nineteenth century'.

Films

Frankenthaler: Toward a New Climate, produced and directed by Perry Miller Adato, 1978, broadcast in the series *The Originals: Women in Art,* produced by WNET-Channel Thirteen.

Jackson Pollock, produced by Hans Namuth and Paul Falkenberg, music by Morton Feldman, narration by Jackson Pollock, 1951.

INDEX